Generational Pra

2022 Edition

Editors:
Paul L. Cox
Brian P. Cox
Barbara Kain Parker

Generational Prayers
2022 Edition

Edited by
Paul L. Cox
Brian P. Cox
Barbara Kain Parker

Published by Aslan's Place

Distributed by Aslan's Place Publications
9315 Sagebrush St
Apple Valley, Ca 92308
760-810-0990
AslansPlace.com

Edited and formatted by Paul L. Cox, Brian P. Cox, Barbara Kain Parker

Cover Art by Oliver Pengilley

ISBN 979-8-4862-6523-5

Foreword

For almost thirty years, prayers from Aslan's Place have acted as starting points as ministers, groups and individuals work to follow the lead of the Holy Spirit in generational prayer. These prayers have been developed during Aslan's Place events, Bible studies, prayer sessions and through revelation. They provide an opportunity to enter into new freedom as you exercise the authority you have through Jesus Christ over your life and family line.

Information about individual authors as well as the theological, biblical, and historical foundations of the prayers are available in our book *Come Up Higher*, and our *Exploring Heavenly Places* book series.

Brian P. Cox
Aslan's Place

TABLE OF CONTENTS
BY PRAYER TITLE

Renunciation of Sins of My Family Line

As a member of this family line, I repent for all of those who suppressed the truth by their wickedness.

I repent for all those who, although they knew God, they neither glorified Him as God nor gave thanks to Him because their thinking was futile and their foolish hearts were darkened.

I repent for all those who became fools and exchanged the glory of the immortal God for images made to look like mortal man, birds, animals, and reptiles.

I repent for the sinful desires of my ancestors' hearts who gave their hearts to sexual impurity for the degrading of their bodies with one another.

I repent for all those who exchanged the truth of God for a lie, and worshipped and served created things rather than the Creator, Who is forever praised.

I repent for the shameful lusts of my ancestors, and for the women who exchanged natural relations for unnatural ones.

I repent for the men in my family line who abandoned natural relations with women and were inflamed with lust for one another, men who committed indecent acts with other men, and received in themselves the due penalty for their perversion.

I repent for those who did not think it worthwhile to retain the knowledge of God, and therefore, were turned over to a depraved mind, to do what ought not be done.

I repent for all those who have been filled with every kind of wickedness, evil, greed, and depravity, and for all those who were full of envy, murder, strife, deceit, and malice.

I repent for all those who were gossips, slanderers, God-haters, insolent, arrogant, and boastful, for all those who invented ways of doing evil, who were disobedient to their parents, who were senseless, faithless, heartless, and ruthless.

I repent for those who, although they knew God's righteous decree that those who do such things deserve death, they not only continued to do these very things but also approved of those who practiced them.

Prayer to Change Inertia

I pray protection for myself, my family, and my household. I command that no astral projections, remote viewing, remote sensing, telluric energies, demonic spiritual fields, ley lines or witchcraft can in any way empower, influence, or have any adverse effect on me.

Father God, I agree with Your purposes to remove all ungodly inertia and the influence of all demonic territorial captivity in my life. Lord, please remove all strongholds, idolatries, afflictions, generational curses, traditions, false teachings and doctrines caused by any person, place, Satan, or any other evil being, above and below this earth. I break all ungodly ties between me and any ungodly dimension.

I ask the Holy Spirit of the True and Living God, to release from captivity all parts of me—heart, spirit, soul and body—from these territories. Lord, please remove and clean off any giftings, callings, resources, blessings and purposes from captivity.

I thank you Lord for now realigning me to Your throne.

I declare that I will be in agreement with:

1. The Spirit of the Lord and all His characteristics, attributes, and benefits including the Spirit of wisdom and understanding, the Spirit of counsel and might, the Spirit of knowledge and the fear of the Lord.

2. My seated position in the heavenly places with the Lord Jesus Christ and to the All-seeing God, El Roi, and His direction for me.

3. The voice and power of the Almighty, El Shaddai, and to the word of God, both the *rhema* word and the living *Logos*, The Lord Jesus Christ, and to the protection and authority of the Lord of Hosts.

4. The grace, authority, rule and dominion of the throne of God and to His right hand, and to His kingdom purposes and divine order.

5. The name of The Lord Jesus Christ that is above every other name in every dimension of the heavens, the earth, and below the earth.

6. The fire of His presence, His sanctifying, purifying, and revelatory attributes, and to all reproductivity and creativity purposed through Him for me.

7. All the covenant promises and blessings given to Abraham and fulfilled in God the Father's Seed, The Lord Jesus Christ.

Please restore me to the image of Yahweh's glory and honor and to every kingdom purpose, calling, and gifting. Please permanently align me to a position where I am seated with The Most High God in His Most Holy Place.

I now thank you Lord, that the Spirit of the Living God brings a permanent godly inertia and that I am now properly aligned to the throne of God and will never again be moved from this position by any ungodly force above, below, or on this earth.

Prayer to Dismantle Powers

I declare that once I was a child in slavery under the elemental spirits of the world. But when the time had fully come, God sent His Son, born of a woman, born under law, to redeem me who was under law that I might receive the full rights of a son. Because I am a son[1], God sent the Spirit of His Son into my heart, the Spirit who calls out, "Abba, Father." So I am no longer a slave, but a son, and since I am a son, God has made me also an heir.

I repent for all current and generational religious activities, and the belief in and practice of all human philosophies and traditions including any ungodly reliance on the law.

I now demand, in the name of Jesus, that all ungodly powers leave and you will remove all magnets, capacitors, cylinders, tubing, antennas, and any other device you have placed on me.

I ask, Father, that You remove all dominions, rulers, and thrones that are aligned with these powers.

I renounce and repent for generational alchemy and I break all generational ties that have empowered that alchemy.

I renounce and repent for the ungodly magical belief in the five basic elements of the creation – earth, air, fire, water, and metal.

Lord, please now bring all magnetic fields back into correct alignment and balance.

Father, please now send Your fire to consume all the evil associated with these powers.

Lord, please clean up and return to me everything the enemy has stolen.

I now declare that I am seated with Christ in heavenly places and that the enemy will be under my feet. I now ask, Father, that You release into me my generational birthright.

---

[1] We are all sons of God. This is a position that is separate from our gender. Galatians 3:26

Prayer to Remove the Roots of Rebellion

In the name of the Lord Jesus Christ, I repent for all generational idolatry.

I repent for all personal and generational rebellion, stubbornness, and disobedience that have contributed to witchcraft in my life and in my generational line.

I repent for all envy and jealousy of the mind, physical bodies, and personalities of others.

I repent for any worship of myself and any need of personal recognition.

I repent for all envy and jealousy of the spiritual giftings and capacities of others.

I repent for myself and for those in my generational line who did not guard the gates of the spiritual and physical senses.

I repent for choosing my will above the will of the Lord.

I choose to owe no one anything, but to love one another.

I choose to cast off the work of darkness and to put on the armor of Light, the Lord Jesus Christ, and to make no provision for the flesh, to fulfill its lust.

I choose to walk only according to the grace and anointing God has given to me.

I choose to walk in unity with my brothers and sisters in the Lord.

I choose to follow Christ, living a life of love, preferring others above myself.

I choose to yield and surrender my personal rights so that I might serve the Lord wholeheartedly.

I choose to be devoted to one another in brotherly love and to honor one another above myself. I will never be lacking in zeal, but will keep my spiritual fervor, serving the Lord. I will be joyful in hope, patient in affliction, and faithful in prayer. I will share with God's people who are in need. I will practice hospitality. I will bless those who persecute me. I will rejoice with those who rejoice and will mourn with those who mourn. I will live in harmony with other believers. I will not be proud, but I will associate with people of low position. I will not be conceited. I will not repay evil for evil. I will have regard for good things in the sight of all men. I will live at peace with everyone. I will not take revenge on others.

Lord, please now remove all ungodly spiritual beings and devices that have been empowered by my idolatry, rebellion, and jealousy, and the idolatry, rebellion, and jealousy of my ancestors.

Lord, please disconnect me from any evil network and I break all ungodly ties between the abode of the enemy and myself.

Lord, please remove the generational tree of the knowledge of good and evil.

Lord, please break the cords of death that entangle me, the torrents of destruction that overwhelm me, the cords of Sheol that are coiled around me, and the snares of death that confront me.

Lord, please return through the blood of Jesus any godly anointing, energy, authority, finances, and health given away and perverted because of my sin and my ancestors' sin.

Lord, please set me as a seal upon Your heart, and as a seal upon Your arm, for Your Love is stronger than death.

I declare that the Lord, Jesus Christ, is the Lord over all.

Prayer of Renunciation – Soul

I transfer ownership of all that I am and all that I have to the Lord Jesus Christ of Nazareth. I now ask You, Lord, to cancel all legal right for evil influences and activity in every domain of my being.

I declare the Lordship of Jesus Christ over every domain of my person including above me and below me, to the left and to the right, and to the front and to the back. Lord, release me from the evil power of all these domains. Please clean up and return to me any part of me that has been removed to any dimension.

I now apply the Blood of Christ, the refiner's fire, and the launderer's soap[2] to the passageways between the domains, so that the anointing of the Lord may flow freely through me.

---

[2] Malachi 3:2

Prayer of Renunciation – Physical Body

Lord, please reverse the work of any evil operators, including thrones, who changed the vibration of my foundation affecting the DNA of the zygote in the womb. Holy Spirit, please now hover over the original DNA in the zygote, so that I will resonate only with the Holy Trinity. Lord, as you do this, please remove any evil matter, evil vibrations, evil oscillation, evil frequencies, evil tones, and evil colors. Lord, please do this in my generational line all the way back to Adam.

Lord, please now move me from the virtual reality created by the enemy to your reality. Lord, take me out of the prison that I am in and set me free. Remove all deception and denial that makes me believe that my current perception is reality. Lord, bring all programming back to nothing and reformat it so that the programming reflects the image and nature of Jesus Christ.

Lord, please do this in every dimension.
Lord, please break all ungodly covalent bonding and any other chemical bonding.
Lord, please seal all of your work with spiritual interferon.

Prayer to Remove the Generational Roots and to Proclaim My Dedication to the Lord

I ask, Lord God, that You come and burn like a furnace and destroy all the arrogant and evildoers in my generational line so that not a root or a branch will be left to them. Lord, destroy all these false roots and all false fruit. Lord, please remove the old nature.

Lord, please set me free and send the Sun of Righteousness with healing in its wings.

I declare that Jesus Christ is the true vine and I desire to be one of the branches. Since I acknowledge that I can only bear fruit as I am in Christ, my desire is to always remain in Him.

Lord, my desire is that I will be like a tree planted by the water that sends out its roots by the stream so that I will have no fear or worries. As I remain in You, I realize that You will satisfy my needs as I am in a scorched land. My desire, Lord, is that I will yield fruit and that I will prosper in everything that I do and I will strengthen Your fame, Lord. I want to be like a well-watered garden, like a spring whose waters never fail.

Lord, I will always have confidence in You.

I desire to be a planting of the Lord so that I can be rooted downward, built up in Christ, established in His love, strengthened in the faith, and overflowing in thankfulness so I will bear much fruit.

Prayer to Replace Double-Mindedness
with the Mind of Christ

In the name of the Lord Jesus Christ, I confess my doubt and the doubt in my generational line. I confess that this doubt has made me unstable and has given me double-mindedness. I confess that the source of this double-mindedness has been pride in my life and in my generational line. I also repent for all intellectualism, ungodly reasoning, logic, and humanism. I repent of caring more about man's approval rather than God's Truth.

I repent of my own self-effort and pride. God, in humility I receive Your love, mercy and grace.

I choose to be no longer conformed to the pattern of this world, but to Your pattern and to be transformed by the renewing of my mind so that I might prove what is the good and acceptable and perfect will of God.

I will do nothing out of selfish ambition or vain conceit, but I will walk in humility, considering others better than myself.

I choose to resist the devil. I choose to submit myself to God as my Lord and Master and to draw near to Him. Lord, please wash my hands and purify my heart.

Father, thank you for giving me the mind of Christ, so I will be like Him, becoming like a servant.

Renunciation of the Janteloven Iniquities
Scandinavian Iniquities

1. I break, shatter, cut-off, dissolve, and destroy the iniquity that says I am not special.

2. I break, shatter, cut-off, dissolve, and destroy the iniquity that says that I do not have the same standing as others.

3. I break, shatter, cut-off, dissolve, and destroy the iniquity that says that others are smarter than me.

4. I break, shatter, cut-off, dissolve, and destroy the iniquity that says others are better than me.

5. I break, shatter, cut-off, dissolve, and destroy the iniquity that says that others know more than I do.

6. I break, shatter, cut-off, dissolve, and destroy the iniquity that says others are more important than I am.

7. I break, shatter, cut-off, dissolve, and destroy the iniquity that says I am not good at anything.

8. I break, shatter, cut-off, dissolve, and destroy the iniquity that says I will not speak or laugh in public.

9. I break, shatter, cut-off, dissolve, and destroy the iniquity that says that no one cares about me.

10. I break, shatter, cut-off, dissolve, and destroy the iniquity that says I cannot be taught anything.

The Blood and Heart

Father, I acknowledge You and Your power. I praise you, Lord Father.

Please remove all evil in my family line from before the beginning of time to the present.

I repent for all the sins of my ancestors and I totally renounce:
All blood covenants and oaths
All communions with demons
All blood sacrifices
All eating of flesh or blood
All blood rites and rituals
All offerings of the heart
All union with demons through blood rites
All eating of organs
All ungodly shedding of blood
All cutting of the dead and self
All blood covenant curses
All sacrifices to Molech
All bloodletting or co-mingling of blood
All sacrifices of children
All drinking or tasting of blood
All belief in vampires
All blood bathing
All false weddings
All blood anointing
All ungodly dedications
All blood sprinkling
All bitterness and unforgiveness
All yielding of blood for a substitute
All hard, calloused and blind hearts
All mixing of wine and blood
All murder and innocent bloodshed

I renounce all evil done in my family line. I renounce all sacrifices to and the worship of other gods. I repent for and I renounce all idol worship. I renounce all ungodly armlets, bracelets, charms, rings, earrings, or other tokens.

In the name of Jesus Christ, I ask you, Father, to cleanse my family line and to break all curses, covenants, and oaths from before the beginning of time to the present.

Lord, please break all curses and iniquity from my family line associated with heart and blood disorders. I apply the blood of Jesus over all the iniquity. All evil, I command you to leave, from before the beginning of time to the present, to my children, to my children's children, to thousands of generations.

Renunciation of the Generational Evil Listed in Deuteronomy 28:15-68

In the name of Jesus—
I break off all evil that has come against me from generational iniquity committed in the city and from all curses in the country.

I break all generational iniquity that has come against my provision for a healthy life.

I break off all generational iniquity that has come against my creativity, my ability to produce and reproduce, my need for food and shelter, the work of my hands, and the capital I have invested

I break off all generational iniquity that has come against me and against my family in the areas of travel and transportation.

I repent for any evil we have done in our family line in forsaking the Lord Jesus Christ.

I renounce all generational iniquity that has resulted in confusion. I renounce all generational iniquity that has resulted in rebuke, and I renounce all generational iniquity that has brought destruction and sudden ruin. Father, please remove all confusion, rebuke, destruction, and ruin that has touched my family line and the things we have put our hands to do.

I repent of all generational sin and iniquity that has resulted in my family line being plagued with diseases and that has brought destruction to my family line to prevent us from taking the land the Lord wants us to have.

I renounce all generational iniquity that has brought wasting disease, fever and inflammation, scorching heat and drought, and blight and mildew to plague us until we perish.

I renounce all generational iniquity that has resulted in the sky above us being bronze and the ground beneath us being iron, thus causing our work becomes fruitless toil.

I renounce all generational iniquity that has resulted in the rain upon our country turning into dust and powder. I renounce all generational iniquity that has resulted in the rain coming down from the skies until we are destroyed.

I renounce all generational iniquity that has resulted in defeat before our enemies. I renounce all generational iniquity that has allowed our enemies to come against us from one direction and caused us to flee in seven directions. I renounce all generational iniquity that has caused my family line to become a thing of horror to all the kingdoms of the earth.

I renounce all generational iniquity that would cause our carcasses to become food for all the birds of the air and the beasts of the earth with no one to frighten them away.

I renounce all generational iniquity that resulted in boils like those of Egypt and in tumors, diseases, festering sores, and the itch from which we cannot be cured.

I renounce all generational iniquity that has resulted in the affliction of madness, blindness, and confusion of mind.

I renounce all generational iniquity that has allowed, at midday, the groping about like a blind man in the dark. I renounce all generational iniquity that has resulted in being unsuccessful in everything we do, day after day being oppressed and robbed, with no one to rescue us.

I renounce all generational iniquity that has resulted in times when the woman we were pledged to be married was taken and ravished by another. I renounce all generational iniquity that resulted in building a house without being able to live in it. I renounce all generational iniquity that has resulted in planting a vineyard, but not enjoying its fruit.

I renounce all generational iniquity that resulted in our oxen being slaughtered before our eyes, and not being able to eat any of it. I renounce all generational iniquity that resulted in our donkeys being forcibly taken from us without being returned. I renounce all generational iniquity that resulted in our sheep being given to our enemies, with no one to rescue them.

I renounce all generational iniquity that has resulted in our sons and daughters being given to another nation and the wearing out of our eyes watching for them day after day, powerless to lift a hand.

I renounce all generational iniquity that resulted in people whom we do not know eating what our land produces.

I renounce all generational iniquity that resulted in our ancestors having nothing but cruel oppression all of our days.

I renounce all generational iniquity that caused many seeds to produce little harvest because locusts devoured the crop.

I renounce all generational iniquity that caused my ancestors to plant vineyards and cultivate them, but not to drink the wine or gather the grapes, because worms ate them. I renounce all generational iniquity that resulted in my ancestors not benefiting from their labor.

I renounce all generational iniquity that resulted in the alien, who lived among us, to rise above us higher and higher, and resulted in our sinking lower and lower.

I renounce all generational iniquity that resulted in others lending to me, and my being unable to lend to them; I renounce all generational iniquity that made others the head, and me the tail.

I renounce all generational iniquity in the family line that resulted in others coming upon me to pursue me and overtake me until I was destroyed, because I did not obey the LORD our God and observe the commands and decrees he gave me.

I renounce all generational iniquity that came upon me because my ancestors did not serve the LORD their God joyfully and gladly in the time of prosperity, and as a consequence, they had to serve the enemies the LORD sent against them in hunger and thirst, in nakedness and dire poverty,

I renounce all generational iniquity that resulted in an iron yoke being put on my ancestors' necks until they were destroyed.

I renounce all generational iniquity that came against my ancestors and me causing fearful plagues, harsh and prolonged disasters, and severe and lingering illnesses.

I renounce all generational iniquity that came against my ancestors and me causing all the clinging diseases of Egypt.

I renounce all generational iniquity that came against my ancestors and me to destroy us and all generational iniquity that brought any kind of sickness and disaster that was not recorded by Moses in The Book of the Law.

I renounce all generational iniquity that caused our family not to be as numerous as the stars in the sky but caused us to be few in number, because we did not obey the LORD our God.

I renounce all generational iniquity that came upon my ancestors and has come upon me to ruin and destroy us and to uproot us from the land that we were to possess.

I renounce all generational iniquity that came upon my ancestors and me so that we would be scattered among all nations, from one end of the earth to the other.

I renounce all generational iniquity that came upon my ancestors and me so that we would find no resting place for the soles of our feet.

I renounce all generational iniquity that came upon my ancestors and me so that we would have an anxious mind, eyes weary with longing, and a despairing heart.

I renounce all generational iniquity that came upon my ancestors and me so that we would live in constant suspense, filled with dread both night and day, never sure of our life.

I renounce all generational iniquity that resulted in saying in the morning, "If only it were evening!" and in the evening, "If only it were morning!"— because of the terror that filled our hearts and the sights that our eyes would see.

Prayer to Break Iniquity Associated with Poverty

Father, I come in the Name of Jesus to repent for the sins and transgressions of my ancestors. I repent for all disobedience of Your commands by turning away and listening to the enemy or to other people. Father, I receive redemption from iniquity by the Blood of Jesus and ask you to break off all iniquity of poverty upon my family line and upon me.

Lord, I repent for anyone in my family line who offered sacrifices that were not favorable and right. I repent for any withholding of the first fruits and the best portions; I repent for all wrong motives and attitudes of hearts. I repent for anger, resentment and bloodshed of my brother. Lord, please forgive any bloodshed and bring peace to the blood that cries out.

Lord, please break all Canaanite curses and iniquity against me, as today I declare, I am my brother's keeper! Lord, please restore the ground to me and please restore Your promise of blessings and fruitfulness. Lord, please remove any marks on me and break any curse or iniquity of wandering. Father, please allow my family to come into Your presence again as a chosen covenant people.

I repent for all my ancestors who denied justice to the poor, for all who held on to ill will, and for all who withheld forgiveness to a brother. I repent for shutting my ears to the poor, for exploitation of the poor, and for crushing them in court. I repent for all who did not forgive, but held grudges and became bitter against those who unjustly exploited them or crushed them.

Lord, please break all curses others have spoken against my ancestors or me because of the guilt of our sins and transgressions. Lord, please remove any curses or iniquity that have put up walls of separation between You and me. Hear my prayers again and please open my eyes, ears, and heart.

I repent for any generational dishonesty, even the smallest hidden, accepted, or self-justified dishonesty.

I repent for any of my ancestors who would not forgive debts in the Lord's timing and who ignored the poor. I repent for all hardheartedness, tightfistedness, and unforgiveness. Lord, please restore mercy and cheerful giving in my family line. Please bless me as You promised in Your Word.

Lord, I repent for generational idolatry, for disobedience, and for not following Your commands. I repent for not serving You joyfully and gladly in my time of prosperity.

Lord, please break all curses and iniquity against us that send locusts and worms. Lord, please break all skies of bronze and ground of iron. Please release any captive sons or daughters and stop the destruction. Lord, please remove all iron yokes, all blindness, oppression, and spirits of robbery. Lord, please break any curses or iniquity of hunger, nakedness, dire poverty, and slavery.

Lord, I repent for any of my ancestors who were unfaithful, greedy, disobedient, thieves or liars. I repent for breaking the covenant and coveting or keeping the things of the pagans and not totally destroying them as commanded.

Lord, please break any iniquities that have come on my family for the evil they did, especially the curse of destruction by fire.

I repent for all ancestors who were evil and tried to control and frustrate the poor. Lord I repent for any in my family line who put up security or pledges for another. Lord, please forgive any unfulfilled debts. I break all ungodly covenants, oaths, and alliances. Lord, please remove all traps or snares from the words of my mouth. Please break all sluggish and slumbering spirits from me and restore wisdom and ambition.

I repent for all my ancestors who unduly withheld from others and for all who trusted in riches rather than in God. I repent for all who ignored discipline and correction. I repent for all greed, bribes, and for idle talk and boasting. I repent for inaction, nonperformance, and not keeping my word.

Lord, please break all iniquities of injustice and shunning and please break any walls between me and others and between me and You. Please restore honor to our family.

Lord, I repent for myself and for all my ancestors for being liars, hasty, proud, arrogant, selfish and lovers of the world and its pleasures. I repent for our lack of diligence, oppression of the needy, exploitation, and favoritism. I repent for all rejection of God and any cursing or blasphemy of God.

Lord, I repent for all my family's sluggishness, laziness, neglect, and lack of judgment; I repent for anyone in my family who charged exorbitant interest. I repent for any and all family concealed sins. I repent for spiritual pride in those who would not repent.

I repent for any ancestors who chased fantasies because they were stingy and greedy. I repent for all who did not fight injustice, were unfair, and closed their ears to the cries of the poor and needy.

Lord, please break all poverty curses and iniquities off of me and change my heart.

Lord, I repent for myself and anyone in my family who followed deceptive words and relied on social or religious identity for salvation. I repent for injustice, for oppressing the aliens, widows and the fatherless. I repent for any idolatry, for all ungodly sacrifices and worship, all innocent bloodshed, and for stealing, adultery, perjury and murder for myself and my family line. I repent for all our backsliding, rebellion, disobedience, pride, and spiritual pride. Lord, please break all connections and control that the queen of heaven has on my family and please restore in me wholeheartedness. Please make my heart pure, noble, faithful, and sensitive to You.

Lord, I repent for all generational idolatry and ask You to remove any spirit of prostitution in my heart. I repent for all corruption, guilt, sin, arrogance and unfaithfulness. Lord, I repent for all illegitimacy in my line.

Lord, please set me free from the spiritual enemies of righteous finances: moths, rot, lions, sickness, and sores. Please restore Your covenant as promised.

Lord, I repent for all my ancestors who were boastful and proud of their position, standing, and authority. I renounce all love of sin or iniquity. I repent for myself and for all in my family line who became comfortable, selfish hoarders and trusted in their wealth. I repent for all who sold their righteousness, for all who enslaved others, and for all who trampled the poor. I repent for all who were stingy and controlling of wealth.

Lord, please remove any curse or iniquity that keeps me from enjoying the fruit of my labor. Please break off from me any poverty iniquities that have been passed on through my generational line, from Adam to me. Lord, please break off from me all curses "that there will never be enough." Lord, please restore to me a new purse without any holes. Please break off from me all curses or iniquities of lack, shrinking, theft, loss, blight, mildew, and hail.

Lord, I repent for myself and for all those in my family line for being controlling, deceptive, and for putting ungodly burdens on others. I repent for trying to please man rather than God and for accepting praise, honor, worship, or ungodly authority and titles from men. I renounce all religious spirits, legalistic spirits, self-exaltation and hypocrisy. I repent for myself and my generational line for not entering the door to heaven and for shutting it on others. I repent for being a blind guide, and I ask You, Lord, to break all ungodly oaths, covenants, pledges, dedications, and alliances. I repent for all ungodly and insincere sacrifices or for any sacrifice on an unholy altar. I repent for being unjust, merciless, unfaithful, greedy, and self-indulgent. I repent for harboring sin or wickedness. I repent for myself and my family line for rejecting, mocking, cursing, or killing the prophets and the messengers from God. I renounce any spiritual pride that rebels against repentance, and I apply the blood of Jesus to all the roots of iniquity. I repent for all my ancestors who would not believe or declare that Jesus was Lord.

Lord, please give me the mind of Christ in the matters of finance.

I repent for myself and my ancestors who committed adultery with the queen of Babylon and enjoyed or benefited from her luxuries. Lord, please break all ungodly ties and connections with the queen of Babylon. I repent for myself and for those in my family line who did not come out of the queen of Babylon. Lord, please remove all consequences and plagues that were a result of any alliances with the queen of Babylon. Please remove all plagues of death, mourning, famine, and judgment fire.

Lord, please guide me by Your Spirit and Your word in the godly use of wealth and teach me to be a faithful servant.

Prayer for Renunciation of Generational Druidism

I renounce any and all participation by my ancestors in druidic worship, sacrifices, or rituals.

I renounce any human sacrifice made by my ancestors. I renounce human sacrifice by burning, drowning in wells, or suffocating in cauldrons, or by slitting of throats over a cauldron to catch the blood.

I renounce the Druid animal gods, especially Baco the Boar, Cernunnos the stag-antlered man, and Epona and her horse.

I renounce the false god Dis, god of night.

I renounce looking to the stars to tell the future or for assistance in decision making. I renounce all divination.

I renounce the tossing of valuables into wells as a prayer or offering for any purpose.

I renounce the annual meetings in the territory of the Carnutes.

I renounce allegiance to the high priest of the Druids.

I renounce the control of the peasant people by the Druidic orders. I renounce the slavery of the average person while Druids held power.

I renounce any religious rites involving mistletoe, oak trees, or acorns, or the gathering of these items. I renounce any spirits of oak trees or other plant life.

I renounce all placing of human skulls or bones into buildings for decorative or foundational purposes.

I renounce the Druidic control of the government of the land.

I command all spirits associated with the above to leave me now in the name of Jesus.

Breaking Ungodly Spiritual Ties

Father I renounce all ungodly spiritual ties with my husband [or wife], my children, friends, mother, father, grandparents, brothers, sisters, uncles, aunts, and sexual partners.

I renounce all ungodly spiritual ties with anyone who has had homosexual relationships, with sexual abusers, with pornography, with any person who has engaged in an inappropriate touch, with emotional abusers, physical abusers; with anyone I've had a romantic relationship with and with any object of fantasy.

I renounce all ungodly spiritual ties with pastors, leaders, other Christians, ungodly prophecies, past churches, denominations, false doctrines, ungodly ministries, employers, fellow workers, ungodly intellectuals, teachers, classmates, entertainers, heroes, musicians, ungodly music, political figures, and gangs.

I renounce all ungodly spiritual ties with the dead, inanimate objects, trinkets, charms, idols, jewelry, any material object, false gods, saints, psychics, fortune tellers, occult leaders, mediums, astrologers, spiritualists, new age individuals, martial arts, gurus, mantras, chanting, yoga, fraternities, secret societies, and sororities.

I renounce all ungodly ties with pets, animals, food, books, law enforcement groups, people I have made blood pacts with, military personnel, doctors, nurses, lawyers, acupuncturists, and healers; with buildings, land areas, anyone who anyone who cursed me because of an accident, anyone who was angry, dishonest people, and foolish people.

Replacing Ungodly Elders

I repent for myself and for those in my family line who only took care of themselves and did not lovingly shepherd the Flock of the Lord. I repent for those who ate well and clothed themselves well but did not take care of the flock.

I repent for myself and for those in my family line who did not strengthen the weak or heal the sick, did not bind up the injured, did not bring back the strays or search for the lost and ruled harshly and brutally.

I repent for myself and for those in my family line who caused the sheep to be scattered over all the mountains and on every high hill and over the whole earth and made them vulnerable to wild animals because there was no shepherd. I specifically repent for those who allowed wolves in sheep's clothing to enter and devour the flock.

I repent for myself and for those in my family line who cared more for themselves rather than for the flock of the Lord and who enriched themselves at the expense of the flock.

I repent for myself and for those in my family line who refused or laid down or fled from any calling of God on our life.

I repent for myself and for those in my family line who brought disunity, disorder, disharmony, and wounding to the flock.

I repent for myself and for those in my family line who, through evil practices polluted the flock.

I repent for myself and for those who accepted or taught the doctrine of demons.

I repent for myself and for those in my family who agreed with unrighteous religious authorities.

Lord, I choose to be a leader who is patient and kind. I choose not to be envious. I choose not to boast or to be proud. I will not be rude or self-seeking. I will not be easily angered or keep a record of wrongs. I will not delight in evil but will rejoice in truth. I will always protect, always trust, always hope, and always persevere.

Lord, please unseat all ungodly elders.

Lord, please now invite and seat all the righteous elders assigned to me.

Prayer to Heal ADD

Lord Jesus, I thank You that Your healing power, purchased through the cross of Calvary is available for me today.

I declare that You created my brain for the purpose of bringing glory to Your name. I do not want my brain to be conformed to the patterns of this world, instead I ask for Your transforming power to enter all areas of my brain so that You might give me the ability to process academic and spiritual wisdom from Your Holy Spirit.

I declare that I believe that You created my innermost being and that my brain is fearfully and wonderfully made by Your hand.

Lord, I repent of all the times I have not regarded my brain and my learning abilities as a gift from You. Lord, please forgive me for the negative thoughts and words that I have spoken against my own brain and learning abilities.

I repent of trying to solve my learning problems through my own efforts rather than turning to You first to receive Your love, grace, and healing touch.

I choose to forgive parents, teachers and friends who have not believed in my mental abilities or who have made learning more difficult for me. In the name of Jesus, I now free them from unreasonable expectations I may have placed upon them.

Lord, please remove all generational sin from my family line that may have played a part in the present learning struggles. As a member of my family line I repent for all those who, although they knew You, did not use their brains to glorify You, but engaged in futile and foolish thinking.

Lord, I repent for those in my family line who used their brains to misuse the spiritual gifts that You had provided for them.

In the name of Jesus, I command the neurons in my brain to function properly. I command in Jesus name that the damaged dendrites in my brain be healed. All axons and synapses will respond to the healing touch of Jesus Christ and function the way they were created to work.

In Jesus name, I command my right and left-brain to function normally and in complete balance, and I command that all my academic and creative abilities to flow like a river.

In Jesus name, I command all electrical and chemical frequencies in every cell of my brain to come into harmony and balance.

In Jesus name, I command my Wernicke's area (speech) and Broca's area (understanding of language) to function normally.

In the name of Jesus, I declare that all lack of impulse control and lack of attention to tasks be healed.

In the name of Jesus, I declare that I have a new academic and occupational future. I break, shatter, dissolve, and destroy the lie that says my brain will always remain the same.

In the name of Jesus, I declare that I will not have a spirit of fear about learning new things. I accept Your gift of the spirit of power, love, and self-discipline into my brain.

Lord, please give me the Spirit of wisdom and revelation that I might succeed in school and that I might know you better.

Prayer of Rest

I thank You Lord, that because of Your grace and mercy, You are the giver of good gifts.

I thank You Lord that Your Holy Spirit dispels chaos and fear everywhere He goes.

I ask You Lord, to forgive me for the times in my life that I have purposefully chosen chaos and anxiety rather than asking You to deal with my worries and fears.

I repent for the times in my life when I have not accepted Your rest, but instead have invited stress, disorganization and confusion.

Forgive me, Lord, for anyone I may have hurt by my words and behaviors when I was under stress and swimming in chaos. I ask You to bless those I may have hurt and place them under the shadow of Your wings.

As a member of my family line I repent for all those who used drugs, alcohol or medications to force rest upon their bodies and spirits rather than turning to You.

As a member of my family line I repent for all those who although they knew You, chose pride and selfish ambition over surrender to Your Sabbath rest.

In the name of Jesus I break, shatter, cut-off, dissolve and destroy all ungodly frequency vibrations, lay lines, tubes and mechanisms that have prevented my brain from receiving your rest. Father please tune my brain to Your heartbeat.

Father, in Jesus name please seal all ungodly dimensions and open up the godly dimensions that lead to You and the revelation of Your purposes in my life.

I declare that You give only light burdens. I welcome Your gentle touch upon my life.

In the name of Jesus, I break, shatter, cut-off, dissolve and destroy the behaviors in my life that have prevented me from observing Your Sabbath rest and remembering Your healing touch.

Father, in the name of Jesus, please come into my brain and transform any thoughts that are not pleasing to You. Seal all cracks in my brain that have allowed chaos and fear to enter.

I thank You Lord, and bless Your name because you carry my problems and teach me to depend on You. Teach me about the peace and joy of Your Sabbath rest.

In the name of Jesus, I accept quietness into my heart.

Thank You Lord that You are the God of rest!

Marriage Prayer

As a man and as a husband, I repent for myself and all the men in my family line who abdicated their responsibility for spiritual leadership and surrendered that responsibility to women. As I stand in for those men and for myself, please forgive me.

I right now extend my spiritual covering and headship over you and I say to the enemy that you will back off and not ever touch her again.

As a woman and as a wife, I repent for myself and for all the women in my family, who because of frustration over lack of spiritual leadership and headship, took spiritual matters into their own hands and went into spiritual error. As I stand in for those women, and for myself, please forgive me.

Prayer to Release the Fullness of the Holy Spirit in My Life

In the name of the Lord Jesus Christ and by the power of His blood I choose to remember my Creator before the golden bowl was broken. I renounce and repent for all those in my family line who did not acknowledge you, Father God, as Creator.

I repent for myself and those in my generational line who committed the seven sins in Proverbs 6:16: A proud look, a lying tongue, hands that shed innocent blood, a heart that manufactures wicked thoughts and plans, feet that are swift in running to evil, a false witness, and he who sows discord among his brothers.

I repent for myself and all those in my family line who have entered into rebellion, defiance, apostasy, and who have entered into unholy covenants, divination, and legalism.

I renounce and repent for all ungodly agreements with leadership and of all recognition and acknowledgement of unholy elders in word, thought, or deed for myself and my generational line.

I repent for myself and my ancestors who prayed against the will of God and spoke false prophecies.

I repent for alignment with any counterfeit holy spirit.

I repent for all allegiance to the ungodly world system; I break all connections to the Queen of Heaven in my life and my generational line; I choose to come out of the ungodly world system.

I repent for any apostasy and abomination which honored the Queen of Heaven, including human blood sacrifice on God's holy altar which is on God's holy mountain.

I repent for myself and for those in my generational line who chose to draw life from the Queen of Heaven. Lord, please disconnect any attachment between myself and the Queen of Heaven. Lord, please remove all evil I received from the Queen of Heaven and cleanse me and reconnect me to You so that I might draw life only from You.

Lord, please close all ungodly portals connected with the Queen of Heaven.

I choose to empty the golden bowl of any ungodly contents and I ask You, Lord Jesus, to sanctify and make the bowl holy.

Lord Jesus, please deal with the Queen of Heaven according to Your Word.

Lord, please fill the golden bowl with everything You have for me.

I come into agreement with all that You have for me through the finished work of the cross.

Prayer for Rapid Inner Healing

If any of the following six things have occurred during the pregnancy, the fetus may respond by having parts in other places.

1) Rejection-not being wanted by the mother or the father
2) Rejection from siblings
3) Illegitimacy, conceived out of marriage
4) Mother has great fear from abuse situations, anxiety, and stress
5) Abortion-even just the talk of abortion, or failed attempts at abortion
6) Parents wanting a child of the opposite gender

These things can give the enemy the legal right to send parts of the fetus to ungodly places. If a person describes cold on one side of their body, this can be an indication that parts of them are in different dimensions. You may feel a tingling in your hands or arms, or you may feel cold on your body as you test them to see if parts of them are in the dimensions.

Steps to be taken:
1. Ask the Lord to take the person back to their mother's womb. (wait a few minutes for the Holy Spirit to take them there…for some people it is easy to go there for others it is hard…give them time)

2. Ask them what they feel there. (It is always important to ask open ended questions-never suggesting anything to them-people are very easily suggestible especially during ministry times.) As you are praying with the person, be aware of what you are feeling within your 5 natural senses as well as being aware of what the one receiving ministry is feeling in their 5 natural senses.

3. Pray something like this," Lord, please bless the sperm and the egg as they are joining together. Lord, please bless the zygote and all the multiplication of the cells through the first month., Lord, please remove all evil and all rejection and the roots of rejection."

As you go through each of the following months pause after each sentence and allow time to see how the team is feeling, to assess the evil leaving and to wait on the Holy Spirit to see if He shows anything to anyone. In each section you may feel lots of heaviness or get a picture or a word. Include that in the prayer time.

If the Lord shows anything ask Him 'to remove any of the consequences of *** in the person's life.

Lord, please bless through the second month.
Lord, please bless through the third month.
Lord, please bless through the fourth month.
Lord, please bless through the fifth month.
Lord, please bless through the sixth month.
Lord, please to bless through the seventh month.
Lord, please bless through the eighth month.
Lord, please bless through the ninth month.

If the person was born premature than ask the Lord to complete what did not get finished due to being born early.

When the time has come for them to be born, ask them a few questions:

Do you want to live? Do you want to be born?

If they answer yes, then you move on to the next stage. If the answer is no, then have them ask Jesus if he wanted them to live and to be born. Have them listen to the Holy Spirit as He speaks truth.

After they hear the truth, ask them if they are willing to receive it and if they choose to be born now? When they say "Yes" to life and to being born then you can move onto the next step.

Have them stand up and take their hands and symbolically pull them out of the womb. Have someone behind them to remove the grave clothes. (This can also be done if you are praying over the phone or internet. For instance, you can say, "As God connects us through the Holy Spirit, I'm symbolically pulling you out of the womb. In Jesus' name, I pull off all grave clothes and send them to the feet of Jesus.")

The person may fall to the floor after that. Let them stay there for a while and sense what is going on for them. (Spiritually it may feel like they are in a bottle and it is fizzing-you are feeling what is going on in another dimension.)

Once you sense that the Lord has finished here, then ask the Lord to pick them up as a newborn baby.

Lead the person in praying, "Lord what would you like to say to me?" (have them listen and report what the Lord said)

Have the Lord take them from birth up to their adult life bringing healing to their childhood. As you go through each year give time for the team to discern what is going on and if there needs to be specific work done in any of the years. When it feels really heavy, ask them what happened in that year. Once they remember what happened in that year, lead the person to pray, "Lord I ask You to remove the trauma off of me from that experience."

Lord, please carry me through age 1 and remove all evil.
Lord, please carry me through age 2 and remove all evil.

Repeat this until you get to age 20

Once you reach the age of 20, lead the person in praying something like this:

Lord, please carry me through my adult years.
Cause everything coming off of me to go to your feet to be sent where You want it to go.
Lord, please seal all that has been done here today.
Lord, what is Your word of blessing to me at this time?

Prayer to Release Sleep

Lord, I repent and renounce for myself and my ancestors for all fear, distrust, disobedience, unbelief, hardening of hearts, and rejection of the Gospel resulting in the inability to enter into the rest of the Lord. I repent and renounce for myself and my ancestors for failing to heed God and rest from works as God rested from His works.

I repent and renounce for myself and my ancestors for not being diligent to enter the rest of God and for not drawing near to the throne of grace to receive mercy and forgiveness.

I break, shatter, destroy and smash the curse that I will find no rest and there shall be no resting place for the sole of my foot and that I will have a trembling heart, failing eyes and despair of soul, no assurance of life, be in dread night and day, and long for evening in the morning and morning in the evening.

Forgive me Lord and my generational line for not perceiving when You spoke to us even though You spoke more than once – in dreams and visions during my sleep. Lord, You were trying to withdraw me from my own purposes and pride. Lord, I repent for myself and my generational line, and I ask Your forgiveness and I ask that You would again speak while I sleep and grant me sound sleep.

I renounce all worship of the serpent and believing any lie of the enemy in my generation line. I disconnect myself from the effects of eating from the tree of knowledge of good and evil. I choose now to draw my life from You, the Tree of Life. I repent for grumbling and murmuring instead of thanking You for all the blessings You have given and want to give to me. I ask You, Lord, to heal me and take me into Your perfect rest and time.

I choose to obey the voice of God and not go to the right or to the left, or follow other gods to serve them. I bind myself to God's wisdom, discretion, and understanding, and I commit into Your hands, Lord, all that concerns me, my family, my household, my finances, my life, my whole body, soul and spirit and all that You are doing in my life. I ask You to give me Your deep refreshing and perfect sleep, I ask You, Lord, to cleanse every part of me from opposition from the enemy and bring me into Your place of safety and rest.

I repent for myself and my generational line for not loving our fellow man. I repent for murdering, stealing, and coveting. I choose to walk in the finished work of Christ. I choose to love my neighbor as myself. At this present time, I put aside the deeds of darkness and put on the armor of light, because the night is over and the day is almost here. I put aside orgies, drunkenness, and sexual immorality and debauchery. I choose not to walk in dissension and jealously. I choose not to gratify the desires of the sinful nature. Rather, I clothe myself in Jesus Christ.

Lord, if I am stuck in time, domains, quadrants, or dimensions because of my sin or sin in my generational line, or due to a life event, Lord, please forgive the sin and release me and adjust my time clock and the natural cycles of my body into the correct creative time order. Lord, please move me into the birthright You have written for me. I demand back from the thief a seven-fold return for everything good stolen from me and my generational line.

Lord, I ask You for my birthright and for my inheritance that You have ordained for me. I repent and renounce for deliberately giving away and handing over my birthright and inheritance to the enemy because of not believing that You would fulfill Your word Lord, please close the unrighteous doors that were opened and to open the doors for righteous blessings to come in, and I request 100-fold blessings. Lord, I choose to receive from You the keys to open and to shut. I choose to receive only from You, Lord, the Tree of Life and not from the tree of knowledge of good and evil. I choose to receive the refreshing dew from heaven. I repent and renounce for myself and my family line for not receiving and using the rod of authority and power that You have given in order for You to receive glory. I now choose to receive and thank You for the rod, power, and authority that you have given to me to use for Your glory, Lord. I choose to receive Your words, Your way, Your wisdom and all that I need to go forth in Your name, authority and power.

Prayer of Agreement to Bless the Jews

Lord, I come to You now asking Your forgiveness for anything I have said or done that cursed the Sons of Israel (name specific sins if known). I understand Your righteous decree that You will bless those who bless them, and curse those who curse them. Lord, please break any curses on my family or me that are there because of these sins against the Jews. I plead the blood of Jesus and asked to be cleansed from all sin and unrighteousness. Lord, I submit to Your plan for my life and ministry that will bless the Jews. I also agree with Your plans and purposes for the nation of Israel. Lord, I want to receive Your heart for Your people and the courage to do Your will no matter what the opposition may be. Lord, help me to humble myself and make the Jew first in my prayers and ministry to the lost. Lord, release to me provisions and favor to bless and protect the Jews. Lord, confirm your message in me with signs and an inner witness of the Holy Spirit.

Prayer to Release Us into
Our God Given Spheres of Authority

I am a bondservant of Jesus Christ who will operate only in my God given spheres of authority under the authority of Jesus Christ…

- I repent for not being obedient and for not yielding to and operating in the sphere of authority in which You, Lord, want me to operate.
- I repent for limiting the sphere of authority in which You, Lord, want me to operate.
- I repent for being jealous of other peoples' spheres of authority.
- I repent for being jealous and not partnering when spheres of authority overlap in the body of Christ.
- I repent for not helping and serving others to succeed in their ministries.
- I repent for not valuing other people's spheres of authority.
- I repent for operating in self-proclaimed spheres of authority in which the Lord did not want me to operate.
- I repent for not trusting You, Lord, to be the Head over other spheres of authority.
- I repent for not believing or trusting that You, Lord, can work through another person.
- I repent for not acknowledging that there is a level of revelation that can only come through unity.
- I repent for yielding to the fear of man and not operating in my sphere of authority.
- I repent for allowing others to exploit my sphere of authority and I repent for exploiting others.
- I repent for not recognizing and valuing the other parts of the body of Christ.
- I repent as a leader for anytime I did not release people into their God given sphere of authority.
- I repent for not waiting on God's timing to place me in my sphere of authority.
- I repent for speaking curses and death over other people's spheres of authority and making bitterroot judgments against them.
- I repent for operating in suspicion and judgment rather than the gift of discernment.
- I repent for not following the biblical guidelines for confrontation and correction in love while dealing with others within our spheres of authority.
- I repent for not casting down every thought that exalts itself against You, Lord, and for exalting myself and my giftings above the knowledge of You, God.
- I repent for self-exaltation, esteeming myself over esteeming You, Lord.
- I repent for operating in pride and false humility instead of true humility.
- I repent for bumping out others and not embracing them.
- I repent for rejecting the new and unusual revelations of You, God.

Declarations – Proclamations

- I declare that I will glorify Your name by finishing the work You, Lord, gave me to do in my sphere of authority.
- I declare that in my sphere of authority, I will have love, joy, peace, patience, kindness, humility, mercy, meekness, goodness, faithfulness, gentleness, and self- control.
- I declare that I will live a life worthy of the calling I have received. I declare that I will always be humble and gentle.
- I declare that I will be patient, making allowances for my own and other's faults.
- I declare that I will operate in the grace of God and His power and not in my own strength and understanding.
- I declare that I will be united with others in the Holy Spirit and bound together with others in peace.
- I declare the truth that Jesus Christ has blessed me with every spiritual blessing in the heavenly places in Christ.
- I declare the work Christ has begun in me will be completed.
- I declare that I will be like-minded with Christ.
- I declare that I will intentionally guard against division.
- I declare that I will be united in purpose, and stand in one spirit and one mind with my brothers and sisters in the Lord.
- I declare to the heavens that as far as it is up to me, I will walk in peace and unity with all men.
- I declare that I embrace the spirit of wisdom and revelation in the knowledge of Him so that the eyes of my understanding may be enlightened, that I may know the hope of his calling and what are the riches of the glory of His inheritance in the saints.
- I declare that I will not reject the unusual and the new revelation of God.
- I declare that I will embrace others and not try to bump them out.
- I declare that I will yield my will to the will of God.
- I declare that I desire to have open heavens and visions of God.
- I declare that I will walk in the spirit and not in the flesh.

Prayer of Release from Chronic Physical, Mental, and Spiritual Disorders

Lord, for myself and my generational line, I repent and renounce for coming into agreement with gossip, slander, critical judgment, envy, strife, holding offenses, accusation, and jealousy.

Lord, please forgive me and my generational line for all agreement with gossip, slander, critical judgment, envy, strife, holding offenses, accusation, and jealousy.

Lord, I repent for myself and those in my generational line who came against You by lying, denying You, speaking accusations against You, conceiving and uttering falsehoods from the heart, speaking oppression and revolt, and entering into witchcraft.

Lord, I repent for coming into agreement with any false accusations that have come against me or my family line. Lord, I break and renounce assignments and agreements with any lying spirit and the generational curse resulting from that. I ask Your forgiveness Lord, and I repent on behalf of myself and my forefathers. Lord, please break all generational curses and release Your blessings. I choose to bring my spirit, soul, and body into agreement with the Spirit of Truth.

Lord, please make null and void and cancel any reinforcement of curses and their assignments in their allotted time. Lord, please disconnect me from all ungodly heavenly places. Lord, please now seat me in Your heavenly places.

Lord, I repent and ask forgiveness for operating in an independent spirit when I came into agreement with gossip, slander, accusation and walked away from You and the Body of Christ, causing disunity and isolation in the Body of Christ. Today, I choose by Your mercy to be reconciled and to be restored into the unity of Your Body.

Lord, I repent for coming into agreement with slander that has been spoken against me. I repent for receiving offenses and for not blessing my enemy.

Lord, I ask that I not conceive trouble. Please destroy the viper and spider eggs that have been placed into me: slander, hatred, self-rejection and gossip. May no adders or spiders be allowed to come forth from this generation forward.

Lord, please remove all cobwebs of false clothing and nesting places that may be covering my body. Lord, please also remove the cobwebs of false identity from my body and soul and remove all deception that clouds my perception of my true identity. And where my past generations and I have allowed the enemy to weave within me a web of false identity, coming into agreement with this illness as who I am, forgive me for gaining my identity from diseases and not from You. Release me, for You wove me in my mother's womb, and I agree that I am fearfully and wonderfully made. Lord, give me Your revelation of my true identity in Christ, which I now receive.

Lord, please completely restore my ability to receive all that I need from You including healing, revelation, and restoration of my spirit, soul, and body.

Lord, I forgive the Body of Christ for reacting in judgment and rejection against those who are being wounded by witchcraft and curses that are being empowered and reinforced over time. Lord, forgive me for making bitter root judgments against those who have harmed me in any way. I forgive the Body of Christ for not accepting, understanding, and protecting me.

Lord, I choose to forgive those who have rejected me and in doing so have further empowered the curses already against me.

I repent for not seeking Your strength, Lord when striving to resist the enemy's assault on my mind. I repent for accepting feeling of helplessness. Lord, please renew my mind so that I can have Your mind, and know that I can take every thought captive to the Lord Jesus Christ. Help me to know and understand that You are my sure defense, and that I am safe in the shelter of Your wings.

Lord, please raise up a standard based upon Ephesians 4:31 and remove all effects of bitterness, rage, anger, brawling, and slander along with every form of malice. Lord, break off all generational curses, the reinforcement of curses in their allotted times in all heavenly places, and all spiritual, mental, and physical retribution. Lord, please protect those who repent and turn from their generational sin, witchcraft, and idolatry.

Lord, please realign me with Your purpose and heal the receptors of the cells that make up my being so my divine calling and birthright will be fulfilled.

I receive the promise that I am no longer a prey of the enemy. You are my good Shepherd. You feed me, and I receive your covenant of peace that I may dwell safely. I choose to be a blessing around your holy hill and receive the showers of blessings You promise in season that there would be fruitfulness and increase in my life. I know that the bands of the yoke are broken, and I am delivered from the hands and words of those who have made me a prey. I know that I belong to You, and You are with me. I embrace my restoration within the Body of Christ and the restoration of receptor sites of my own body.

Lord, thank you for considering my cause and my affliction and for delivering me and my generational line. Lord, thank You for pleading my cause through the generations and reviving me and my family line according to Your Word. Lord, I hold on to Your promise that, as I trust in You, I am like Mt. Zion which cannot be moved, but abides forever. I thank You, Lord, for delivering me and my family generations—past, present, and future. Thank You for redeeming me and reviving me and my family line according to Your Word. For as the mountains surround Jerusalem, so You, Lord, surround me and my family generations— past, present, and future from this time forth and forever.

Thank You, Lord, that the scepter of wickedness shall not rest on the land allotted to the righteous, because the entirety of Your Word is Truth; and every one of Your righteous judgments endures forever. Lord, thank You for restoring the Scepter of Righteousness.

Lord, please forgive me and my generational line for closing the doors of Your anointing and blessing. Lord, please now bless me and open the doors of Your anointing and blessing; and release the generational blessings, gifts, callings, and goodness that you have for me and my family line.

Prayer to Release Me into the
Fullness of Intimacy with the Lord

Lord, I repent for and renounce the sin of transgressing Your will and command by partaking of the tree of the knowledge of good and evil.

I repent for disobedience to Your known will, which stopped me from being fruitful, filling the earth and subduing it and having dominion as You intended. I repent for surrendering the authority You gave to me.

I repent for the lust of my eyes, the lust of my flesh, and the boastful pride of life. I repent for the desire to make myself wise and for taking the fruit of the tree of knowledge of good and evil.

I renounce and repent for allowing my senses to be perverted by the deception of the enemy. Lord, I repent for surrendering my senses by seeing, hearing, tasting, touching, and smelling the fruit from the tree of the knowledge of good and evil.

I repent for believing that You were withholding good from me. I repent for believing the enemy's lie about Your character. I repent for not trusting in Your love and forgiveness by not submitting to You.

I repent for fear and for separating myself from You by hiding and covering up my transgressions against You.

I repent for feasting on human knowledge rather than on Your life.

I repent for a rebellious spirit against Your command to not eat of the fruit of the tree of the knowledge of good and evil.

I repent for listening to another voice and not trusting the voice of the Lord.

I repent for trading God's truth for a lie.

I repent for taking and accepting any seed of doubt from the enemy; and I ask You, Lord, to crush any seeds of doubt, to destroy any growth from them, and to now replace all doubt with the implanted Word of God.

I repent for seeking to be like You, God, and for trying to steal Your Glory.

I repent for and renounce abdicating responsibility and blaming others, hiding and covering up my sin.

I repent for rejecting my inheritance as a son of God.

I repent for listening to the voice of the enemy, for embracing the wisdom of man and for believing, agreeing with, and embracing the enemy's lies.

I repent for the sin of independence from God in seeking wisdom apart from God.

I repent for the sin of covetousness.

I repent for the sin of independence from God in my responsibilities in relationships.

I repent for the sin of independence from God in my responsibility as a caretaker of creation.

I repent for choosing independence from God in the exaltation of my own knowledge, wisdom, and understanding above and apart from the life of God.

I repent for myself and all those in my family line who allowed Satan to cheat us through philosophy and empty deceit; and allowed Satan to capture or influence our thinking according to the traditions of men and the basic principles of the world.

I repent for acting like an expert in the law and taking away the key of the knowledge of God, and shutting out the Kingdom of Heaven from men.

I repent for not entering into the Kingdom of Heaven and for hindering others from entering into the Kingdom of Heaven.

I renounce the sin of boasting great things and of allowing my tongue to curse and not bless. I repent for gossip, backbiting, malice, slander, lies, and all evil speaking. I repent for judging others. I repent for using my tongue to set on fire the course of nature.

I repent for trying to walk in the world and in the Kingdom of God at the same time.

I repent for allowing others to defraud me of the prize of my full calling and inheritance in Christ. Lord, I repent for not holding fast to You as the Head of Your Body, the church.

I repent for agreeing with the doctrines of men in legalism and asceticism, and not walking in the fullness of life.

I repent for myself and all those in my family line who chose to serve other gods and broke all covenants with You.

Father, I ask for the sevenfold Spirit of the Lord. I ask for the release of the Spirit of the Lord, the Spirit of Wisdom, the Spirit of Understanding, the Spirit of Counsel and the Spirit of Strength, the Spirit of Knowledge and the Spirit of the Fear of the Lord.

Lord, I declare that You are the Way. You are the Life. You are the brilliance of the Light that shines and pierces through the darkness. You are the Door and the Center of all. You are the Key.

I declare, in the name of Jesus, that I will rise up and take my place. I declare my authority in Christ. I declare that no one can come against me. I will fight and prevail. I declare I am the head and not the tail.

I declare that the enemy is crushed beneath my heel, and I am seated with Christ at the right hand of the Father.

Grant me according to the riches of Your glory to be strengthened with might through Your Spirit in my inner man.

I take my place and authority, the place and authority that You have given me in Christ, and I choose this day to stand firm and be strong so that no one can come against me.

Lord, in all my relationships, please restore male and female partnership according to Your perfect design.

Lord, please cleanse my senses from all defilement and enhance them for the glory of God.

Lord, please restore my relationship with You; make it like Adam's relationship was in the Garden before the Fall so that I can enter into the intimacy with You that You have always intended for me to have with You.

I declare that in You dwells the fullness of Deity and in You, I have been made complete. You are the Head over all rule and authority.

Lord, please restore the wisdom of the fear of the Lord.

I declare that I will hear You above all other voices.

I declare that I will acknowledge You in all my ways.

Lord, please remove from me all curses in Deuteronomy 28; Lord remove Your anger against the land. Lord, please heal the land.

I declare that the secret things belong to You, Lord, my God, and that You will reveal what You want to reveal to me and to my sons and daughters forever.

I choose to be circumcised, buried with Jesus in baptism and raised with Him through faith in the working of God, who raised Him from the dead. Lord, I choose to be encouraged; I choose for my heart to be knit together with others, in Christ through love, attaining full assurance and understanding in the knowledge and mystery of God, and of the Father and of Christ in whom are hidden all the treasures of wisdom and knowledge. I choose to make every effort to keep the unity of the Spirit through the bond of peace.

I declare that I will know You, Jesus, as the Son of God who has come to give me understanding so that I may know You. I declare that You are true and that I am in You.

Lord, please bring me into oneness with You and with the Father, even as You are one in the Father.

Prayer to Release Us into Financial Freedom

I repent that I have not treated and valued the Kingdom of Heaven as I should and that I have exchanged the value of the Kingdom of Heaven for the desires of my heart in the form of an earthly Kingdom. Lord, I repent for worrying about life, food, and clothing. I repent for laying up treasures on earth where moths and rust destroy and where thieves break in and steal. I repent for robbing You, Lord, and not freely and cheerfully giving my offerings to You out of a heart of love.

Lord, I repent for loving money, for serving Mammon, for greed and for covetousness.

I repent of the belief that money is the answer to everything in my life. I repent of expecting money to be my answer and my friend. I repent for forsaking You as my life source and for focusing my eyes on the pursuit of wealth to my own harm and the harm of others. I repent for choosing to serve Mammon in preference to You and thereby filling my life with darkness. On behalf of my ancestors and myself, I renounce every agreement made with Mammon by using money in ungodly ways and for ungodly purposes. I repent for being double-minded with money and unstable in all of my ways. I choose to hate Mammon and to love you, Lord, with my whole heart. I choose to place my treasure where my heart is, in the Kingdom of Heaven, for You to use as You choose.

I repent for making money my defender, security, and protection.

I repent for believing that chants, spells, fate, superstition, and luck will provide the money I need.

I repent for myself and my family line for using diverse weights and measures and not paying employees their due. I repent for making money, not You, Lord, the center of the universe.

I repent for pride, gaining wealth by dishonest means, and vain striving for silver and gold. I repent for myself and my family line for not exercising my responsibility to pay money that was owed to governmental agencies. I repent for defrauding, cheating, lying, and stealing from the government. I also repent for a begrudging and bitter attitude in paying my taxes. I repent for not recognizing Your anointing on government to provide for the basic necessities of our corporate life. I repent for criticizing, complaining, and cursing my government for not providing enough for the people.

I repent for myself and my generational line for seeking, accepting, treasuring, profiting from, and spending blood money. I also repent for adding blood money to my children's inheritance. On behalf of my ancestors, I choose to forgive those financial institutions that have foreclosed on mortgages and stolen property which rightfully belonged to me and my descendants as an inheritance.

I repent across my generational line for abandoning and sacrificing family and relationships, land, culture, and even faith in God to seek gold and earthly treasures. I choose to seek after the ultimate treasure of my Lord Jesus Christ with all my heart.

I repent on behalf of myself and my ancestors for believing in a poverty mindset and for being stingy with the body of Christ. I declare that Jesus came to give us abundant life. Father, in your mercy, please free me and my future generations of the consequences of this. I repent and confess the lie that godliness implies poverty, lacking in basic necessities, living in poverty, always being in need, and that the children will never procure their education. I choose to believe and accept that God will supply all of my needs, that there will be an inheritance for a thousand generations, that my descendants will not have to beg for food, and that all my needs will be met.

I repent for being disconnected from the River of Life of God's endless supply. I choose to be connected to the River of Life where God will grant me the ability to acquire wealth for His Kingdom. I repent for spending money on that which does not satisfy and for not coming to God's living waters to drink.

I repent for myself and my generational line for hardening my heart and shutting my hand against my poorer brothers in their need. I repent for not feeding the poor or taking care of the widows and orphans. I repent of holding back my possessions and services to get higher prices from those in need. I declare that I will open my hand and heart to the poor, sharing my resources as You lead, so no one will lack, Your power will not be hindered and Your grace will remain. I repent for not bringing unity in the body of Christ. I choose to not hold back from the needy. Jesus, please break the curses and evil that have come against me and my generational line for demanding unfair prices from the needy. Lord please release Your blessings and grace on my selling and trading, especially to those in need.

I repent for myself and my family line for not receiving the inheritance that You had for us; and I choose now to receive the inheritance, abundance, and gifts that You have for us. I ask that they will come in such abundance that we will be able to leave an inheritance for our children and grandchildren.

Lord, please disconnect my ancestors, me, and my descendants from money that was tied to freemasonry, secret societies, secret agendas, covert operations, ungodly funding of churches and institutions and from money tied to the building of ungodly altars and funding prostitutes.

Lord, break off the curse of sowing much and bringing in little, of eating and not having enough, and of earning wages only to put them into a bag with holes.

Lord, please destroy the connectors and cleanse the ley lines attached to earthly treasures.

Lord, connect me to You alone. I choose not to hold on to anything but You. I give everything I have to You.

I repent for myself and my family line for the belief that the gifts of the Holy Spirit could be purchased or sold. I break the curse that the money in my generational line and in my life will perish with me. I repent for my wickedness and my generational wickedness and ask that my heart be restored into a right relationship with You.

Lord, I repent for making my giving an obligation to You and not a free act of my love. Lord remove the canopy of law and the canopy and yoke of obligation from me. Lord, allow me to live in your grace and your provision.

I ask You, Holy Spirit, to be the One who directs me in what to give. Lord, make my giving come from an attitude of gratitude and love. I choose to seek and follow Your guidance in my giving.

Lord, I repent for not trusting You and not trusting You to provide.

On behalf of my ancestors and myself and for future generations, I choose to forgive those who have swindled me, especially banks, financial institutions and government agencies; I forgive those who have charged me and my ancestors usurious interest, and who have tried to keep us in poverty and have disinherited our children.

I declare that I will be content in You and in my wages in whatever financial state I am in.

Lord, thank You for giving me the creativity to produce wealth in seed. Holy Spirit, teach me what to sow, what to reap, and what to harvest for your purpose.

I declare that I will eat of the bread of life and delight in your abundance.

I declare that I am one of many members of the body of Christ in whom are all the hidden treasures of wisdom and knowledge.

Lord, please release into me the blessing and joy of giving freely in accordance with Your will for my life.

Lord, help me to see money with spiritual eyes, knowing it is Your resource and belongs to You. Lord, please release the treasures that the enemy has stolen from me and my family line.

I declare that your Word says: You will go before us and make the crooked places straight; I will break in pieces the gates of bronze and cut the bars of iron; You will give us the treasures of darkness and hidden riches of secret places; You are the One who gives power to get wealth that You may establish Your covenant which You swore to our fathers, as it is this day; The blessing of the Lord makes one rich, and You add no sorrow with it; The generous soul will be made rich, and he who waters will also be watered himself. Thank You for enabling me to leave an inheritance to my children's children. Lord, please give me a circumcised heart, so You can release Your treasure from heaven.

Prayer to Break Hard Heartedness

Father, I come to You in the Name of Jesus Christ and I repent for myself and all of my ancestors who hardened their hearts to You. They rebelled and stubbornly turned away and did not listen to Your Word, Your Spirit or Your prophets. I repent for all generational hardheartedness, calloused hearts, blind hearts, resentment, blasphemy, bitterness and all unforgiveness. Lord, please break the curse of ignorance, all futile thinking, all darkened understanding and any lost sensitivity to Your Holy Spirit. I repent for all my ancestors who gave themselves over to sensuality and impurity with a continual lust for more.

Lord, I repent for all that trusted in works rather than faith and Your grace. I repent for any rebellion, disobedience, doubt and unbelief, betrayal, hatred of others, following deceptions and false prophets.

I repent for wickedness, being lukewarm, love gone cold and oppression of the weak and poor. I ask You to break the curses and uproot the iniquity in my family line that has caused spirits of stupor, blind eyes, deaf ears, deceptions, snares, traps, stumbling blocks, retribution for evil and all bent backs. I repent for all stubborn and evil inclinations of our hearts that cause us to go backwards.

Lord, please sprinkle clean water on my entire generational line and cleanse us from our impurities, idols and uncleanness. Please remove our hearts of stone and give us new hearts of flesh and a new spirit that moves us to follow and keep Your laws. Lord, please now listen to my plea and restore in us a heart after Your heart, a heart that administers true justice, mercy, love and compassion instead of unfeeling sacrifice. Lord, I ask for a restoration of the covenant in our family line. Please restore all birthrights, inheritances, blessings, lands, provision, protection and the relationship and intimacy with You. Lord restore in us the belief that with God nothing is impossible. Revive our faith in miracles and the fact that Your supernatural things are for me. Help us to stand firm until the end and let our wholehearted devotion to You bring honor, praise, thanksgiving and glory to Your Name.

I repent for all my ancestors that were grudging, grumblers, hardhearted, tightfisted and harbored evil thoughts towards the poor. I repent for all generational love of money, greed, self-reliance, bitter envy, selfish ambition, pride, arrogance and denial of the truth. I repent for all generational doubt and unbelief that replaced love, trust and reliance on You. I repent for those that built their house on sand and did not put Your words into practice.

Lord, please restore feeling in our hearts so we would give and lend cheerfully, willingly, generously and thankfully. Lord, I ask today for godliness with contentment and a thankful attitude for my daily bread. I ask for humility and Your wisdom from above which You give generously. I ask for fire, passion and a burning heart that would move me into action for the things of God. Lord please restore in us a trust and a love of Your Word. Bring it alive and activate it in our hearts so it would once again penetrate, divide and judge the attitudes of our hearts. I ask for another chance for my family, that we would build a new foundation on the cornerstone, Jesus Christ. I ask for the restoration of our hearts, so we have the ability to love God with all our heart, soul, mind and strength. I ask for a broken, contrite, pure and noble heart. Help us consider it pure joy when we face trials, knowing that they develop perseverance which brings completeness and maturity.

Lord, I apply the Blood of Jesus to wash away all the bitter roots of iniquity in my family line. Father, forgive us for all this wickedness and iniquity. Lord please remove all generational reproach, blame, shame, guilt, scorn, disgrace and dishonor. Today I make a choice to forgive myself.

Prayer to Establish Us as Living Stones

Father, in the name of Jesus, I come before Your throne. I repent for being so stuck and focused on the past that I have been unable to see Your calling for me.
I repent for not rightly discerning Your presence.
I repent for not acknowledging Your presence when you have acknowledged mine.
I repent for asking you for things that You have already done and are doing.
Lord, I repent for not using my keys to unlock the mysteries of the Kingdom of Heaven.
Father, I repent for looking to man for wisdom, knowledge, understanding, and counsel, and for looking into my flesh for might, strength, and ability. Forgive me for being arrogant, disrespectful, and for not honoring Your Spirit even as it comes forth through others. As You forgive me, Lord, please restore the reverential and obedient fear of the mighty God.

Lord, I want to repent for myself and for anyone in my past generations who spoke harshly against Your body and the brethren. Lord, I repent for coming into agreement with anybody who spoke against the body of Christ. Lord, I choose now to bless Your entire body and to speak health and wholeness to those things I don't understand of Your body.

Jesus, I repent for agreement with the spirit of slavery, for choosing to be subject to the law and for not choosing to be free as a son and daughter. I choose to birth forth the promises of God and His inheritance in me. I declare that this is the set time of the Lord, and I will be realigned with the New Jerusalem.

Lord, I repent for grasping onto the world instead of You. Lord, I repent for getting caught up in generational addictions rather than in Your generational blessings. I ask You for Your forgiveness and Your redemption for the rest of my days.

Father, I repent for myself and my generational line for often being people pleasers rather than God pleasers. I declare for me and my household, that today, right now, we are stepping over the line to serve You. From this day forth, I am, and I will continue to be a God-pleaser rather than a man pleaser.

Lord, please forgive me for not trusting You. Lord, I ask You to untangle my feet. Lord, please forgive me for not being able to jump over the fences of offenses. I ask that You continue to show us our inheritance so that we can receive all that You have already given.

I choose to repent for and to forgive all of those in my family line who were involved in Satanism and corporate mind control in efforts to pervert and abort God's plans and promises.

Father, I forgive all offenses of those who have traumatized me and my past generations. I thank You for cleansing all pathways and ungodly heavenly places so that I can be seated with Christ in heavenly places.

I thank You for redeeming me from my past. The past is not my identity. I leave the past at Your feet and choose to pursue the calling and inheritance You have for me.

I choose now to take the key of faith to unlock my inheritance so that I may step forward into my birthright, my calling, and my anointing. I choose to be a restorer of all things.

I want to have faith like Abraham who searched diligently for the city whose builder and maker is God. Help me fix my eyes on Your purpose, Your will, and Your plan for me.

I thank You that You have made me Your son.

Lord, please disconnect me from the things of the earth and remove the sin and the snares that so easily entangle and hinder me from running the race marked before me.

Father, please establish Your glory on me and be my rear guard. Lord, please establish Your plumb line between my inner man and Your throne.

Lord, I remember Your body that was broken for me and Your blood that was shed for me. I accept the sacrifice that You gave for me on the cross.

Lord, please remove all contamination on the elemental spirits. I recognize that this contamination has come from the human traditions and the basic principles of the world rather than from Christ.

Lord, please realign my spirit, soul, and body to Your plumb line.

Lord, as You created Adam from the dust of the earth and breathed into him Your breath of life, so breathe on the elements of my life.

I choose to die to myself and die to the world and to lay down my life as a living sacrifice.

I declare that my heart will be encouraged and knit together in love with other believers and that my heart will attain all wealth that comes from the full assurance of understanding that results in the true knowledge of God's mystery, which is Christ Himself.

I declare that I am a living stone and will operate in unity with the body of Christ.

Prayer to Release Me into My God Given Influence

I choose to forgive those who have come against my spiritual authority and influence. I forgive those who declared that I was not operating in the Spirit because they wanted to restrict me to a dimension of their understanding in the natural realm. I forgive them for coming against the influence that You chose for me to have.

I choose to forgive those who have suppressed women and children and limited their potential for growth. I forgive those who have silenced women and children and placed barriers over women and children that have hindered them from coming into their birthright. Lord, forgive me and my ancestors for suppressing, limiting, silencing, and hindering women and children from their birthright.

I repent for myself and for those in my generational line who have limited authority to those who express themselves logically and have shut out those who express themselves emotionally, intuitively, and through their spiritual giftings.

I ask now, Jesus, that You bring my wheel of influence into proper balance, put the spokes back into place, repair the rim, and repair all the dings and damage. Lord, please remove all influence of ungodly elders.

Lord, please put the hub in the right place and center it in Jesus Christ. I am choosing to be in the center of Jesus' will and only have the influence that Jesus wants me to have. Lord, please remove any evil attack against the wheel, and align the wheel to Your kingdom purposes.

Lord, please place the anointing that You want me to have on the hub. Lord, please destroy any birds, especially ravens, that would seek to attack this wheel and the influence You want me to have.

Lord, please bring the speed of the wheel back into balance.

Lord, please bring the wheel back into right alignment within the dimensions and within time. I demand that Kronos get off my wheel. Lord, please release Your power on this wheel.

Lord, may the wheel only operate under Your power, not mine or the enemy's. I draw strength only from You. I choose to have my influence totally guided by You and affected by You. If, Lord, in any way, the wheel is out of control or other people are trying to control my wheel, Lord, please break that off. I declare again that my godly influence will only be affected by You. I demand all man-fearing spirits to leave, all co-dependency to leave, all manipulation to leave and all control to leave.

Cellular Memory Prayer

Father God, I have been hindered from appropriating the fullness of my inheritance in the Kingdom that You sent your Son, Jesus, to die for and purchase for me. Lord, I ask that Your Holy Spirit would be released in and through me now to reverse this state and condition so that I may fully experience every one of the benefits of my salvation.

Now, with the authority and power I have been given as a priest of the Most High God, through the blood purchased work of Jesus Christ of Nazareth, I command my spirit, soul, and body to be activated and empowered by the Holy Spirit so as to cast down and remove all unholy strongholds, all ungodly encoded and consolidated memories, fears, images, idols, doubt and unbelief, resulting from subconscious post-traumatic stress, anywhere that they are latently affecting me in the cells of my body.

I also command that I be physically and spiritually cleansed in my spirit, soul, and body from every work of the flesh that has at any time manifested in me, through me or towards me, in my lifetime or through any former generation, including all: immorality, impurity, sensuality, idolatry, sorcery, enmity, strife, jealousy, outbursts of anger, disputes, dissensions, factions, deception, malice, envy, drunkenness, carousing, adultery, fornication, uncleanness, lasciviousness, witchcraft, hatred, violence, ambitious rivalry, wrath, strife, sedition, heresy, murder, reviling, sensuality, double-mindedness, impatience, lovelessness, bickering, lying, wicked imaginations, false witness, sowings of discord, mischief, uncleanness, hypocrisy, stubbornness, rebellion, hardness of heart, foolishness, injustice, despising, shame, impatience, lust, grief, fear, control, corruption, reprobation, pride, selfishness, manipulation, affliction, confusion, disobedience, chaos, rejection, bruising, seduction, enticement, abandonment, captivities, disease, vain glory, provocation, gossip, demonic wisdom, fornication, doubt, denial, judgment, unforgiveness, unholy vows and oaths, witchcraft, curses and any other sin or work of the flesh that came against me from others or from myself toward others.

I command my body to purge me from all accumulated metabolic waste, pollution, byproducts of improper chronic stress responses, and resulting toxins in the cells of my body. I also command that all resonant frequencies, oscillations, including their amplitudes and phases and all spectrums, polarities, electromagnetic fields, and harmonics at a cellular level be brought into their intended godly order.

I command my immune system and all biological and chemical systems in my body to return to their optimum state of full health so that my body is in a completely balanced state of homeostasis (*healthy function*) according to the Lord Jesus Christ's originally designed intention and purpose.

I command each of my body systems to apprehend their full healing and be submitted and yielded to the finished work of Jesus Christ, the slain Lamb of God. I command my body to be in perfect union, harmony and accord with the Voice of His blood, the power of His resurrection, the purity of His Love and the truth of His Living Word. May my body now be fully illuminated with the Light of my Savior the Lord Jesus Christ and be brought into the full knowledge and understanding of the power of an endless Life. I decree that my spirit, soul, and body be in full covenantal agreement with the Lord's intended mercy and goodness toward me through salvation. I now command my soul to not forget any of the Lord's benefits so that every cell of my body, especially my mind, will and emotions can testify and declare:

Bless the LORD, O my soul;
And all that is within me, bless His holy name.
Who pardons all my iniquities;
Who heals all my diseases;
Who redeems my life from the pit;
Who crowns me with loving kindness and compassion;
Who satisfies my years with good things,
So that my youth is renewed like the eagle.
The LORD performs righteous deeds,
And judgments for my oppression.
The LORD is compassionate and gracious,
Slow to anger and abounding in loving kindness to me.
He has not dealt with me according to my sins,
Nor rewarded me according to my iniquities.
For as high as the heavens are above the earth,
So great is His loving kindness toward me, who fears Him.
As far as the east is from the west,
So far has He removed my transgressions from me.
Just as a father has compassion on his children,
So the LORD has compassion on me
For He Himself knows my frame;
He is mindful that I am but dust.

Lord Jesus, I now willingly yield my body, soul and spirit, especially my heart and mind, to the knowledge of the truth that God's love for me includes my manifesting every fruit of the Spirit, which are love, joy, peace, long-suffering, gentleness, goodness, and faith so that I may prosper and be in health even as my soul prospers.

I choose this day to yield to the indwelling Holy Spirit and put on as the elect of God, holy and beloved, the armor of light, bowels of mercies, kindness, humility, meekness, long-suffering; forbearance, righteousness, godliness, thankfulness, faith, patience, meekness and forgiveness. I choose to believe that Christ has given me a new mind and a new heart, so that I may live from a pure heart, a good conscience and a sincere faith. I also choose to apply and increase in all diligence, faith, moral excellence, knowledge, self-control, perseverance, godliness, and brotherly kindness, so that I am neither useless nor unfruitful in the true knowledge of my Lord Jesus Christ.

Above all these things Lord, I put on love, which is the bond of perfection. Now, let the peace of God rule in my heart so that Christ may dwell in my heart by faith so that I may be rooted and grounded in Your love and be filled with all the fullness of God. May the God of peace sanctify me wholly as I draw near to You, Lord, with a true heart, in full assurance of faith. May my heart be continually conscious that it has been sprinkled from an evil conscience by the blood of the Lamb and may my whole spirit, soul and body be preserved blameless unto the coming of my Savior, the Lord Jesus Christ.
I thank You, Lord, that You bless me, and keep me; You make Your face to shine upon me, and are gracious to me. You lift up Your countenance upon me, and You give me peace. You put Your name upon me and bless me.

I now seal this work in the precious name of my Lord Jesus Christ, Son of The Most High God and I thank you, Lord, that you have heard my prayer and that you will reward my diligence in seeking you.

Prayer for those who Were Involved in Transcendental Meditation

Lord, God, please forgive me, and I repent for and renounce any and all of my participation and involvement in The Transcendental Meditation / Sidhi Program whether I knew or did not know what I was getting myself into.

I renounce and repent for the following evils:

- The giving of my time and money and talent towards this movement.
- Being used as a spokesperson for this movement, encouraging and causing others to be snared into a movement designed to usher in the Age of Enlightenment, the Anti-Christ, his one-world religion, one-world government and one-world monetary system.
- Grieving the Holy Spirit.
- Engaging in the Hindu religion's false belief system.
- Participating in the Puja ceremony, and allowing myself to become involved in it, including bowing down to all gods invoked.
- Calling countless times on my personal mantra, a Hindu deity and for obtaining any blessings from this familiar spirit.
- Being present and bowing down to all evil the TM teacher invoked, including;
- The Hindu trinity, the Lord Narayana, Brahma, the false creator, and Vashista.
- Agreeing with the TM teacher's request that the Hindu Trinity enter my heart.
- Worshiping Vashistha, Shakti , Parashar, Vyasa, Shukadeva, Gaudapada, Govinda and to his disciple, Shri Shankaracharya, Padma-Pada, Hasta-Malaka, Trotakacharya, and Vartika-kara, the teacher of Karma.
- Believing the traditions of the masters, the wisdom and the ultimate evil authorities, the Shrutis, the Smritis, the Pranas, Shankara, Shakarya, Badarayana, Brahmanada, and Indra
- Worshiping of Soma, Shiva, Kali, Ganesh, Lakashimi, and Krishna, Guru Dev, and Vendanta

I renounce and repent for all participation in the following techniques:
- Japa, the repeating of a mantra;
- The checking procedure, hypnotism, and all of the reinforcement of evil planted, especially during the post-trance state of mind;
- Any faith in karma and its laws of enforcement;
- Tm-sidhi "age of enlightenment" techniques, described in Patanjalis' Sutras according to the Dharan Tradition;
- The nineteen sutras I practiced to develop supernormal abilities: friendliness, compassion, happiness, strength of an Elephant, bronchial tube, inner light, sun, moon, polestar, trachea, navel, the distinction between intellect and transcendence, intuition, transcendence finest hearing, transcendence finest sight, transcendence finest taste, transcendence finest touch, transcendence finest smell, and the levitation/flying technique, the relationship of body and Akasha and the lightness of cotton fiber;
- The laws of Manu;
- The practice of Soma Veda to gain supernatural powers from Indra;

- The reading of the Mandala;
- Listening to Hindu monks chant;
- Receiving the title "citizen of the age of enlightenment" and accepting the card with a crown on my head;
- Yogic asanas, holding a certain body position that leaves the body open
- to demons;
- Pranayama, breathing exercises designed to clear a channel in my body for soma to enter;
- Reading of the 9th and 10th Mandal, which resulted in inviting gods to feast on the soma in my stomach;
- Any bond between me and the ancient Aryan cultures;
- The watering of the Tree of Wisdom in the garden and its branches of knowledge;
- The attunement of myself and my mind to any energy or wisdom from Satan.

I repent for opening my intellect to create divine unity with myself and Satan. I repent for believing and proclaiming that by practicing the techniques I learned from the TM and TM Sidhi Programs, that I would attain a gift of Supreme Knowledge and that Supreme Knowledge would fulfill my life.

Lord, please break all links, chains, bonds, and any connection between me and all TM teachers and the TM movement.

Lord, God, please break any lines connecting me to the generational lines of the ancient tradition and the masters of antiquity.

Lord, please heal my mind from being put on the field of the Absolute.

Lord, please free me from the counterfeit harmony of my thoughts, speech, and action or my ego, intellect, mind, and senses.

Lord, please take from me any gifts, anointing, knowledge, and powers gained by my involvement in the TM-SIDHI program.

Prayer to Release Evangelistic Healing

Heavenly Father, I lift up the land. I lift up myself as a keeper and tiller of the land. I lift up myself as an employee and an employer. Forgive me, Father, forgive me for not giving the land a Sabbath rest. Forgive me for not giving myself a Sabbath rest. Forgive me for not giving our employees a Sabbath rest. Forgive me, because in disobeying your commands to rest I have rejected your holy principles and ordinances. I have turned away and gone my own way. I have done what is right in my own eyes. Forgive me for unrighteousness and turn me so that I will be turned back to you. Lord, break off all consequences on me and upon the land from any curses related to not taking a Sabbath rest and not giving the land rest.

Heavenly Father, forgive me for not entering into the rest of God. Forgive me for not allowing my giftings and calling to enter into Your rest. Forgive me for not allowing Your healing gifts, as you originally planned for them to be expressed through me, to enter into Your rest. I acknowledge that You give these healing gifts so that the work of evangelism will function in Your rest. I acknowledge Your Ways as greater than my ways. Forgive me for not choosing Your ways and Your rest, for You have given the healing gifts so that the work of evangelism might be effortless, so that it might be accomplished not by my might, not by my power, but by Your Spirit. I regret that rather than receiving Your way, I have leaned on my own understanding. I have chosen to formulize and institutionalize both healing and evangelism. I repent for thinking that evangelism and healing can be done according to man's methods. Forgive me, Father.

Father, remove from me anything that absorbs your Spirit and everything that insulates me from Your Spirit. I renounce any elemental spirits that absorb or block the workings of your Holy Spirit both to and through me. Remove any and all contamination from the elemental spirits and return them to neutrality.

Father, I humbly repent for and renounce turning evangelism and healing into methods, and formulas and I repent for not allowing Your power to flow through me according to Your will. Forgive me, Mighty God. I ask that You be placed in the Highest Place, for You are the Lord, my God. You and You alone can accomplish true evangelism and healing. I desire that you bring these forth so that Your holy, worthy, wonderful name be glorified.

Father, I ask to be open to fully receive Your grace and Your rest. Father, in Jesus' name, give me an ability to no longer work in the flesh or to lean on the arm of the flesh. Thank you.

Father, I repent for and renounce any way in which I or my generations past have manifested an ungodly gift of healing or have relied on or called upon any powers for healing other than Your own. I repent for and renounce any rejection of Your authentic healing gifts by myself or by anyone in my family line—including all my ancestors. Lord, please remove from me and my family line all curses and iniquity against the gift of healing. Remove from us all thorns and nettles.

Father, I receive Your callings and the giftings, even those I have previously refused, for the gifts and callings from You, God, are without repentance. I accept that it is not necessary to rely on my own methods. I do not need to know how to make this work. I need only say "Yes" to Your gifts and Your callings.

I agree with the Word which states, "But those who wait on the LORD SHALL renew their strength; they shall mount up with wings like eagles, they shall run and not be weary, they shall walk and not faint."

Lord, I want to soar like eagles, catch the heat vents, fly, and have an eagle's eye to see afar. I want to know where to go after food and provision. I thank You that I can run and not be weary.

Lord, I declare this to be the time of running and renewing strength. I want to disciple the next generation so that they will fly higher than I can fly. I will not shut them down in the way I was shut down. I will disciple them in Your power and might. They will move into the unusual, the far beyond; and that which was unusual for me will be normal for them.

Help me to make every effort to walk into Your rest. Father, on the seventh day you rested. You ask me to rest. You ask me to separate myself one day a week from all that is profane—to come apart and be Holy, to focus on You and gather together with those who are Holy. You are my God who makes a distinction between the Holy and the profane, between the sacred and the vile, between the clean and the unclean.[3]

When I enter the world, as I must, oh Lord, separate and mark the holy from the profane. You pardon my transgressions, great and slight. You multiply my seed as the sand. I call upon You to fill all my needs.

Cause me to enter into Your rest, that Your name may be glorified. Turn back my enemies so that Your name will not be mocked. Let none say, "Where is the God who created you?" Arouse in me Your love to save a people who live in Your rest.

Bring forth Your healing gifts; bring forth Your Life to raise the dead. Bring forth evangelism that Your glory may cover the earth. Cause Your kingdom to come and Your will to be done. And in all these matters, cause me to move in the might of Your rest.

I declare the truth of Your Word, "For as the heavens are higher than the earth, so are My ways higher than your ways, and My thoughts than your thoughts, for the rain comes down, and the snow from heaven, And do not return there, but water the earth, and make it bring forth and bud, that it may give seed to the sower and bread to the eater, so shall My word be that goes forth from My mouth; It shall not return to Me void, But it shall accomplish what I please, and it shall prosper in the thing for which I sent it. For you shall go out with joy, and be led out with peace; The mountains and the hills shall break forth into singing before you, and all the trees of the field shall clap their hands. Instead of the thorn shall come up the cypress tree, and instead of the brier shall come up the myrtle tree; and it shall be to the LORD for a name, for an everlasting sign that shall not be cut off."

Heavenly Father, I love You. Lord Jesus, I love You. Holy Spirit of the living God, I love You. Yahweh, I must have You at the center of everything.

---

[3] Leviticus 10:10, Ezekiel 22:26, 44:23

Lord, please now to take all that is pleasing to You and to build me up—with You as the center and with me within Your confines. Please take all that remains and do what You want with it. Take it as far as the East is from the West, for I only want what pleases You.

Lord Jesus, I renounce and repent for all those in my family line, all the way back to Adam and Eve, who, because of their sin, released thorns and thistles into the ground placing a curse on reproduction—the reproduction of the land, the reproduction of business, spiritual reproduction, and human reproduction.

As a parent, I renounce and repent for myself and my family line for provoking my children to anger and not blessing them to walk in son ship. I now release them to walk in godly inheritance, authority, and as sons properly placed within a redeemed family tree. As a son, I renounce and repent for myself and my generational line for not honoring my parents. I ask for Your realignment of our redeemed family tree. I receive the parental blessing and move forward in freedom.

For myself and my family line:

I repent for and renounce those who focus on the moon, fear the moon and worship the moon rather than the Son of God. Lord, please break all curses related to moon worship.

Lord I repent for those who denied the gift of healing, spoke against the gift, and cursed the gift of healing. Please break all curses that came against me. Lord, please destroy the ungodly reflection of the Sun of Righteousness with healing in her wings— that ungodly reflection, that imposter, who is like a bramble bush, who brings the counterfeit healing gift and the one that brings sickness and disease— the anti-healing one.

Lord please heal the damage done to my back. Please break all the curses on reproduction that have come against me. Lord, disconnect me and my family from all fertility cults and sacrifices that have brought curses, barrenness, and thorns into our lives and upon our land.

Father, I repent for and renounce choosing to drink the water of affliction rather than drinking from the River of Life. Father, I repent for and renounce silencing the seed, shutting the truth within my bowels, allowing the moons of unrighteousness to overshadow the righteousness within me.

Lord, for myself and my family line, I repent for and renounce any who have spilled their seed on the ground or caused the seed of others to be spilled upon the ground. Lord I repent for and renounce blocking the seed of evangelism.

Father, forgive me and my family line for covering Your light and not bringing it forth for all to see. Forgive me for hiding Your light under a bushel. Cause Your light to shine through me that others might see You and come to know You.

Lord, please burn up the bramble bush—that ungodly misrepresentation of the evangelism and healing You desire to bring forth. On behalf of myself and my family line, I repent for and renounce hiding my light under a bush. I repent for and renounce those in my generations who hid their lights in any way. We submit to Jesus, the burning bush, the all-consuming fire. Lord will you burn away the things that entangle, and release me to fly in the fullness of my inheritance.

Lord, please turn the wilderness and wasteland into streams in the desert and the parched land into a pool. I receive the healing of the land and of my body. Lord, please open the blind eyes, unstop the deaf ears, heal the lame and release the mute to shout for joy.

I want to be like trees planted by the rivers of water that bring forth the fruit of the season.

Moreover, the light of the moon will be as the light of the sun, and the light of the sun will be sevenfold, as the light of seven days, In the day that the LORD binds up the bruise of His people and heals the stroke of their wound.

I repent for and renounce the Rahab spirit-that "do nothing" spirit.

I renounce and repent, on behalf of myself and my generational line, for all ungodly plantings, for not being grounded and rooted in love, and for receiving nourishment and strength from the land and not from You. I renounce and repent for receiving and relying on the ungodly fruit that was produced from this ungodly planting. On behalf of myself and my generational line, I renounce and repent for all ungodly dependence on the land. I renounce and repent for all worship of the land. I break all ungodly ties for me and my generational line with the land.

Father, I renounce and for trying to reap fruit from thorns and from bramble bushes. Cause me to see and discern the trees from which I pick fruit. I want only fruit from Your hand—from what and from whom You have ordained for me – not from any imposters. I acknowledge that good fruit comes only from good trees. Thorns and bramble bushes yield only bad fruit and desolation.

Reach deep, clean out, and wash the cisterns of our hearts and lives.

Father, I renounce and repent for all false gifts of healing. I repent and renounce for myself and for anyone in my generations who declared that healing was not of God, but came from my enemy. I repent for and renounce any false healing gifts or the misuse of any healing gifts both for myself and for my ancestors. I repent and renounce for turning away from, or discrediting the healing gifts.

Lord, please break the curse off of the Land. Please heal the land. Please break the curse off of the gift of healing. Please break the curse off of me. Please appropriate Your blood over the land and over me and over the healing gifts in these specific matters.

I now accept and receive Your healing, Your healing gifts, callings, and mantles. Help me not to look to myself to make the gifts work. Grant me faith that You will do all that needs to be done. You alone are God.

I ask that all healing and healing giftings and mantles from You come forth to move evangelism forward. Even as the Sun of Righteousness, with healing in her wings. flies or moves by means of wings, so sweep evangelism forward through healing, let it take wing and fly – even according to Your will. Glorify Your name. Cover the earth with Your glory.

Prayer to Break all Ties to the Incubus and Succubus Spirits

Although not in the Bible, the names incubus and succubus have been used throughout history to represent evil sexual spirits, spiritual sexual attacks and evil involved in ungodly sexual behavior. When we use these terms, we are asking God to remove evil associated with these concepts.

Father, in the name of Jesus, I repent on behalf of myself and those in my family line who had sexual relations with evil spirits, familiar spirits, or with any spirit represented by the terms incubus or succubus. I renounce and break any covenants or dedications to the Nephilim, Baal, or Belial.

I repent for anyone in my family line who has had any connections, ties, pacts, or allegiances to the Harlot spirit and the Queen of Heaven. I repent for all who participated in any fertility rites or rituals, and who sacrificed, worshipped, danced before, or gave offerings to any gods or goddesses.

Lord, I repent for myself and all those in my family line who had night or spirit husbands, night or spirit wives. Lord, forgive us for rejecting You as our husband and forgive us for our unfaithfulness towards You. Forgive us for finding comfort from these spirits and for looking to them to fulfill our desires and needs. I choose to rely upon You and to trust in You for everything I need. Please restore my joy and faithfulness to Jesus Christ, the Bridegroom.

Lord, I repent of every contact, personal and generational, with all night-husbands and night-wives and I and renounce all night husbands and night wives which have been assigned to function specifically within my family. I repent of the blood covenants which opened the door to this family night-husband and night-wife. I cut every soul tie with this family spirit. I repent of the deception adopted by my ancestors that polygamy is acceptable and for any deception which was one of the ways in which the door was opened to incubus and succubus and mare.

I repent for those in my family line who were involved in astral travel, dark practices such as the occult, and new age practices. I repent for any involvement with witches, sorcerers, magistellus, or familiar spirits. I renounce all night spells, charms, enchantments, or allurements used by witches and warlocks at night. I renounce any positions, possessions, powers, or any secret knowledge that have come from darkness. Please close all ungodly pathways, gateways, portals, cracks, or seams into ungodly realms or the underworld. Remove all defilement and tainting, and as Your child, please restore my godly dreams from heavenly places.

I repent for myself or any of my ancestors who have visited sangomas, witches, or warlocks for their "love witchcraft." I repent of buying, accepting, and using their love potions. I repent of rituals performed, invocations offered up, and any using of baths, washes, charms and psychic prayers. I repent of having my body rubbed with ungodly ceremonial liquids or allowing ungodly ceremonial or commercial liquids to be poured over my body.

I repent for the breaking up of marriages, covenants, divorces, and the destroyed relationships that resulted from having relations with these spirits. Lord, please break off from me and my family line all false love, lust, hatred, impotency, frigidity, sickness and disease that have been caused by these spirits.

I repent on behalf of myself and my family line for all fornication, adultery, incest, orgies, sodomy, homosexuality, and sexual addiction. I repent for all pornography, rape, abuse, ungodly masturbation, lust and fantasy lust, and any ungodly sexual contact with other people, any bestiality, and all sexual perversion and sex for money.

I repent on behalf of myself and my family line for shedding innocent blood through abortion and human sacrifices. I repent of murder, pride, greed, rage, hate, jealousy, pretense, falseness, cursing, and lying.

Father, on behalf of myself and my family line I repent of having been involved in acts that showed worship and obedience to Satan and his demons through having sexual relations outside of marriage. Lord, forgive us for not following Your commands.

In the Name of Jesus, I renounce all ungodly soul ties with every person I have been sexually involved with, physically or spiritually. Father I ask You to break these soul ties from my spirit, my mind and my body. Break in Jesus Name. I now apply the Blood of Jesus Christ over all ungodly ties.

Father, I repent for allowing these evil spirits to reduce and control my will. I now choose to put my spirit, will, emotions, mind and body under the Lordship of Jesus Christ.

Now in the name of Jesus Christ I renounce and demand that all evil represented by incubus, succubus, incubi, succubi, eldonna, mare and all evil connected to ungodly sexual behavior to come out of my body and my physical and spiritual conscious, subconscious and unconscious mind. I break off these spirits from my tongue, hands, fingers, breasts, sexual organs or any part of my body.

I renounce any reliance with evil. I specifically renounce Satan and all his works. I stand in the authority that I have as a believer, and in the name of Jesus I cast out any spirits that have been residing in my body.

I command all confusion to leave and I call back all parts that have been scattered or fragmented.

Father, please forgive me, wash me and cleanse me and I ask You to restore my innocence. Please increase my love for You and give me the ability to be truly faithful and intimate with You.

Prayer for Divine Intervention and Release into Your Birthright

For myself and my family line, I repent for and renounce:

- Forgetting You, Lord, and exalting myself as lord of my life
- Misusing godly supplies and money
- Worshiping Your gifts instead of You, God, the Giver of the gifts
- Not guarding my heart with all diligence towards You, Lord
- Not reading and acting upon the Word of God
- Not spending time with You
- Not sowing with an attitude of righteousness and therefore not reaping the fruit of unfailing love
- Not breaking up my unplowed ground which has resulted in hardheartedness
- Not extending and receiving mercy for myself and others
- Plowing wickedness and reaping injustice
- Eating the fruit of lies and deception
- Trusting in my own ways and my own strength

For myself and my family line, I repent for and renounce wearing a crown of pride.
I choose to exchange the crown of pride for Your crown of glory and a diadem of beauty.

For myself and my family line, I repent for and renounce being apathetic and passive towards our governmental inheritance and not being partakers and stewards of prayer concerning the government and the battle at the gate. I choose now to be a gatekeeper and a watchman of prayer concerning the government of my home, neighborhood, city, county, state, country, and the world. I have a longing for justice and righteousness. I receive Your wisdom for strategies that will bring victory to Your Kingdom on earth.

For myself and my family line I repent for and renounce not seizing the opportunity to pray and speak into the realm of influence into which You placed us. I now choose to be obedient and redeem the time. Please now bring me out of man's time and into Your *kairos* time, into the present moment of Your presence and will, and please establish Your authority in me on earth as it is in heaven.

For myself and my family line I repent for the priests, prophets, and leaders who have erred in vision and stumbled in judgment and were partakers in generational addictions. I repent for and renounce those teachers who did not teach godly precepts and did not develop line upon line, but gave milk instead of true discernment. I repent for not receiving with an open heart the godly precepts of the Lord and for closing the door to the blessings. I renounce and repent for hardheartedness and for allowing my heart to become dull.

For myself and my family line I repent for and renounce putting up walls that keep us from hearing and receiving Your Word. I ask You to remove the walls that keep me from hearing and receiving Your godly precepts. I ask You, Lord, to break off the curse of hearing but not understanding, and of seeing but not perceiving.

For myself and my family line, I repent for and renounce not hearing Your call to enter into Your rest. I repent for myself and all those in my generational line who strived in an attempt to minister to the flock. I repent for the leaders in my family line who did not offer Living Water but offered human wisdom and knowledge as the answer for spiritual matters. I repent for leaders in my family line who chose to bear the sin of the people rather than allow Christ to be the sacrifice.

For myself and my family line, I repent for those who were in positions of spiritual leadership and did not shepherd or feed the sheep but fleeced them. I repent for myself and those in my generational line who ruled by force and hardhearted harshness, who did not strengthen the diseased and the weak, who did not heal the sick, who did not bandage the hurt, and who did not bring back the lost who had gone astray. I repent for receiving and holding offense against unholy shepherds. Lord, I ask You to restore the scattered sheep. I ask that You return godly shepherds' hearts to this generational line. Lord please break off all the consequences that came as a result of being weak, exhausted, and poor leaders who caused Your sheep to be led astray.

For myself and my family line, I repent and renounce all attempts to satisfy our spiritual thirst by going to broken cisterns and drawing from poisoned wells instead of the fountain of living water and for using human methods to accomplish the purposes of the Spirit.

For myself and all in my family line, I repent for forsaking You, the Lord of Hosts, through weakness and backsliding. I did not consider or realize what an evil and bitter thing it is to forsake You, Lord. I realize now that I did not fear You, Lord.

For myself and my family line, I repent for and renounce being unwise, impatient, and going here and there to increase knowledge instead of seeking You first.

Please fill me with Your Holy Spirit so I can move in Your love; illuminate me with Your revelation. Please release me as a leader to walk in the fullness of Your wisdom and to shine like the stars of heaven, leading many to righteousness.

For myself and my family line, I renounce and repent for calling You, "Lord" but not obeying Your words. I repent for not healing the sick, casting out demons, and raising the dead as You commanded Your followers to do. I invite You to do these works through me by Your Spirit. I choose to obey Your commands.

For myself and my family line, I repent for and renounce building on a refuge of lies and deceptions and striking agreements with the god of death to avoid the grave and the coming destruction. Please annul this covenant with death and break this curse off me. I choose to build on You, Lord Jesus, the true foundation, the Living Stone in Whom I will never be shaken.

For myself and my family line, I renounce and repent for being intoxicated with the world instead of being filled with the Holy Spirit.

For myself and my family line, I repent for and renounce not following Your command to submit to the Father and to one another.

For myself and my family line, I repent for and renounce not abiding in Your light and partaking in unfruitful works of darkness. Lord, please free me to awaken and to arise to do Your will.

For myself and my family line, I repent for and renounce all hidden sins and ask You to reveal them in the light of Your presence. Help me discern my error and the error of my generational line. Cleanse me from hidden faults; uncover any lies which hide my sin and any deceptions I have concealed from myself and others.

Lord, help me to confess my faults to others and to pray for others so that I may be healed and so that You may present me faultless before the presence of Your glory.

For myself and my family line, I repent for and renounce disobeying You and not keeping Your commandments. Lord, please remove all the consequences that have come upon me and my generational line: sickness, depression, despair, oppression, mental illness, loss, debt, lack, famine, slavery, fear, barrenness, fruitlessness, and failed marriages.

Lord, I choose to obey you. Holy Spirit, please help me to obey the Father. Please command all of Your blessings to come and overtake me and my generational line: fruitfulness, fertility, divine health, increase in the storehouses of finances and goods, harvests, blessings in all my ways, rain to the land in the right seasons, godly rulership and authority, a sevenfold victory over my enemies, and establishment as a part of Your Holy people.

For myself and my family line, I repent for and renounce all selfishness, self-centeredness, self-protection and decisions not to love myself and others. I choose now to live in all the fullness of love which will lead me to my birthright ordained by Jesus Christ. Lord, please disconnect me from the tree of the knowledge of good and evil and connect me to the Tree of Life so that Your love will flow through me and touch others.

I confess that in Christ, I am free from the spirit of slavery and I am adopted as Your son. I agree with You that I am Your child and Your heir according to Your promise. I pray for Your divine intervention in my life. I also ask You to reveal Your glory in me, so that I can take my place as a son of God and so that I will rule over creation according to your original call.

Lord, please break the seal of the revelation of Daniel in my life and release me into the fullness of my birthright.

Lord, I choose to turn towards You. I ask that You remove from my face the veil that separates me from You. Lord, please remove all ungodly devices and religious spirits and disconnect me from all ungodly heavenly places that keep me from Your glory. Please reveal Your glory in me. I receive freedom from Your Holy Spirit and please transform me into Your likeness with ever increasing glory.

I declare I will:

- Remember all the blessings and faithfulness of You, God, with a thankful heart
- Be a good steward of everything You give me as You direct me
- Keep my eyes on Your face and not on Your hands
- Guard my heart with all diligence by being careful to protect my eye gate, ear gate, and heart gate
- Seek You
- Extend mercy to myself and others and receive mercy for myself
- Sow righteousness and reap justice and the fruit of unfailing love

- Eat of the fruit of the Tree of Life which is Jesus Christ
- Trust in Your Word, Your Ways, and Your Strength
- Be an over comer through Your grace and take back dominion over the land and over all creation

I declare I will enter into Your glory. I declare I will no longer allow my sin to separate me from Your glory. I declare I want to come and sup with You, Lord. I declare I want You to disclose Your Face to me. I declare I will no longer hide from You. I declare this is the time to move into Your realms of glory. I declare this is a new time, a new period, and a new season. I declare that this is the time of a directional shift into Your birthright for me.

Prayer to Release Supernatural Favor and to Proclaim the Favorable Year of the Lord

Father God, I repent for myself and for those in my generational line for seeking fortune, wealth, health, and prosperity using all evil forces and powers like *feng shui*, fortune telling, palmistry, face reading, divination, astrology, numerology, Ouija boards, *I Ching*, the Chinese almanac, tarot cards, and all superstitious practices.

I repent for myself and for those in my generational line for seeking false destinies, magical healings, and good fortune.

I repent for myself and for those in my generational line for financing the worship of idols and the building of temples. I repent for all false burning of candles, oil lamps, joss sticks, paper money, paper material-assets, and incense.

I repent for myself and for those in my generational line for the practice of false spiritual cleansing and purification using flowers and water blessed by ungodly beings.

I repent for myself and for those in my generational line for the worship of all false gods and any allegiance with demons. I repent for all attempts to communicate with false idols for the purpose of prosperity, fertility, longevity, health, protection, and destiny.

I repent for myself and those in my generational line for consulting mediums, witch doctors, shamans, bomohs, and false healers.

I repent for myself and my generational line for dedicating families, possessions, land, and ourselves to other gods and idols of the land and water.

I repent for myself and for those in my generational line who received names for their children from leaders of false religions. I repent for myself and my generational line for dedicating and associating our names to the dragon and other ungodly deities.

I repent for myself and for those in my generational line for marrying and communicating with the dead.

I repent for myself and for those in my generational line for worshipping the gods and goddess of the sun, moon, heavens, and stars.

I repent for myself and for those in my generational line who relied on the cycles of the moon for all ungodly festivals and religious activities.

I repent for myself and for those in my generational line who denied and spoke against Your Word and offered burnt sacrifices and flowers to the Queen of Heaven.

I repent for myself and for those in my generational line for discrediting You because we relied on our own prosperity, strength, and abilities, and we assumed we lacked nothing.

I repent for myself and for those in my generational for temple prostitution, sexual immorality, bestiality, licentiousness, and its associated vices.

I repent for myself and for those in my generational line for the worship and manipulation of the five elements—metals, wood, water, fire, and earth.

I repent for myself and for those in my generational line for practicing other forms of religion in conjunction with the Christian faith.

I repent for myself and for those in my generational line for all ancestral worship and all belief in reincarnation.

I repent for myself and for those in my generational line for all practice and worship of Buddhism, Hinduism, Taoism, Confucianism, Islam, and Shintoism.

I repent for myself and for those in my generational line for trading our birthright for ungodly gains.

I repent for myself and for those in my generational line for forsaking You Lord and Your Holy Mountain and setting a sacrificial table for fortune and filling cups with mixed wine for destiny. Lord, please remove the curse of the sword and slaughter.

I repent for myself and for those in my generational line for any misuse and manipulation of the prophetic gifts for self-gain and for following the ways of Balaam.

I repent for myself and for those in my generational line for all participation in the martial arts, *tai chi*, meditation, *yoga*, and *qigong*.

I repent for myself and for those in my generational line for bowing to and honoring our ancestors and bowing to and honoring all who called themselves masters or gurus, exalting themselves above You God, rather than honoring and bowing to You, Lord.

I repent for myself and for those in my generational line for all worship of animals according to Chinese zodiac signs and for trying to take on the spirit, personality, and characteristics of animals.

I repent for myself and for those in my generational line for binding our children to animals and gods.

I repent for myself and for those in my generational line for receiving impartations of skills of power from an ungodly source.

I repent for myself and for those in my generational line for ungodly animal expressions of the body.

I repent for myself and for those in my generational line who tied their coins and paper money to the signs of the zodiac and thus caused their funds to become defiled.

I repent for myself and for those in my generational line for all ungodly medical practices based on the zodiac and the spiritual realm.

I repent for myself and for those in my generational line who, even though we knew God's invisible attributes and divine power, did not honor Him and give thanks to Him. On behalf of my generation line, I repent for exchanging the truth of God for a lie and for worshipping and serving the creation rather than the Creator. I repent that I became futile in my speculations and my foolish heart was darkened. I repent that instead of being wise, I became a fool. I repent for exchanging the glory of the incorruptible God for images in the form of corruptible men, birds, crawling creatures, and animals and I repent for all in my generational line who worshipped them.

I repent for myself and for those in my generational line for all ungodly use of colors, sounds, objects, symbols, numbers, and fragrances to attract supernatural and ungodly powers for prosperity and control over people for prosperity and control over nature and people.

I repent for myself and for those in my generational line for all ungodly chanting, dancing, prayer wheels, and trances.

I repent for myself and for those in my generational line for believing we could have eternal life by other means than Jesus Christ.

I repent for myself and for those in my generational line for putting our birthright under the ungodly oaths and covenants in friendships, family relationships, and relationships with authority and with our country.

I repent for myself and for those in my generational line for all compromises in the house of the Lord, for perverting the word of the Lord and manipulating the people in the house of the Lord in order to build a personal kingdom rather than the Kingdom of God.

I repent for myself and for those in my generational line who manipulated and controlled people in order to build with bricks and mortar rather than allowing Christ to build His church with Living Stones.

I repent for myself and for those in my generational line who were leaders who boasted that they did work when it was really the work of others and of the Lord.

I repent for myself and for those in my generational line for choosing to listen to the voice of the enemy and calling it the words of God.

I repent for myself and for those in my generational line for worshipping water spirits, and for calling upon them to make a way in the water to go through.

I repent for myself and for those in my generational line for all forms of fire worship, including sacrifices by fire and fire walking.

I repent for myself and for those in my generational line for the ungodly association of wealth with water and the ungodly use and acquisition of wealth.

I repent for myself and for those in my generational line for ungodly mixing of God's creation in the physical and spiritual realms.

I repent for myself and for those in my generational line who based decisions on man's honor rather than on the Word of God.

I repent for myself and for those in my generational line for all abortions and rejection of fetuses, and babies, especially female babies.

I repent for myself and for those in my generational line for exalting evil.

I repent for myself and for those in my generational line for not thinking about You, Lord, or noticing what You are doing. I repent for calling evil good and good evil, darkness light and light darkness, and bitter sweet and sweet bitter, and mocking You, the Holy One of Israel, by saying "Hurry up and do something quickly. Show us what You can do. We want to see what You have planned." I repent for dragging my sins behind me and tying myself with cords of falsehood. I repent for taking bribes to pervert justice and letting the wicked go free and for punishing the innocent.

I repent for myself and for those in my generational line for all ungodly blood covenants and oaths, ungodly blood sacrifices, all drinking of blood and blood anointings made to achieve fame, prosperity, and success.

I repent for myself and for those in my generational line for rejecting and despising Your law and work.

I repent for myself and for those in my generational line for idolizing church and ministry leadership rather than You, Jesus Christ, as the Builder and Cornerstone of my faith.

I repent for myself and for all those in my generational line who supported religious leaders who hindered and criticized the true, free and lavish worship of You, Jesus.

I repent for myself and for those in my generational line who, as religious leaders, were stumbling blocks and shut out the Kingdom of Heaven to others.

I repent for myself and for those in my generational line for all attitudes of pride and rebellion against God's righteous authorities, and for calling what is holy, profane.

I repent for myself and for those in my generational line who did not seek Your heart, Lord, for our family, church, and nation. I repent for not seeking after Your Kingdom's will.

I repent for myself, religious leaders, and my generational line for the spirit of anti-Semitism and the ignorance of Your purposes for the nation of Israel. I choose to bless and pray for the peace of Jerusalem, according to Your Word.

I declare that my leaders will lead God's people into true and intimate worship of the Living God.

I declare that the Lord knows me by name and I have grace in His sight.

I declare that the Lord Jesus Christ is the only true leader of my church and ministry.

I declare that I only have purpose in You, Jesus Christ, and I will walk in Your purposes.

I declare that You, Jesus, are the Alpha and Omega, the beginning and the end, the first and the last. I choose to obey Your commandments. I declare that I will have the right to the Tree of Life and enter through gates into the City of God.

I declare that I shall no longer be called forsaken, nor shall my land be called desolate. From henceforth I shall be called Hephzibah and Beulah.

I declare that I will always give thanks for all the saints who are increasing more and more in love and the power of faith.

I declare that I will look to the Lord God Almighty and be radiant, and my face will never be covered in shame.

I declare that I will overcome by the Spirit of God, and the name I receive is the name connected to the Lord my God. Lord, give me my new name written on the white stone.

I declare that my desire is to buy Your gold, refined in fire, the true wealth of the Kingdom of God.

I declare that You, God, will call me by name, and I will follow Your voice and Your direction for my life. I will not follow the voice of the stranger, but I will follow the Good Shepherd of my life.

I declare I will pray for the saints and my leaders to preach the gospel in regions beyond my nation, and I will continue to grow in godly activity and allow You, Lord, to produce Your fruit in me.

I declare my allegiance and submission to the Lordship of Jesus Christ of Nazareth, the root and offspring of David, the Bright and Morning Star.

I declare that I will be a fool for Your sake knowing that this is Your wisdom.

I declare that although I am weak, in You, Christ Jesus, I am strong.

I declare I will cry out for wisdom and understanding. I will look for wisdom and understanding as if they were silver or hidden treasure. I will look to You, Lord for wisdom.

I declare that from Your mouth comes wisdom and understanding.

I declare that I am now in You, Christ Jesus, and I am a New Creation. The old has passed away and the new has come.

I declare that my will shall come into alignment with Your will for my life.

I declare that You, Lord, have saved Your best wine for the last and that You will manifest Your glory. As for me and for my family, we will believe in You, and we will fear and serve You, Lord, in sincerity and truth.

I declare that I, and the children that You, Lord, have given me, have names that reveal the plans that You, Lord Almighty, have for us.

I declare that I will only accept the true prophetic, which is like a lamp shining in a dark place and like the rising of the Morning Star and the beginning of a new day.

I declare that You, the Lord God Almighty, have redeemed and restored salvation to Your creation and established Your Throne in the Heavens. Your sovereignty rules over all the earth and all it contains.

Lord Jesus, I honor You and exalt You as You reign over my nation. I ask You this day to establish Your plumb line of righteousness and holiness over my nation.

Lord, shepherd Your people, the flock of Your heritage, with Your staff. Who is like You, God, pardoning iniquity and passing over the transgressions of the remnant of Your heritage? Lord, You do not retain Your anger forever because You delight in mercy. I pray that You will again have compassion on me and will subdue my iniquities. I pray You will cast all my sins into the depths of the sea. Lord, please give truth and mercy to all nations. Please extend mercy, which You have sworn to my fathers from the days of old.

Prayer to Rescind the Evils Associated with Buddhism

In the name of Jesus Christ, I repent for myself and for those in my generation line who asked for the ascension process to start. I repent for those for calling forth their soul to fully descend into their consciousness and four-body system.

I repent for myself and for anyone in my family line who proclaimed and declared that they were the great "I Am."

I repent for myself and for those in my family line who spoke the sound Aum, as if it were a sacred sound.

I repent for myself and my family line for calling forth our so-called glorified "lightbody" to descend into our consciousness and four-body system.

I repent for myself and for my family line for calling forth the "ascension Flame" to descend and enter into our consciousness and entire four-body system.

I repent for myself and for my family line for calling forth the full activation of our "alpha and omega" chakras.

I repent for myself and my family line for calling forth the Amrita, fire letters sacred geometries, and key codes from the "keys of Enoch" to become fully activated.

I repent for myself and for my family line for calling forth the full activation and creation of the potential twelve strands of DNA within our physical vehicle.

I repent for myself and for my family line for calling forth the full activation of our pituitary gland to create the life hormone and to stop producing the death hormone.

I repent for myself and for my family line for calling forth the activation of our monadic divine blueprints in our conscious, subconscious, and super conscious minds and four-body system.

I repent for myself and for my family line for calling forth and trying to fully activate the kundalini energy to guide our monad and mighty "I Am" presence.

I repent for myself and for my family line for calling forth the matchstick-sized spark of "cosmic fire" from the presence of "god himself" to illuminate and transform our entire beings into the light of god.

I repent for myself and for my family line for calling forth the full axiatonal alignment as described in "The keys of Enoch" to perfectly align all our meridian flows within their consciousness and four-body system.

I repent for myself and for anyone in my family line who called forth and fully claimed our physical immortality and the complete cessation of the aging and death process.

I repent for myself and my family line for claiming we were now "youthing" and becoming younger every day.

I repent for myself and my family line for calling forth the full opening of our third eye and all our psychic and channeling abilities, to use them for the glory and service of a false most high god and their brothers and sisters in the false Christ on earth.

I repent for myself and for my family line for calling forth perfect radiant health to manifest within our physical, emotional, mental, etheric, and spiritual bodies.

I repent for myself and my family line for asking and commanding that our bodies now manifest the health and perfection of the false christ.

I repent for myself and my family line for calling forth our sixteenth chakra to descend and move our chakras down our chakra column until the sixteenth chakra resides in our seventh, or crown chakra.

I repent for myself and for my family line for calling forth our fifteenth chakra to descend, enter into our sixth, or third eye chakra.

I repent for myself and for my family line for calling forth our fourteenth chakra to descend and enter our throat chakra.

I repent for myself and for my family line for calling forth our thirteenth chakra to descend and enter and reside in our heart chakra.

I repent for myself and for my family line for calling forth our twelfth chakra to descend and enter and reside in our solar plexus chakra.

I repent for myself and for my family line for calling forth our eleventh chakra to descend and enter and reside in our second chakra.

I repent for myself and for my family line for calling forth our tenth chakra to descend and enter and reside in our first chakra.

I repent for myself and for my family line for calling forth the rest of their chakras, nine through one, to descend down their legs and into the earth in a corresponding fashion. I break all ungodly ties with the earth that were made because of that evil.

I repent for myself and for my family line for calling forth the complete stabilization of our new fifth-dimensional chakra grid system within our consciousness and four-body system.

I repent for myself and for my family line for calling forth our chakra column to light up like a Christmas tree with our first chakra becoming a large ball of pearl-white light.

I repent for myself and for my family line for calling forth our second chakra to become like a large ball of pink-orange light.

I repent for myself and for my family line for calling forth our third chakra to become a glowing ball of golden light.

I repent for myself and for my family line for calling forth our heart chakra to light up with a pale violet-pink light.

I repent for myself and for my family line for calling forth our fifth chakra to light up with a deep blue-violet light.

I repent for myself and for my family line for calling forth our third eye chakra to light up with a large ball of golden-white light.

I repent for myself and for my family line for calling forth our crown chakra to light up with a violet-white light.

I repent for myself and for my family line for declaring that our entire chakra column has now been ignited with the fifth-dimensional ascension frequency.

I repent for myself and for my family line for calling forth with all their heart, soul, mind, and might the collective help of the eleven other soul extensions in our ascension process.

I repent for myself and for my family line for calling forth the combined collective help of the one hundred forty-three other soul extensions of our monadic group in their ascension process.

I repent for myself and for my family line for calling forth the complete descension and integration into our being of the rain-cloud of knowable things·

I repent for myself and for my family line for calling forth the trinity of Isis, Osiris, and Horus, and all pyramid energies that were aligned with "source" to descend into our consciousness and four-body system and to become fully activated.

I repent for myself and for my family line for calling forth the "ascended master Serapis Bey" and his ascension temple energies from Luxor to descend and become fully activated within their consciousness and four-body system.

I repent for myself and for my family line for calling forth our ascension column of light to surround our entire being.

I repent for myself and for my family line for calling forth the complete balancing of our karma from all our past and future lives.

I repent for myself and for my family line for calling forth the raising of our vibration frequencies within our physical, astral, mental, etheric, and spiritual bodies to the fifth-dimensional frequencies.

I repent for myself and for my family line for calling forth the light of a thousand suns to descend into our being and raise our vibration frequencies one thousand-fold.

I repent for myself and for my family line for calling forth the sacred sound of "aum" to descend and reverberate through our consciousness and four-body system.

I repent for myself and my family line for calling forth a complete and full baptism of the ungodly holy spirit.

I repent for myself and for my family line for calling forth the perfect attunement and completion of our dharma, purpose, and mission in our lifetime service of the ungodly plan.

I repent for myself and for my family line for calling forth the ability to descend into our "christ overself" body.

I repent for myself and for my family line for calling forth our fifth-dimensional ascended self. I repent for believing that we had already ascended within the understanding of simultaneous time, to now meld our consciousness with our unified field and aura.

I repent for myself and for my family line for calling forth any spiritual teacher to descend through our crown chakra and meld his or her ascended consciousness and light into our consciousness and four-body system.

I repent for myself and for my family line for calling forth the great "god flame" to descend and integrate and blend its greater flame within our lesser flame on earth.

I repent for myself and for my family line for calling forth the monad, the mighty ungodly "I am presence and spirit" to fully descend into the consciousness and four-body system and transform them into light. I repent for those who said they were the "ascended master."

I repent for myself and for my family line for declaring:
- Be still and know I am god!
- I am the resurrection and the life!
- I am the mighty "I am presence" on earth forever more.
- I am the "ascended master."
- I am god living in this body.
- The mighty "I am" presence is now my real self.
- I am the "ascension in the light."
- I am the "truth, the way, and the light."
- I am the "open door which no man can shut."
- I am the "divine perfection made manifest now."
- I am the revelation of God.
- I am the light that lights every man that comes into the world.
- I am the cosmic flame of cosmic victory.
- I am the ascended being I wish to be now.
- I am the raised vibration of my full Christ and "I am" potential.
- I am the "aum" made manifest in the world.
- I am a full member of the "great white brotherhood and spiritual hierarchy."
- I am the realized manifestation of the eternal self.
- I am the embodiment of divine love in action.
- I live within all beings and all beings live within me.

- I am now one with the monadic plane of consciousness on earth.
- I am now living in my glorified body of light on earth.
- I repent for myself and my family line for affirming our ability to transform our four bodies into light and travel anywhere in god's infinite universe.

I repent for myself and my family line for calling forth Helios, the "solar logos," to send forth into our consciousness through our crown chakra, the sixty-four "keys of Enoch" in all five sacred languages, so they would be fully integrated into our being on earth.

I repent for myself and my family line for affirming our identity as the "eternal self," "the christ," "the Buddha," "the atma," the monad, the "I am Presence" on earth in service of humankind.

I repent for myself and for my family line for affirming that we could remain on earth indefinitely without aging.

I repent for myself and for my family line for seeing every person, animal, and plant as the embodiment of the "eternal self."

I repent for myself and for my family line for believing we were the perfect integration of the monad, soul, and personality on earth.

I repent for myself and for my family line for declaring that salvation has come because of what we have done.

I repent for myself and for my family line for saying we were united with the "creator" because of our own effort.

I repent for myself and for my family line for saying we were the "light of the world" because of our own efforts.

I repent for myself and for my family line for saying that were a fully ascending being who had chosen to remain on earth to be of service to all sentient beings.

I forgive anyone who has made any of these proclamations over me or any member of my family and break all ungodly power released by these proclamations over us, sending all that is ungodly to the feet of the true Son of God, Jesus of Nazareth.

Prayer of Release from Being a Sacrifice

Father forgive me and my generational line for placing our sins and blame on others and chasing them away or making them scapegoats.

I repent for myself and my family line for wittingly or unwittingly receiving the sins and blame of others or allowing myself to be the sacrifice or the scapegoat. Forgive me and cleanse me from all assigning or giving to others the sin that Jesus died for or from taking on myself and receiving any sin that Jesus died for.

I confess that I am no longer willing to be the sacrifice. I am no longer willing to be the scapegoat. I ask that all sins and blame of others which have been placed upon me be removed. Break them off. I will not bear them. I refuse them.

Father, remove the consequences of this sin from me and from my generational line. I ask that the reaping of the consequences and all related curses be broken off of me from this time forward. I ask they be broken off my family line for all future generations. I ask they be removed from me and removed from my children based on Your righteousness which You have imputed to me through the blood of Jesus. I ask that they also be removed from all of my grandchildren, all of my future grandchildren, and all future generations, from this time forward throughout eternity.

Father, right now in the name of Jesus, remove the scapegoat from me and my children and please remove every evil thing related to all ungodly sacrifices.

Lord, please replace these vacated areas with your Holy Spirit and with your blessings. Thank you for pouring your Spirit into me and into my descendants.

Prayer to Repent for Ungodly Intercession

For myself and my generational line I repent for and renounce all ungodly prayers ever uttered, including controlling witchcraft prayers and prayers birthed out of fear instead of faith. Lord, please remove all that evil from my life, and from my DNA, and please restore Your presence and the power of Your Holy Spirit to my life.

Lord, please forgive me for misunderstanding the high calling and privilege of intercession.

I repent for myself and those in my generational line who left their watch and station and did not wait on You. I choose now to be stationed on the rampart, to wait upon You and to hear what You will say to me. I will wait until I am reproved. Lord, I choose to write down the vision, so future generations can run with it. I choose Your timing so that the vision will not be delayed.

For both myself and my generational line, I repent for and renounce relying on our own understanding instead of Yours, Lord. I repent for praying our will instead of Your will. I renounce and repent for not relying on Your living Word and for speaking death over my loved ones instead of the life which You so richly give.

For myself and my generational line I repent for and seeking and praying our own will and desires and not Yours. Lord, I repent for and renounce limiting You and all that is possible through You. I repent for and renounce not receiving Your dreams and praying them into reality because they are so big. Please release the gift of faith and expectancy in me, so that I will know with confidence that You are able to do more than I can think or imagine. I choose to receive the dreams and desires that You have given me and to believe that all things are possible with You, Lord.

Lord, I repent for and renounce not acknowledging You, Your power, and the time of Your visitation; I repent for not knowing You and for not praying what is on Your heart. Lord, I desire to know You and to pray what is on Your heart and to receive Your blessings.

I repent for and renounce stepping out of my own realm of authority and fighting battles that You never told me to fight.

For myself and my generational line, I repent for and renounce looking at my circumstances and praying from a soulish perspective and a worldly view. Lord, forgive me for being misled and for trusting in a system that has failed me because it was not based on truth or relationship with You. You paid the price of my sin in full.

For myself and my generational line I repent for and renounce praying prayers of doubt, unbelief, self-righteousness, pride, jealousy, envy, fear, hardheartedness, strife, selfish ambition, judgment, and deception. Lord, please remove all bitter-root judgments that I agreed with. Please remove all ungodly intercession based upon these sins. I ask for the angel, Breakthrough, to break, shatter, dissolve, and destroy all ungodly intercession, all ungodly prayers, all self-righteous prayers, all soulish prayers, and unsound mind prayers. I choose to walk in power, love, and a sound mind.

I repent and renounce, for myself and my generational line, all jealousy, envy and attempting to steal the giftings and callings of others. I repent for shutting the door on the children of God so that they would forfeit their callings. Lord, I admit that these things have interfered with my intimacy with You and my intercession for others. I choose to completely forgive those who have been jealous of me or tried to steal my giftings and callings or tried to shut the doors to my birthright or interfere with my intimacy with You and intercession for others. Lord, I now chose to freely give what You have given to me so that You may rebuke the thief in my life and in the lives of others. I chose to lay down my life so that You may raise it up again.

For myself and my generational line, I repent for and renounce praying controlling manipulative prayers out of a selfish motivation for the purpose of controlling others for selfish advantage. Father, please remove and cancel the effects of all the soulish prayers, ungodly intercessions, prophecies, and declarations that have released curses against me, my family, and others. I forgive those who have knowingly or unknowingly brought curses upon my family by praying their will instead of Yours.

For myself and my generational line, I repent for those who rejected the identity of sonship with You and rejected the spirit of adoption and walked according to the futility of their minds. Lord, I receive the spirit of adoption, crying, "Abba, Father." I choose to walk and pray by faith and not by sight. I come into agreement with the truth that as Your child I have direct access to You, and I can approach Your throne by faith in the blood of Jesus.

For myself and my generational line, I repent for and renounce praying striving, compulsive prayers from a state of anxiousness and unrest instead of praying from a state of rest by being seated with You in heavenly places. Lord, I choose to have my eyes focused on the victory that You intend for me to have.

For myself and my generational line, I repent for and renounce taking on the yoke of religious, organizational, and manmade intercession instead of taking on Your burden of intercession. I ask You to break off all ungodly yokes and false burdens of intercession from me and my family line. I break all agreements made to ungodly religious and governmental authorities.

Lord, please break off of me and my family line the consequences of fatherlessness, abandonment, rejection, and the consequences of allowing a false spirit of Elijah to have power over my intercession and prayers.

For myself and my generational line I repent for and renounce withholding prayers and intercession that would release the sons and daughters of God.

For myself and my generational line, I repent for and renounce all ungodly intercession directed to idols, gods, goddesses, objects, heavenly and earthly bodies, and the dead. Father, please break the consequences of ungodly intercession that hindered Your answers to prayer from Your throne.

For myself and my generational line I repent for and renounce all ungodly chanting, ritualistic, and repetitive prayers. Lord, please remove the curses that were activated and the ungodly spiritual forces that were empowered by these unrighteous prayers. For myself and my generational line I repent for and renounce trusting in manmade formulas. Lord, I repent for not surrendering to the Holy Spirit allowing Him to make intercession through me according to His mind and the will of God.

Father, please remove from my heart, mind, and will all deception and wrongful motivations and intents that would cause me to pray misguided prayers.

Father, please remove the brass heaven. Father, please release an open heaven and pour out the bowls of the prayers of the Saints according to Your will.

For myself and my ancestors, I repent for not honoring the godly priests and priestesses who have prayed Your heart, Lord God. Please pour out the godly bowls of intercession prayed by the saints before me.

 Lord, I repent for not seeking Your kingdom first and for not trusting that You know and will fulfill my needs. I receive Your promise that when I seek Your kingdom first, all these things will be added to me.

Lord, I repent for not asking from You as You have commanded me, so that I may receive from you and my joy may become full.

Lord, I repent for not continuing to travail in prayer as Elijah did until Your purposes have been joyously fulfilled, until heaven gives rain and the earth produces its fruit.[4] Lord, please establish me as the trees planted by rivers of water which bring forth fruit in season, so that whatever I do will prosper.

Lord, for both myself and my ancestors, I repent for and renounce praying faithless prayers and not having faith for You to heal the sick. Lord, I desire to please You by praying in faith that all things are possible to those who believe. I believe You are good and all good and perfect gifts come from You, the Father of Lights.

I repent for and renounce, for myself and my generational line, any agreement with the enemy's trickery or deceptive schemes that caused me to yield my God given authority thus affecting my prayers, decrees, proclamations, and myself. Thank you for bringing the revelation of truth, so I can repent and take back my authority.

For myself and my generational line I repent for and renounce listening to or using flattery which causes deception and ruin, and for misrepresenting God's truths in order to control others for my personal gain.

Lord, I repent for and renounce, for myself and my ancestors, any coming to the altar of incense before being cleansed and confessing sins, faults, and offenses to one another.

On behalf of myself and my ancestors, I repent for not seeking You daily and delighting to know Your ways; I repent for doing as we pleased on the day of prayer and fasting. For myself and my ancestors I repent for believing that the outward works of fasting and prayer would bring results when we inwardly held on to strife and dissension that resulted in cursing, hitting, and exploitation of Your children. Lord, I choose the fast You have chosen—to lose the chains of

---

[4] John 16:21, James 5:17,18

injustice, to break the yokes of the oppressed, to feed the hungry, to provide for the homeless, and to clothe the naked. I choose to do right, to seek justice, encourage the oppressed, defend the cause of the fatherless, and plead the case of the widow.

I repent for myself and for the women in my generational line who took it upon themselves to act as if they were the Holy Spirit to men. I repent for those women who did not allow men to be the spiritual leader in their marriage but tried to take on that position.

For myself and the men in my generational line, I repent for all inconsideration, for all dishonoring, and for not recognizing our wives as joint heirs by the grace of God. I choose to live in consideration of my spouse and honor her as a joint heir of God's grace.

I repent for myself and the men in my family line who, because of fear and passivity, relinquished their responsibilities as leaders. I renounce and break all agreements with the spirit of Jezebel and Ahab in myself and my generational line.

I repent for myself and for those in my family line who did not know and or care to know their responsibility for intercession. For myself and my generational line, I repent for those who did not value intercession, said it was for others, and did not pray. Father, forgive me for prayerlessness.

Lord, I ask forgiveness for not recognizing the creative arts as intercession. I repent for restricting dance, painting, music, and visual arts from worship and intercession to You. Lord, break the consequences off my family line of legalistic mocking, limiting, and restricting passionate worship and intercession through dance and the arts.

I choose to forgive all those in the body of Christ who shut down and limited creativity in me as a worshipper and an intercessor. I choose to recognize and bless the creative arts in others as the word of God in the anointing of truth.

Lord, I choose to enter into Your courts with praise and to worship You for Who You are in Spirit and in truth.

For myself and my generational line I repent for and renounce being narrow minded and not embracing all of You and Your Kingdom. I repent for a narrow view of Your Kingdom. I ask You to remove all the limitations that I have agreed with and replace them with Your wisdom, Your knowledge, Your Understanding, and the fullness of Who You are.

I repent for myself and my generational line for not praying for leaders and those in authority that You have placed over us. For myself and my generational line, I repent for and renounce not submitting to governmental authority; I also repent for and renounce any praying against the President and other government officials; they have been appointed by God. I repent for using liberty as a cloak for cursing and speaking evil in my prayers against the established government. I repent for not honoring the leaders of my nation. I repent for not praying for and seeking the peace of the city, state, and nation where You have caused me to live.

I repent for letting false prophets, diviners, and the news media deceive me and cause me to bring negative prayers to You. I repent for not seeking Your divine insight. I renounce generational terrorism, treason, insurrection, and murder. Lord, please remove all judgments that I have brought against me, my family, and Your people through unrighteous prayers.

Lord, please go before me as my King, please go before me with the breaker anointing so that I can pass through the gate, breach the womb and break out and burst forth in multiplication and spread in all directions.

For myself and my generational line I repent for and renounce believing lies, walking in discouragement, pain, suffering, disappointment, hopelessness, and allowing these circumstances to negatively affect my intercession.

For myself and my generational line, I repent for and renounce praying prayers to look or sound righteous or spiritual in front of others rather than praying in the humility of true relationship and coming into Your presence and communing with You, Lord.

For myself and my generational line I repent for and renounce praying and bowing the knees to any man, angel, idol, or image rather than to You, Lord God. I repent for not relying on You to strengthen my feeble knees. I repent for confused, faithless, and complaining prayers during a time when You were chastening me. I acknowledge that Your desire was to strengthen my feeble knees, but my attitude and prayers hindered me from receiving Your correction. Lord, forgive me for not exalting You in prayer as the Lord to Whom every knee should bow.

I repent for myself and my ancestors for prolonged kneeling, self-abasement, flagellation, and striving in prayer, and for going beyond the leading of Your Holy Spirit so that we could boast of our prayers. I repent for not strengthening the weak hands and feeble knees of others.

For myself and my generational line I repent for and renounce praying out of a place of disunity with Your body and praying out of a heart filled with selfish desires, envy, and jealousy. This has caused me to miss the mark. Forgive me for every time I have been pulled off course, either by the enemy or my own unyielding will. Forgive me for wanting to promote my own self-will rather than You. I repent for and renounce idolatry. I choose to set my face to know You and Your heart of mercy and compassion, and I will pray Your heart and not my own.

Lord, release Your sound as a war cry in me and others so that we may worship with one accord with your Spirit in such a way that will breach the walls, break through the brass heaven, and pierce the canopy that holds back generational blessings.

Lord, on behalf of myself and my ancestors, I repent for and renounce everything that has allowed the enemy to steal my prayers. Lord, please remove all generational curses and evil assignments against intercession.

Father, in Jesus' name I choose to empty myself of fleshly emotions and desires and ask you, Yahweh, to fill me with Your mind, Your Heart, and Your will.

Lord, please forgive me and my generational line for not accurately perceiving Who You are and for not approaching You in the true intercession that comes from worshipping You in the totality of Who You are.

I repent for and renounce, for myself and my generational line, coming into Your presence with meaningless offerings; I repent for having evil assemblies, having unclean hands, unrepentant hearts, pride, and for doing wrong.

Lord, please remove all ungodly powers, authorities, rulers, elders, and all ungodly spiritual devices that are a consequence of ungodly intercession.

Lord, please break off of me all guilt and condemnation for not interceding correctly. I choose to forgive myself for this false guilt. Lord, I now receive your true intercession and any godly mantles of intercession You choose to give me.

Lord, please remove all deception from me and my family. I repent for and renounce, for myself and for those in my generational line, all who squandered talents, gifts, resources and money from the beginning of time to the present.

I declare that I will not lean on my own understanding, but in all my ways, I will acknowledge You in intercession. Lord, I declare that as I sit in the heavenly places with You, I will release Your decrees and they will come into existence. I declare Lord that I will allow You to teach me how to pray.

Prayer to Restore Compassion and the Fear of the Lord

Lord, I repent for myself and for everyone in my family line who failed to have godly compassion toward others.

I repent for myself and my family line for being impatient or angry with You, Lord, and for blaming You for our suffering and the suffering of our loved ones.

For myself and for my family line, I renounce and repent for all false acts of compassion and all substitutionary acts of compassion.

For myself and my family line, I renounce and repent for condemning and judging instead of showing mercy and compassion.

For myself and for my family line, I repent for all those who did not heed the voice of compassion from the Lord but silenced the cries of those who were ill, hurting, injured, or in pain.

For myself and for my family line, I renounce and repent for mistaking compassion as weakness. I forgive those who have mistaken my compassion as weakness.

For myself and for my family line, I renounce and repent for not showing compassion for others who were in pain. I forgive those who did not show compassion while I was suffering.

For myself and for my family line, I renounce and repent for submitting to any ungodly authority which required us to suppress mercy and compassion.

For myself and for my family line, I renounce and repent for not having the Fear of the Lord and therefore ignoring Your promptings to show mercy and compassion to the least of Your children because it would have been too inconvenient, uncomfortable, or costly to do so. Lord, please forgive me for willingly disregarding Your words and grieving Your Holy Spirit. Lord, please forgive me for failing to show mercy and compassion to others as You have shown mercy and compassion to me.

For myself and for my family line, I renounce and repent for not recognizing and acknowledging that You have blotted out our transgressions and the transgressions of others through Your great compassion.

For myself and my family bloodline, I renounce and repent for rejecting those who were not healed after prayer. I renounce and repent for believing the lie that God does not care when the pain does not leave, and others do not show mercy and compassion.

For myself and for my family line, I renounce and repent for agreeing with being stuck in our own pain or understanding and for not expecting the Lord's compassionate acts of mercy for those who were suffering.

For myself and for my family line, I renounce and repent for being impatient, judgmental, frustrated, and angry with those who don't get healed, and with those who don't seek to be healed but find their identity in their problems.

For myself and for my family line, I renounce and repent for embracing self-righteousness and legalism, for denying the Fear of the Lord and for not acknowledging our need for compassion.

For myself and for my family line, I renounce and repent for not showing mercy and compassion because we were convinced that the illness, disease, or affliction was a judgment sent from God, that it was for a person's own good and that God was trying to teach them something.

For myself and for my family line, I renounce and repent for embracing illnesses, diseases, and afflictions as God's will for our lives.

For myself and for my family line I repent for and renounce hard heartedness and passing by those in need. Lord, remove the heart of stone, and give me a heart of flesh so that I can feel what You feel and carry Your heart.

For myself and my family line I renounce and repent for loving our own comfort, selfish lives, and ease of living more than we loved offering compassion to others.

For myself and my family line, I renounce and repent for believing that excellent health and abundant provision are signs of God's blessings and approval and that pain and suffering indicate God's withdrawal and disapproval.

I renounce and repent for the idea that pain and suffering may be a person's own fault and that and might be a sign that they aren't even saved.

For myself and for my family line, I renounce selfishness and repent for valuing money and the cost of caring more than the healing and comfort of those in need. Lord, please forgive me if I withheld charity because I did not trust in Your timing and provision.

For myself and for my family line, I renounce and repent for being fearful of allowing compassionate healing in the church because it would upset the status quo.

For myself and my family line, I renounce and repent for withholding our own compassion and for stopping others from showing compassion—I repent for stopping emotional expressions of compassion, acts of compassion, and for blocking any demonstrations of empathy.

For myself and my family line, I renounce and repent for not allowing ourselves to be vulnerable in compassionate acts because we believed that it would hurt our social standing in the church.

I forgive all of those who seemed not to care and offered advice instead of prayer.

I forgive all of those who, rather than showing mercy and compassion, offered to sell CDs, DVDs, nutritional supplements and other products to me and my family while we were in need,

I forgive all those who were selfish and stingy with resources, compassion, and mercy in my time of need.

I ask forgiveness for condemning and accusing others for lack of faith because they remained sick. Lord, forgive me for coming into agreement with the accuser of the brethren.

I choose to forgive those who have not listened to my soft-spoken voice as I have shared the compassionate heart of the Lord.

I now reject the lie that Job's suffering was from God.

Lord, please tear down the walls that I have put up that keep me from experiencing the pain around me and from knowing Your heart.

For myself and for my family line, I renounce and repent for not believing and trusting that You, God, would bring us out of the wilderness times of our lives.

For myself and for my family line, I renounce and repent for refusing, rejecting, burying, or compromising our identity as compassionate people of God who are agents of God's healing.

For myself and for my family line, I renounce and repent for being unwilling to persevere in long term compassion for the deeply wounded.

For myself and for my family line, I renounce and repent for caring more about schedules, programs, and decorum rather than stopping to help the ones in need.

For myself and for my family line, I renounce and repent for carrying compassion burdens that were not from You, Lord, and for not giving back to You the prayer burdens You gave us. I repent for and renounce carrying false burdens and heavy yokes instead of Your yoke which is light and easy.

For myself and for my family line, I renounce and repent for enabling others in their sin, not setting godly boundaries as Jesus did, and for taking on the role of "Savior" that only Jesus Christ can fulfill.

For myself and for my family line, I renounce and repent for embracing the belief that "I must burn out" for the Lord in exercising compassion. I repent for not resting from times of ministry and seeking the Lord for rest and refreshment.

For myself and for my family line, I renounce and repent for those who responded to compassion by taking on responsibility outside our sphere of authority.

For myself and for those in my generational line, I renounce and repent for abusing those with the gift of mercy and compassion to the point of exhaustion.

For myself and for my family line, I renounce and repent for seeing and hearing through our physical eyes and ears instead of the compassionate eyes and ears of Christ.

For myself and for those in my generational line, I renounce and repent for despising true wisdom and discipline, and for hardening our hearts and abandoning the Fear of the Lord, which is the beginning of wisdom.

For myself and for my family line, I renounce and repent for not being motivated with the love of Christ and for believing that acts of mercy were a duty and an obligation to fulfill. I renounce and repent for teaching duty and law instead of compassion and the Fear of the Lord.

For myself and for my family line, I renounce and repent for ignoring the hurting and being too busy to show compassion.

For myself and for my family line, I renounce and repent for not showing mercy, justice, and compassion for the poor, the weak, the oppressed, the downcast, and the rejected. I ask You, Lord, to show me who to minister to and when. Lord, I ask you to pierce my heart with Your love, compassion, grace, and mercy.

For myself and my family line, I renounce and repent for giving tithes and offerings and fulfilling Christian obligations, while lacking the Fear of the Lord in the more important matters of holiness, character, righteousness, justice, mercy, and faithfulness.

For myself and my family line, I renounce and repent for not keeping the commandments, statues, or judgments You have commanded. Lord, I desire to fear Your name and ask that You would prosper me as Your servant and grant me mercy so that I can complete the work that You have prepared for me.

For myself and my family line, I renounce and repent for receiving the compassion of the Lord but not extending that compassion to others.

I declare that the mercy and compassion of the Lord is with those who fear Him and with their children's children.

For myself and my family line, I repent for those who did not choose to be taught the fear of the Lord. I choose to delight myself in the Fear of the Lord and to gain understanding, so I may operate in true mercy and compassion.

For myself and my family line, I renounce and repent for those who hated true knowledge, coming from a fear of the Lord, but sought a false knowledge, wisdom and understanding, coming from ungodly sources.

For myself and my family line, I renounce and repent for those who did not fear the Lord and hate evil, but instead practiced evil, and were proud and arrogant and perverse in speech.

For myself and my family line, I renounce and repent for those who did not walk uprightly, but despised the Lord by walking in devious ways; and for those who did not shun evil, but were foolish, hotheaded and reckless·

For myself and my family line, I renounce and repent for those who feared man instead of You, God, which led them into evil bondage.

I choose to honor You, God and to be like Daniel, who feared the Lord and did not obey an unrighteous law, trusting God with his very life. I trust You to be my help and shield.

I choose to be like Shadrach, Meshach, and Abednego, who feared the Lord over man's decree, would not worship a false god; they were willing to die in the fiery furnace, yet trusted in God's ability to rescue them."

I choose to fear You, Lord, to follow Your precepts, and find great delight in Your commands.

I declare that the one who fears the Lord will not harden his heart towards those in need.

I choose to be zealous for the Fear of the Lord.

I declare I will be God driven rather than need driven and be God fearing rather than man fearing.

I declare that my delight is in the fear of the Lord, and therefore, I trust the Lord to lead me in compassion.

I declare that I will have compassion on the members of the traditional church as they learn to walk in the true fear of the Lord, learn to recognize and accept the manifestation of the mercy and compassion of the Lord, and allow God to be God in His Church.

I declare that I will approach You, Lord, with a contrite heart, a humble mind, and a heart for the lost.

I declare I will not live by the rules for being a Christian, but I will live in the fear of the Lord and His compassion.

I declare that the Fear of the Lord compels me to show compassion to others. I receive Your grace to love others as You love them. I receive Your showers of mercy to run the race set before me.

Prayer to Release Me into Abundant Life

I repent for myself and for my generational line for blaming God for wronging us.

For myself and for my generational line, I repent for blaming God for bringing us into shame by stripping us of our glory and removing the crowns from our heads.

For myself and for my generational line, I repent for blaming God for surrounding us with His net, destroying us, and demolishing us on every side, thus destroying our hope.

I repent for myself and for my generational line for blaming God for being our enemy and blaming God for being furious with us, and for sending troops against us or sending troops to build up pathways to attack us and camp all around our bodies and dwelling places. I repent for myself for my generational line for blaming God for blocking and walling up our way and plunging our path into darkness.

I repent for myself and for all those in my generational line who had fearful and unbelieving hearts that caused us to depart from the way of holiness. I ask for the restoration of the ancient paths where gladness and joy overtake us. I embrace my birthright and choose to walk knowing the Lord.

For myself and for all those in my generational line, I repent for using ungodly wisdom, for operating out of futile mindsets, and for trying to work things out by ourselves. I choose, Lord, to work out of Your knowledge understanding, wisdom, and discernment. I choose to work with You, Lord, to change my ways so that I can walk in the ancient paths established before the Fall. I choose to walk in Your healing and allow Your strength which flows from your life-giving water.

For myself and for all those in my generational line, I repent for using our God given physical and spiritual senses in ungodly ways and for choosing to operate from our natural minds. Lord, please break off all the iniquity that flowed from those decisions to ignore Your mind, heart, and will. Lord please remove all iniquity from my God-given senses.

I ask You, Lord, to restore my ability to use all of my senses to discern Your mind, heart and will.

For myself and for all those in my generational line, I repent for blaming God for removing friends, family, and employees from us and for blaming God when people turned against us and despised and hated us to the point of death.

 For myself and for all those in my generational line, I repent for blaming God's hand for striking us and persecuting us.

For myself and for all those in my generational line, I repent for wishing that our accusations against God and our suffering could be recorded forever in stone.

Lord, for myself and for all those in my generational line, I repent for not looking for Your path and Your ways. I repent for not being willing to walk on Your path and find rest for my soul.

For myself and for all those in my generational line, I repent for believing that God was withholding good from us and for believing that we could become like God, knowing good and evil.

For myself and for all those in my generational line, I repent for rejecting the law of the Lord and the testimony of His Spirit, for departing from His wisdom and truth and entering the kingdom of our own soul.

For myself and my family line, I renounce and repent for relying on the knowledge of the Tree of the Knowledge of Good and Evil. I repent for relying on our own thinking.

For myself and for all those in my generational line, I renounce and repent for forsaking the Lord, the Fountain of Living Water, and for creating for ourselves broken cisterns that could hold no water.

On behalf of my ancestors and myself, I reject receiving the seed of Satan that was received in our minds with the fall of man, and I reject and repent of believing the lie that we could become like God.

For my ancestors and myself, I renounce and repent for rejecting our birthright of being children of the Most High God and relying upon Him.

On behalf of my ancestors and myself, I renounce and repent for receiving Satan's evil seed, for conceiving mischief and trouble, and for having wombs which prepared deception and birthed iniquity and evil intent into our generational line.

Lord, please remove and seal every access within my womb and the wombs of my ancestors that the enemy gained to take others into ungodly heavenly places.

Lord, please remove and restore by the blood of Jesus any elemental part of me, including my inheritance and birthright, that is trapped in any ungodly or contaminated place. Lord, please close all ungodly doors to any ungodly place.

I repent for myself and for all those in my family line who relied upon the natural wisdom of man and rejected the Spirit of God. I choose to rely on the precepts of truth and the Spirit of God to give me the mind of Christ to direct my mind on His righteous pathway.

I reject the wisdom of man, and I repent for the pride in my family line that saw the wisdom of God as foolishness. I declare that I will be born of the Spirit and of water through Jesus Christ who calls me, justifies me, and glorifies me. I declare this truth of rebirth by the Spirit of God was established before the foundation of the earth and before the elemental spirits were created.

I claim my spiritual birthright of being conceived in love, of being given the Spirit of God who reveals wisdom to me, and of being given spiritual eyes in my heart to see the riches of God's glorious inheritance. I claim that I am being formed in the image of His Glorious Son. I reject the seed of Satan and I reject my position as a child of the father of lies and murder. I ask You, Abba Father, to close the ungodly eyes that were opened when the first man and woman ate fruit from the tree of the Knowledge of Good and Evil.

I renounce and reject any ungodly rights or authorities that were given to my soul to direct my mind along ungodly pathways.

I agree with God's original plan for all spiritual wisdom about good and evil to originate from His throne and be revealed to the spirit of men by His Spirit. I receive the seed of the Holy Spirit into my spirit, and by His power I cry, Abba, Father. I give the Holy Spirit permission to direct my spirit and to lead my soul and body.

Lord, on behalf of myself and my family line, I repent for questioning God's Word and therefore inviting the influence of Leviathan, the king of pride, into my life.

Lord, I choose to be directed by Your commandments so that You might enlarge my heart.

I declare that my redeemer lives and while I am yet alive, I will see God for myself with my own eyes.

I declare that my hope is in You, my redeemer. I ask You now to restore the ancient pathways to me and shine Your light on me so that I can see You with my eyes. I ask You to restore my stolen birthright, my glory, and my crown.

Father, I thank You that before You formed me in my mother's womb, You had pre-determined my birthright, the path of glory I should walk in.

On behalf of myself and my generational line, I repent for and renounce rejecting the truth that You formed us in our inmost being, and that before we came to be, You wrote in Your book all the days pre-ordained for us.

Father, on behalf of myself and my generational line, I repent for and renounce rejecting the ancient paths that You chose for us to walk in.

Father, on behalf of myself and my generational line, I repent for and renounce listening to and aligning our thinking with the wicked. Lord, I reject them and their pursuit of bloodlust.

Father, I declare that I am fearfully and wonderfully made and that You will lead me in the way everlasting. I declare that all Your works are wonderful.

Lord, I agree with Your Word which says that the weapons of my warfare are not carnal but mighty through You to the pulling down of strongholds. I choose to cast down imaginations and every high thing that exalts itself against the knowledge of God, and I choose to bring into captivity every thought to the obedience of Christ.

Lord, please release the resurrection power of the Holy Spirit to restore me to the path of holiness. Lord, please cause your Perfect Love to run through my entire being, casting out all fear. I ask You, Lord, to repair or replace any part of my brain or neural pathway required to establish Your godly attachments with my Heavenly Father and my fellow man.

Lord, please cause me to dwell in the Secret Place of the Most High. I declare my birthright is to walk with Abba Father in the garden, where I can hear His voice and enjoy intimate fellowship with Him. I believe that Jesus Christ appropriated this intimacy for me when He yielded up His spirit on the cross and the veil in the Holy of Holies was ripped in two. Lord, I repent for my generational line because we tried to earn by works that which You had given freely by grace. Lord, please now usher me into that place of rest and perfect peace.

Prayer to Retune and Realign the Heart

On behalf of myself and my generational line, I repent for and renounce viewing ungodly images, listening to ungodly sound in the airwaves, and coming into agreement with ungodly sights and sounds. I repent for not taking every thought captive and meditating on things that are true, noble, just, pure, lovely, of good report, excellent and praise-worthy.

On behalf of myself and my generational line, I repent for and renounce satanic and demonic agreement with any demonic movie or media or the production of it. Lord, forgive me for rejoicing in the triumph of evil as portrayed in movies and books. I repent for reading any books and comic strips and for watching any films that exalted darkness or the bat in idolatry. I repent for idolizing bats or other creatures. Lord, please cut all ungodly ties between me and these dark images and movie characters.

On behalf of myself and my generational line, I repent for and renounce worshipping bats. I renounce the belief that the worship of bats will avert disaster, bring abundance, and bring long life. I also repent for all generational vampirism. Lord, forgive me and my generational line for opening up the door to the spirit of death, sleep apnea, and night terrors. I repent for and renounce our giving access to Lilith, the spirit of night terrors, and I command in the name of Jesus, that Lilith and the spirit of death leave my generational line. I repent for all generational witchcraft, lawlessness, and rebellion. Lord, please disconnect me from the night watches of the witches.

On behalf of myself and my generational line, I repent for and renounce being irritated, angry, and jealous of family, the brethren in Christ, and those who have yet to embrace Christ's way. By the grace and enabling that You, Holy Spirit, have given me, I choose to respond with Your Spirit of love and to dispense your Living Water. I declare that You will supply all my needs according to Your riches in glory. I declare that the place You have chosen for me to occupy within Your body is the best place for me. I will rejoice in the successes of others.

On behalf of myself and my generational line, I repent of and renounce giving place to the devil and coming into agreement and aligning myself with his ways. I repent of and renounce embracing an ungodly vigilante spirit and trying to correct injustice by humanistic means. Lord, I repent for all perversion of justice by unrighteous enforcement of it. I acknowledge that you have said, "Vengeance is Mine." I declare that I will wait for Your justice and for Your restoration and recompense for every injustice to myself and my family line.

On behalf of myself and my generational line, I repent of and renounce coming into agreement with ungodly spiritual rulers who have used lies and fear to stop me from walking in Your ways. Lord, please disconnect me from the consequences of believing these lies and fear. I declare that the end does not justify any means. I declare that true justice is found only in You Lord. Your cross, Lord Jesus, provides the answer to all trauma and injustice.

Heavenly Father, please tune me to Your vibration, sound, frequency, and heartbeat, so that my heart beats in accord with Yours. Let all the sounds that come out of my mouth be in harmony with Your sound. Lord, please replace the life-sucking fear the enemy has attached to me with peace, rest, and confidence in Your eternal unshakable love. Lord, please restore the righteous sound of all creation.

On behalf of myself and my generational line, I repent for trying to control others and for not releasing them to You Lord to deal with. I repent for causing suspicion, disunity, fear, and darkness to come on them by my choices. I repent for operating in collusion with the spirit of Jezebel. I repent for not trusting in others revelation by the Holy Spirit. I repent for misguided intercession motivated by fear, jealousy, insecurity and envy.

I repent for false discernment from a lack of love. I repent for harsh words that stir up anger, foolish words that are opposed to true wisdom, and for not using a wholesome tongue which is the Tree of Life. I repent for speaking perverseness, distortion, and foolishness instead of wisdom. I repent for and renounce on behalf of myself and my family line all negative speech and harboring resentment in our hearts.

Lord, on behalf of myself and my generational line, I ask Your forgiveness for backbiting and reproaching our friends. I repent for not honoring those who have the fear of the Lord. Lord, when our brothers may have sinned against us, I repent because we have taken action based on our suspicions and not checking our facts and not going to You before acting. When they have wronged us, I repent because we have not always gone to our brothers in love to show them their faults in private, but ignoring your command, we have taken action before giving them the opportunity to repent. I repent for allowing religious and legalistic spirits to come against me and stop Your designed purposes. I repent for not trusting You and my brothers.

Lord, on behalf of myself and my generational line, I repent for and renounce criticizing, murmuring, complaining, speaking, and listening to gossip and the lies of the enemy. I repent for listening to the ungodly whispering of humans and demonic beings, allowing the whispering to cause division. Lord, please drive out the murmuring, complaining and critical whispering spirits.

Lord, I forgive all those who have spoken evil against me and my family and I release them to You. I ask that You break all ungodly ties and connections between me and those coming against me. Lord, I forgive those who have offended me and I choose to not hold on to or harbor offense. I ask You to give me an unoffendable and childlike heart.

Lord, on behalf of myself and my generational line, I repent for accepting the enemy's lies and not being a lover of the truth. I repent for not listening to the discernment of others. I repent for not humbling myself to listen to what others are saying and for not being willing to submit to others. I acknowledge that a lot of times I was trying to help but I was in deception and did not use discernment. I ask for a release from deception so that I can intercede appropriately. Lord I repent for not loving the way that You love.

I renounce and repent for giving my body over to darkness and to lust, for being fascinated with darkness and for worrying and not trusting in You Lord. I repent for and renounce reacting to violence out of fear and suspicion. For myself and my ancestors, I renounce and repent for hatred, strife, bitterness, unforgiveness, jealousy, envy, division, doubt, and unbelief. For myself and my ancestors, I repent for and renounce the pride of life, the lust of the eyes, and lust of the flesh, which has empowered hardness in my heart and produced fear, doubt and unbelief.

For myself and my ancestors, I renounce and repent for turning a deaf ear to the poor. Lord I choose to surrender to Your will to honor the widows and orphans.

For myself and my ancestors, I renounce and repent for not ministering with a pure heart of love. I repent for giving and receiving soulish revelation. Lord I submit to and delight in Your Spirit of the Fear of the Lord and I ask you to convict and correct me before I speak. I ask that you would release the gift of discernment and Your Spirit of Counsel, Might, Wisdom, Understanding and Knowledge upon me so that I will know both the words and the timing of when and if I should speak.

Lord I choose to surrender to Your will and I declare that I will come into absolute surrender to Your ultimate lordship of my whole being surrendering my whole heart. For myself and my ancestors, I renounce and repent for being afraid of man and evil and for succumbing to the fear of man which is a snare.

I renounce and repent for myself and my ancestors for listening to the enemy's sound; it is a false breastplate producing a false sense of security. Lord I ask that You would remove the sound and sonar used by the enemy to send vibrations to track my path, identity and inheritance. Lord please remove the all sonar, sounds, frequencies and vibrations being sent to me or being emitted from me that would give the enemy insight into my birthright and place in the world.

For myself and my ancestors, I renounce and repent for having a heart that has grown fat with spiritual plaque. I repent for hard heartedness and for allowing my heart to grow dull, my ears to become hard of hearing and my eyes to be become dim and blind. For myself and my family line, I repent for and renounce hardening our hearts to the voice of God. I repent for and renounce saying any words to suggest or declare that God doesn't hear, see or care about our situations.

On behalf of myself and any of my ancestors who sold our birthright, Lord, I repent for making agreements with the enemy and giving away our original birthright, the birthright You intended for us. I receive life back from You Lord.

For myself and my ancestors, I renounce and repent for spiritual adultery, for giving our hearts over to other lovers and not putting You first in our lives. Lord remove all idolatry in my heart. I renounce and repent for everything and anything that I've placed in my heart above You Lord Jesus.

For myself and my ancestors, I renounce and repent for accepting false responsibility for others and usurping Christ's role as Lord of their heart. Lord forgive me for accepting that responsibility of heart ownership that only belongs to You.

I repent for exposing myself to any graven image or object that would affect my substance or being. Lord, please cleanse my DNA from all transducers. I repent for and renounce all our stagnation of spirit and all thinking in our hearts that the Lord will not do good.

On behalf of myself and my family line, I repent for and renounce releasing ungodly sounds from the heart. Lord remove the ungodly sounds, frequencies and vibrations of the heart, cleanse my blood and regenerate it by the water of the Holy Spirit.

I repent for and renounce all words; prayers and utterances that my ancestors and I have spoken that have given power and dominion to the prince of the air. Lord please remove all sound frequencies and spoken words that have stopped and held back the children of God. Lord please remove all cloaks of invisibility, shame, blame, disgrace and reproach.

Lord I repent for finding my identity in who others say that I am rather than in whom You say I am. Lord remove all identity chips that the enemy has planted in me that I have come into agreement with regarding who I am. I repent for seeking man's approval over Your approval and for trying to build my kingdom instead of Your kingdom. I repent for looking to myself and not keeping my eyes on you. Lord I ask you to remove pride, selfishness, insecurity, rejection and fear of rejection so that I can love You and Your children whole-heartedly. Lord break my heart with all that breaks Your heart, remove my heart of stone and give me Your heart of flesh.

Father, I repent for limiting You and for limiting all that You desire to do in my life and all that You desire to do through me. I repent for rejecting Your dreams as being too grandiose. Lord reawaken Your visions and Your dreams in me, reawaken all that You called me to partake in before the foundation of the earth. I choose to call into being that which is not and to partner with You in creation declaring Your purposes and will.

Lord You have tried my heart. You have visited me in the night. You have found no wickedness in me. I have avoided the ways of the violent. My feet have held fast to your paths. Lord before You I am a baby, an infant trusting in Your care. As a babe in arms, I praise You. Your works and Your name are majestic above all the earth.

Lord You establish the universe by Your word and all creation is Yours, yet You are mindful of man having made him a little less than God crowning him in Christ Jesus with glory and honor. Vindicate me, oh Lord, with Your presence. Destroy your enemies in my life oh God. Restore Your dominion and victory.

Lord, please break off of me the consequences of negative words and curses that others and I have pronounced over my life. I break all agreements with negative thinking and the lies of the enemy and I choose to walk in truth.

Lord, please remove all ungodly spiritual rulers, authorities and shields that have operated in my life. I ask that You release Your godly spiritual rulers, authorities and shields to operate in my life. I receive Your breastplate of righteousness and Your righteous spiritual rulers. Holy Spirit, I ask You to reveal to me Your truth and remove all distorted vision and thinking.

Prayer for Releasing the Gift of Discernment

Father, for myself and my generational line, I renounce and repent for all sins, iniquities, and transgressions that have blocked the gift of discerning of spirits from being activated and used in a way that is godly and anointed for the Glory of God. I renounce and repent for all wrong uses for the gift of discernment for selfish manipulative personal gain. I also renounce and repent for using the gift of discernment with help from the power of darkness.

Father God, please forgive me even as I ask for Your forgiveness. I receive Your forgiveness and I choose to forgive myself for all misuse and abuse of the gift of discernment
.
Father God, I pray that You will release the gift of discernment so that I can grow up and be on the cutting edge and listen sharply and clearly to the voice of Your Spirit.

Lord, right now I repent and renounce all spirits assigned against the gift of discernment. Deaf and dumb spirits, passivity, unbelief, accusation, intimidation, religious spirits, torment, greed, doubts, blockages, condemnation, destruction, fears, unforgiveness, pride, shame, control, deception, uncertainty, dullness, distractions, procrastination, laziness, victimization, legalism, timidity/intimidation, mockery, oppression, repression, suppression, rebellion, inferiority, inadequacy, limitation, failure, double binding, double mindedness, confusion, rejection, abuse, loss, stupidity, occult lust, insecurity, seduction, jealousy, envy, malice, anger, murder, pain, resistance, rebellion, disobedience, poverty, unworthiness, sabotage, criticalness, wanting, helplessness, spirit of death, violence, mistrust, gossip, lying, slander, infirmity, manipulation, dissention, and spiritual autism.

Give me ears to hear You and words from You to speak; help me be proactive, believing, trusting, encouraging, courageous, bold, spirit-filled, peace-filled, quiet, generous, content, open and flowing in Your Spirit, praiseworthy, edifying, forgiving, humble, pure, innocent, not controlling, honest, without guile, true, sure of the truth, alert, clear, bright, resonant, quickened, focused, quick to obey, hard-working, diligent, overcoming, grace-giving, merciful, real, authentic, free, obedient, adequate, unlimited in Your resources, successful, single-hearted and single-minded for You, filled with understanding, rightly ordered and aligned, coherent, connected, accepted, loved, cared for, provided for, wise, accurate, self-controlled, secure, loving, joyful, vulnerable, rich, worthy, trustworthy, helpful, life-filled, strong, stable, sound, direct, awake and alert.

Lord Jesus, I renounce and repent for all activities that have opened up my third eye to deceptive vision and opened all the different chakras. Lord, please blind all powers of darkness that have utilized my third eye in all its various dimensions and in all my different parts that are trapped, lost, and enslaved in the dimensions.

Lord please cut off all connections that watchers have with my third eye to gain information and monitor my movements. Lord please remove all evil powers associated with my third eye.

And Lord, please assign angels to remove the third eye from all parts of my being, in all its various dimensions, in the past, in the present, and in the future.
Lord please fill me with Your presence and replace evil with good. I remove all occult influences and pressures over my life to try to attempt to plant and to activate the third eye from now and forever.

Lord Jesus I receive the eyes of Your Spirit, and ask that I will only see what You want me to see. I ask that all the strategies of the enemy will be exposed by divine revelations of Your will. Lord please open my eyes to see Your power and glory and all Your glories in heaven.

Father God, thank You for giving me the gift of discernment so that I can have complete knowledge of Your will in all manners of life. Thank You for spiritual wisdom and understanding to apply all that You've shown me. Thank You for teaching me how to live a life that will always honor and please You. And Father God, thank You for giving me the discernment to produce a good harvest, every time, in all my investments and in every manner of life.

Father God, thank You for showing me how to receive Your resources in all situations, with all kinds of people. Father, thank You for letting me know Your divine timing, Your opportunities, and Your open doors to supply all that is necessary in my life—in all spiritual, physical, and emotional abundance, so that all I do and all I say, will be a sweet smelling aroma and sacrifice that is acceptable and pleasing to You.

Father God, I thank You. You help me to begin to understand the incredible greatness of Your power to all who believe in You, the same mighty power that raised Christ from the dead and seated Him, at God's right hand in the heavenly realms.

God thank You for giving us a way to access Your incredible wealth of grace and kindness even as we walk in unity.

Father God, thank You for showing by discernment to walk in love, joy, peace, patience, kindness, goodness, faithfulness, gentleness, and self-control. Father God, thank You that there are no limitations to all You have called me to do.

Father God, thank You for showing me the lust of the flesh, the lust of the eyes, and the pride of life, so that I will be able to flee from temptation and live in spiritual truth and freedom.

Father God, I want to know what You want me to do. I am asking You now for Your wisdom. I thank You that You will gladly give me what I ask for and will never resent my asking.

Father God, thank You for teaching me how to submit to my leaders and to fellow believers, biblically and spiritually. Give me the attitude and faith that produces breakthrough, healing miracles, growth, and fruitfulness so that I will reach the full potential of my birthright. Teach me how to live in the harmony of the unity of faith that will glorify You.

Father God, thank You for giving me the ability to discern all the spiritual gifts and callings that You have given to me. Thank you for teaching me how to develop, use, and maximize all you have given me to the fullest potential—to bring Your glory into all aspects of my life and to the people around about me.

Father God, please give me the discernment to receive the right spiritual impartation from the specific people that You have sent into my life. Give me the wisdom to flee, escape, avoid, and refuse any wrong impartation from the servants of Satan. Please teach me to recognize all false servants from afar, even at the sound of their voices. Please protect my ears, my eyes, and my five spiritual senses from the assault of the enemy camp. Lord, please surround me with the songs of deliverance, with the presence of Your Holy Spirit, so that even when darkness comes, it shall not come near me.

Father God, You have given me the ability to hear the voice of Your Spirit. I will not follow the voice of the stranger, but I will follow You all the rest of my life. Thank You that I have the ability to hear Your voice in all my decision making—for my family, for my work, my ministry, investments, business, studies, relationships, marriage, church. May all I that I do and say pertain to life, be filled with life, release life, and be life-giving. Lord, thank You that I can hear Your voice clearly and sharply like the prophets of old.

Father God, thank You for showing me the crisis of the land rather than letting me become a victim to it. I will become a protector and encourager of those in need. Help me flee from all works of darkness upon the land and economy. Secure my properties and all my possessions by Your Spirit.

Father God, will You teach me how to live in peace and harmony with all people to bring about Your will. Teach me how to walk with tenderness, mercy, kindness, humility, gentleness, and patience. Teach me how to forgive every fault and how to walk in love and perfect harmony. Father God, thank You for teaching me how to give and receive counsel perfectly, with all the wisdom of heaven, so that I can be whole in spirit, soul, and body.

Father God, thank You for teaching me how to receive all Your provisions so that I will have everything that I will ever need. Teach me how to share all that I have received. Father God, thank You for teaching me how to increase the resources that You have provided to produce a great harvest of generosity in my life.

Father God, thank You for teaching me how to share Your work in my life effectively with the people I love in ways that demonstrate Your mercy, kindness, and goodness. Thank You for teaching me how to walk in Your peace at all times.

Prayer to Release the Morning Star

Father God, I repent and renounce for allowing my light to become dull, preventing me from allowing Your glory, Lord, to shine through me. Lord, forgive me for not becoming a partaker of the divine nature of Christ but instead allowing the corruption of the world to dull the reflection of Christ within me.

I thank You Lord that You are light and in You there is no darkness at all. I repent and renounce for myself and my ancestors for claiming to have fellowship with You, yet walking in darkness, lying, not practicing the truth, and being blinded by the light. Holy Spirit, teach me to walk in the Light of my Lord Jesus. Father God, cleanse me by the blood of Jesus from all sin so that I may have fellowship with You and the body of Christ.

I repent and renounce for myself and my ancestors for claiming to know You, but not keeping Your commandments, for hating my brother, yet not helping him in his time of need, and closing my heart against him. Teach me to love in deed and in truth so that I may abide in the light. Remove the darkness that has blinded my eyes.

I repent and renounce for loving the world, and the things of the world keeping out the love of the Father. I repent and renounce for myself and my ancestors for the lust of the flesh, the lust of the eyes, and the boastful pride of life. I choose to do the will of the Father, and I pray Lord for discernment to not be deceived in these last days by the spirit of antichrist. I ask You Holy Spirit for a revelation of the truth that I may practice righteousness, abide in Your light and not be deceived.

I repent and renounce for myself and my ancestors for holding on to the letter of the law instead of embracing the Spirit. I ask that my faith be dependent upon the demonstration of the Spirit and power and not just human wisdom, but the wisdom of God revealed by the Spirit of God so that I might know Him.

I repent for myself and my ancestors for practicing sin, lawlessness, and deceit. As a child of God, I ask You, Holy Spirit, to teach me to keep my eyes fixed on You that I may become pure and an imitator of my Lord Jesus.

Father God, Your word says that You are a jealous God and that I am to have no other gods before You.

I repent on behalf of myself and my generations for:
- forsaking Your commands
- making idols
- making Asherah poles
- bowing down to all the starry hosts
- worshipping Baal
- erecting altars to Baal
- building altars to all the starry hosts in both courts of the temple of the LORD
- consulting mediums and spiritists
- sacrificing our sons and daughters in the fire
- practicing divination and sorcery

- selling ourselves to do evil in Your eyes LORD, provoking You to anger
- swearing by Molech
- turning back from following You, LORD, and neither seeking You nor inquiring of You
- practicing violence and deceit
- following the ways of Lucifer by: seeking to ascend to heaven, building my own kingdom, raising my throne above the stars of God, seeking to sit enthroned on the mount of assembly, on the utmost heights of the sacred mountain, ascending above the tops of the clouds, and seeking to make myself like the Most High.

Lord, please break off the following consequences of these sins:
- isolation from You, God
- affliction
- effects of being plundered
- removal from Your presence
- wandering from the land you gave my forefathers
- lawlessness
- fighting between fathers and sons

Father God, I repent on behalf of myself and my generations for:
- not showing and seeking goodness
- not seeking knowledge
- not having self-control
- not having perseverance
- not acting in godliness
- not having brotherly kindness
- not having love

Lord, break off the consequences of these sins in ineffectiveness, nearsightedness, blindness, and unproductiveness in my knowledge of the Lord Jesus Christ.

Father thank You:
- That every good and perfect gift is from above, coming down from You the Father of the heavenly lights. You do not change like shifting shadows.
- That the morning stars sang together and all the heavenly beings shouted for joy.

I repent and renounce for myself and my ancestors for worshiping heavenly bodies, hosts, stars, planets and especially Venus, called the morning star.

I repent and renounce for myself and my family line for
- wishing on stars
- making decisions by stars
- trying to read the times by the star
- trying to find wisdom in the stars
- worshipping stars
- practicing astrology

Father God, I repent on behalf of myself and my generations for:

- tolerating Jezebel
- committing adultery with Jezebel
- holding to her teaching
- embracing Satan's so-called deep secrets

Father, remove from me the consequences and intense suffering of coming into agreement with Jezebel and tolerating her.

Lord Jesus, teach me to hold on to what I have until You return. In overcoming Jezebel, I will receive authority over the nations to rule them with an iron scepter and to dash them to pieces like pottery just as You received authority from Your Father, and I will receive You, the Morning Star. Give me ears to hear what You, Spirit of God, say to Your church.

I repent and renounce on behalf of myself and my ancestors for having and being the light of the world, yet hiding the light under a bushel. Forgive me for not letting my light shine before men, so they may see my good works and glorify my Father in heaven.

Father God thank you that:

- Your divine power has given me everything I need for life and godliness through my knowledge of You Who called me by Your own glory and goodness.
- You have given me Your very great and precious promises, so that through them I may participate in the divine nature and escape the corruption in the world caused by evil desires.

Father God I ask You to teach me and empower me to make every effort to add:

- to my faith goodness
- to goodness, knowledge
- to knowledge, self-control
- to self-control, perseverance
- to perseverance, godliness
- to godliness, brotherly kindness
- to brotherly kindness, love.

I declare that if I possess these qualities in increasing measure, they will keep me from being ineffective and unproductive in my knowledge of You, Lord Jesus Christ. If I do these things, I will never fall.

Father, thank You, that I have Your Word through the prophets. Teach me to pay attention to Your Word as to a light shining in a dark place, until the day dawns and the morning star rises in my heart. Lord restore to me Your presence and raise the morning star in my heart.

Lord, I repent and renounce for myself and my family line for coming into agreement with the enemy and accepting the enemy's ungodly covering that hides the light of the Lord. Please remove ungodly coverings, brandings, and fire from me. I renounce all agreements with Lucifer, and I ask You Father God to remove the dark gauze and shadow placed over me which keep Your light from shining in my being. Burn away the darkness and corruption with Your fire and Your light.

I repent and renounce for allowing a veil of unbelief and doubt to overcome me. Lord, please remove veils from my heart that keep me from understanding and receiving Your truth and from shining Your light before men.

Lord, please lift off the garment of heaviness and replace it with a garment of praise; lift off mourning and replace it with Your oil of joy; lift off ashes and dashed hopes and replace them with beauty. Therefore, I will be called an oak of righteousness, displaying the splendor and light of the Lord.

Lord, please remove all ungodly coverings and cover me with Your feathers and hide me under the shelter of Your wings that I might find refuge.

Lord, please remove the veil that lies on my heart keeping me from receiving Your truth. Lord, remove the veil that covers Your light and Your glory that shines through me.

Lord, remove all ungodly vibrations, sounds, numbers, sequences and lights of the enemy, and I ask for a seven-fold return and redemption of all that the enemy has stolen from my family line.

Lord, please redeem, adjust and align the music, equations, colors, lights, vibrations and DNA that the enemy has tampered with and used for his purposes.

I repent and renounce on behalf of myself and my ancestors for building ungodly structures such as the tower of Babel, pyramids, ziggurats, high places, pinnacles, temples and Stonehenge in order to become like God, to build their kingdom and to worship the heavenly hosts. I repent for ungodly alignment with the stars and planets. Lord, I ask you to tear down the ungodly structures and build Your godly structures on the cornerstone of Jesus Christ and the foundation of the apostles and prophets.

Lord, I ask you to disconnect me from the ungodly structures and land defiled by my ancestors. Cleanse me from walking on defiled land. Lord, decontaminate the multi-dimensional lay lines and reestablish Your highways of holiness.

I repent and renounce on behalf of myself and my ancestors for elevating celebrities, ministers, worship leaders, politicians and movie stars to idol status and worshiping them as stars and heroes. Lord, forgive me from drawing from people in ungodly dependence, and I release them to You. Lord, I forgive those drawing from me and I break ungodly connections that have been put on me that drain my energy and anointing. Lord forgive me for drawing my identity from others instead of seeking and finding my identity in You as a son of God with privileges of a son.

Lord, I ask you to remove and disconnect me from ungodly dimensions, wormholes, portals, including time portals and time dimensions that enable me to build the enemy's kingdom. Please disconnect me from ungodly stones and structures building the enemy's kingdom. Please bring me into alignment with godly magnetic fields.

I repent and renounce for myself and my family line for embracing the age of Aquarius that opened the door to star and planet worship and to the new age.

Lord, align and reconfigure my body, soul and spirit to Your sound, colors, vibrations, frequencies, and notes that create matter and destroy impurities.

Lord, adjust the elements in my physical body and brain to function as You created them to function at creation. Lord, remove all defilement from the elements in the land that my ancestors and I have been connected to. Lord, please take me to Your heavenly places and remove all defilement from me and the land I have been connected to.

I repent and renounce for myself and my family line for allowing the enemy to take over the airways and sending into the atmosphere negative sound waves through words of discord, negative speech, and gossip and for not coming into unity in one accord.

Lord, forgive me for speaking and tolerating profanity. I repent and renounce for playing and listening to ungodly music containing negative speech and profanity. I repent for releasing sounds into the atmosphere which empower negative forces and foreign gods. I repent for watching movies and television programs influenced by the spirit of the antichrist. I repent for passing on corrupt communication by allowing the transmission of information to pass through the atmosphere and the ground through frequencies and signals through computers, I-pods, I-phones, I-tunes, U-tube, Facebook, and other means. Lord, I ask you to dismantle the control stations of the airwaves that have been empowered by negativity and ungodly sounds released into the air. Lord, I ask You to redeem the airwaves so that godly, life releasing sounds, can be transmitted through the airwaves.

Lord Jesus, You are the Root and the Offspring of David, the Bright and Morning Star. I keep my eyes on You, so that I may be a reflection of Your light and beauty. Shine Your light in me and through me so that there will not be any darkness in or around me and that You may be magnified and glorified.

Prayer to Release One from the Ungodly Depth

Father, I repent and renounce for myself and my family line for all sins that have brought on the consequence of being entrapped in the ungodly depth, Sheol, the pit, the snare, and the trap and have kept me bound and unable to fulfill my God given purpose.

Father, have mercy on me, for I have endured much contempt and ridicule. Lord, break off the contempt and ridicule that has been put on me by the proud. Wash me from the arrogance and arrogant ways that brought the contempt upon me.

Lord, forgive me for not forgiving those who have come against me and entrapped me. I choose now to forgive those who have spoken contempt against me, and I release them to you.

Lord, on behalf of myself and my ancestors I repent for making vows, covenants, and promises to You and others which I broke. Lord, even as I have repented, and You have forgiven me, in Your mercy, please cancel these promises, vows and covenants. Lord, please break off any evil or ungodly consequences of these broken vows, promises and covenants.

Lord, I choose to cancel and forgive all broken vows, promises and covenants made by others to me and members of my generational line. I trust in Your words that You will repay. I now choose to forgive them freely and release them.

I repent on behalf of myself and my generational line, for all those who forgot, or turned away from You God, and for all those who even though they saw Your awesome works, they were ungrateful and unthankful, and complained instead of thanking You and being grateful for all You have done. Lord, please break off these consequences from me and my generational line.

I repent and renounce for all those in my generational line who tried to ascend above the stars or above God.

I repent for all generational fear, especially the fear of man, and I repent for all those who ran from fear, thus causing them to fall into the pit.

I repent for all those in my generational line who caused conflict, strife, or disunity, especially in the body of Christ.

I repent for myself and those in my generational line for pride, arrogance, deceit, anger and fury. I repent for all generational adultery, harlotry, immorality, sexual perversion, ungodly bloodshed, and for all murdering of the innocent. I repent for those in my family line who used ungodly seduction, enticement or allurement to lead the upright and the righteous astray.

I repent for all those who had foolish lips and did not watch the words of their mouths.

I repent and renounce on behalf of myself and my family line for all who cursed father or mother.

I repent and renounce for myself and my family line for hatred, racism, and slavery. I repent for putting others in the ungodly depth by hating, despising and discriminating against them because of different skin color, culture, gender, and beliefs. I choose to forgive those who came against my family line because of different skin color, culture, gender, and beliefs. Lord, break the consequences of these sins off my family line and restore love that goes beyond racial, cultural, economic, gender and diversity boundaries.

Lord, please break the consequences of these sins off of me and my family lines, and Lord, please remove me and my lamp from any ungodly secret place, and deep darkness.

Lord, please release me from any ungodly contracts that my ancestors or I agreed to and entered into that have brought me into the spirit of poverty. I pray that You would redeem what the devil has taken away and restore to me Your riches and Your glory.

Lord, I repent for and renounce all generational curses that come with seeking worldly riches. Lord please restore me to seek riches in You alone. I repent for myself and my family line for robbing the poor, swindling, gambling, cheating and using witchcraft to gain wealth. Father, I repent for myself and my generational line for being greedy to gain wealth, power, knowledge, titles, position, mantles, and wisdom from any source other than from You.

Lord, I renounce and repent on behalf of myself for all those in my family line who were destroyed through lack of knowledge because they did not seek You, Your knowledge and Your wisdom, and for all those who did not seek your guidance in their walk, their business, their work, their ministry, their family or other circles of influence. Please remove my family and ministry from any ungodly depth, pit, trap or snare. Please restore to me all the blessings, and benefits that have been held in the ungodly depth for my family line.

Lord, I declare that the enemy will now fall into the trap and snare he had set for me.

Lord, I repent and renounce for myself and all those in my family line who did not walk in true spiritual unity, but allowed bitterness, jealousy and envy to be in our midst, causing us to fall into a trap and a snare. I repent for all those who did not guard their friends and family or the body of Christ and watched them fall into ungodly depths.

Lord, on behalf of myself and my ancestors, I repent for casting an evil eye on others because of envy and jealousy, thus placing them into ungodly depths. Lord please remove and restore any parts of me that were placed in ungodly depths due to the evil eye.

Lord, on behalf of myself and my ancestors, I repent for all ungodly passivity that caused me to come into agreement with unjust accusations, ungodly perceptions, ungodly images, word curses, limitations, gossip and slander that were sent against me or anything that belongs to me. Lord, please disconnect me from all these and cancel them. Lord, I now choose to come into agreement with Your perception of me.

Lord, in your mercy, please break off any ungodly work of my hands. Lord, I repent and renounce on behalf of myself and my family line for worshiping foreign gods, idols, and ungodly beings putting me in ungodly depths, especially through drugs and the spirit of Pharmacia. Lord, please remove any part of me that has been trapped in the dimensions and cleanse it in Your blood.

Lord, I repent and renounce for myself and my family line for uttering false prophecies, ungodly prayers, witchcraft curses, or incantations that have placed me into any ungodly depths. Please remove all consequences of these actions.

Lord, please disconnect me from any ungodly physical touch, trauma, or assault that has trapped any part of me in ungodly depths.

Lord, I repent and renounce on behalf of myself and generational line for all those who committed acts or harbored emotions that would place us into any ungodly depth. I repent for all dishonest or unjust covenants made by my ancestors or me. I forgive those who committed injustice against us, and who brought false accusations against us.

I repent for myself and my ancestors for all fear of man, for not caring for the widows and fatherless, and for declaring that no one would restore us from the pit, Sheol, Hades or any ungodly depth. I choose now to believe and declare that You are the one true God and will restore me.

Lord please now rescue me and my family line from any and all places in the ungodly depth that trapped us, and restore us to Your True and Righteous depth and height- Your plumb line.
Father, in Jesus name, my desire is to be rightly related to You, to have all that You intend to give me and to receive everything that is in my inheritance. I ask You to open my eyes, and correct my perceptions. Show me how to work out my salvation daily. Show me what to let go of and whom to extend forgiveness, so my position will change. Lord, I repent for self-righteousness and wrongly judging others. Lord, please remove the shackle, trap, and snares from my legs.

Lord, I repent for myself and my generational line for denying miracles, power, and the resurrection that You purchased. Lord, remove any balls and chains on me and set me free from the grave.

Lord please shatter the glass walls of deception and ungodly perception that keep me from hearing, speaking, and seeing clearly with Your perception.

Lord, I repent for not acknowledging that the sins of my ancestors and their belief systems affect me today. I repent for blind ignorance and passivity keeping me from taking the kingdom by force. I choose to awaken to righteousness. Lord, please give me a heart of humility and position me rightly before You.

Lord, fill my heart with Your love and give me a revelation of who You are and what my walk is supposed to look like.

Father God, I repent for putting others into the pit through judgments, selfish ambition, and jealousy, especially against my brothers and sisters in Christ. Lord, I repent for choosing to live in the victim mentality.

I repent and renounce on for all idolatry and ungodly worship of man, man's ways and not truly worshipping and exalting You, Lord God.

Lord, please disconnect me from the ungodly star, and ungodly elders, rulers and powers that are holding me and chaining me to the pit, and take off the ungodly cummerbund, the knots and cords that have trapped me there.

Lord, please break off, shatter, destroy, remove and cut off any witchcraft which has empowered my entrapment in any of these ungodly dimensional places such as Sheol, death, fear, Hades, the snare, ungodly depth, perdition, the pits, the darkest place, utter darkness or the deep darkness. Lord, I repent and renounce on behalf of myself and my generational line for all those who used seduction, or any sexual practice as a means to entice and entrap people into ungodly dimensions.

Lord, remove me from the deep darkness of Sheol, the ungodly depth, fear, the snare, the trap, perdition, the pit, the darkest place, utter darkness or the deep darkness. Lord, please remove me from the snares, traps and nets that have bound my soul, my spirit, my body and my health in the ungodly depths.

Prayer to Release the Treasures of Darkness

Lord, I repent for myself and my ancestors for coming into agreement with Satan and seeking riches at all costs and lusting after our own glory, wealth and position at the expense of others and future generations.

I repent for myself and my family line for receiving and agreeing with the sounds, words and songs of Satan and asking him to make us rich and famous no matter the cost. I repent for lusting after my own glory on this side of eternity, instead of waiting on God to justly, generously, graciously and extravagantly care for and reward me in this life and the next.

I repent for myself and my family line for manipulating sound and words in order to make us look good and come out on top at all costs. I repent for puffing myself up, instead of seeking to lay down my life for others. I repent for stealing God's glory, proclaiming myself to be a self-made ruler instead rightfully honoring God alone as the only King of all kings.

I repent for myself and my ancestors for wanting to be the center of the universe and having everyone look and pay attention to me, instead of praising, honoring and giving glory to God, the only wise and true King of kings.

I repent for myself and my family line for trading all that we own and cherish, including parents, siblings, spouse and children in order to receive earthly riches, praise and adoration. I repent for sacrificing my children for riches and promotion and leaving them emotionally starved of parental leadership, protective boundaries, hugs, cuddles and affection that only a parent's love can supply to them. Lord, break the consequences of these actions off of me.

I repent for myself and my family line for passing negative pronouncements, shame, and curses on family and others instead of blessing them. I repent for coming into agreement with the curses and lies of the enemy spoken over me and my family by ungodly leaders, and wolves in sheep's clothing. I ask you, Lord, to break off of me and my generational line those curses, shame, and victimization. I repent for receiving my identity from man, and what others think of me instead of from you, Lord.

I repent for only seeing me, my needs and wants, instead of seeing You, God, and the needs of others. I repent for lavishly adorning myself while not covering the naked and caring for the homeless.

I repent for not guarding my heart or rightly discerning my emotions and responding in the soul rather than in the spirit. I ask You, God to be King over all that I think and feel. I repent for not asking You to seal and protect me, and to close off entrances to the enemy.

I repent for not honoring Your wisdom, Your creation, Your design at an atomic and sub atomic level, so that Your glory could come forth and Your light could be seen through me before conception and up until now. I repent for not correctly stewarding God's creation and having godly dominion over the earth instead of greedily abusing God's resources.

I repent for myself and my generational line for coming into agreement with the spirit of greed and worshipping mammon instead of You. I repent for desiring the power and control that money brings and not submitting to Your control, Father God. I repent for desiring Your blessings, but not wanting to position myself in You to be blessed and a blessing to others.

Lord, I repent of the greed of my ancestors that gave away my inheritance. I repent for their lies, avarice greed, and for stealing from future generations.

I repent and renounce for my ancestors illegally trading future generation's inheritance and blessing for their own immediate gratification and for not having faith in the King of kings to provide for them. I ask you, Lord, to cancel the obligation that my ancestors put on me to pay back what is owed for future trading in the past.

Lord, break off of me the consequences of my family line trading the blessings of future generations for instant gratification. I appeal to Your justice and Your bloodshed on the cross, and I ask You to declare in Your heavenly court that the agreements are illegal, null and void.

I repent for myself and my ancestors for loving money more than You, Lord, and clinging to the things of this world. I break agreements with the love of money, and let go of the things of this world. I ask you, Lord, to cut off the ungodly strings to wealth.

I pledge my love to You, Jehovah Jireh, and I look to You for provision. I declare that You are the Great I Am and the source of all that I have, all that I am, and all that I am to become. You are my Lord and my Redeemer.

Lord I pray the prayer Abraham Lincoln prayed: "we have forgotten You, Lord. We have forgotten the gracious hand which preserved us in peace and multiplied and enriched and strengthened us, and we have vainly imagined, in the deceitfulness of our hearts, that all these blessings were produced by some superior wisdom and virtue of our own. Intoxicated with unbroken success, we have become too self-sufficient to feel the necessity of redeeming and preserving grace, too proud to pray to the God that made us." Lord, I repent for pride, self-sufficiency, and not giving thanks for the abundant blessings You have given to me.

I repent and renounce for myself and my ancestors for valuing time and my schedule more than you, Lord. I repent for loving time and the control of time, "me" time, my time, quality time, instead of getting into Your time, God, and asking You to order my day according to Your desire. Please forgive me for allowing time to control me, for not seeking You first, or Your rest and restoration. Lord, please release me from any ungodly time warps or places where I've been stuck in time.

Lord, reestablish my generational timeline according to Your Kairos timeline. Please reconcile me to your correct Kairos timeline. Lord, remove me from any ungodly timeline that the enemy has placed me on that may be in the depth.

Lord, please purify my time with your living water. Wash away all the old timelines. Lord, align my inner clock to synchronize with Your heartbeat, sound and movement.

Lord please cleanse the elements of my physical body and the body of Christ. I declare that I will be a living stone properly fitted together in the body of Christ in timeless eternity with You, Lord.

Lord, please return to my DNA, all components that were given away or stolen from my ancestor's line. Lord, please correctly align the order and sequence of all the components of my DNA. Lord, please restore, the health, wealth, blessing, and favor that should be inherent in my DNA structure. Lord, please reverse the curse on my DNA when Adam sinned and return to me the original blessing that was designed in my family's DNA. Lord, release all the inherent blessings that were given to my family's DNA.

Lord, release the components of my DNA that were trapped by the stealing and illegal trading and giving away of my ancestors with the enemy for instant gratification. Lord, reestablish, the vibration of the electrons that connect the elemental parts of my DNA. Reestablish the correct frequency and vibration to the chemical bonds in my DNA.

Lord, please remove me from ungodly places in the heavens, the depth, the length, the width, and the height. Lord, I declare that all the earth belongs to You, and please reestablish the correct grid on the earth, above the earth, and under the earth.

Lord, please unearth the treasures of darkness stolen from my generational line and from the kingdom of God. Lord, please remove the ungodly guardians over the ungodly places in the depths that hold back what belongs to me and to Your kingdom. I declare that all I have and all that is owed to me belong to You, Lord God, and to Your kingdom.

Lord, right now I appeal to Your written word and to the spiritual laws that You have set up in Your kingdom, Your kingdom laws. Where the King's law rules, there will be a year of Jubilee. Lord, since You honored that law thousands of years ago, I declare there has been multiple jubilees.

Lord right now, in my family line, I lay claim for all jubilees, and I declare that today is my Day of Jubilee. I declare that all ungodly trading of the past by my ancestors, and the debt that I have been paying, to become null and void; it is cancelled and is no more. I ask for a seven-fold return at current market price for all that has been lost, stolen, or given away in my generational line.

Lord, I anticipate through faith, and declare that my trading will now be done in faith. My trust is in you Lord. Lord, I trade by faith and say You have my life. I trust in You, and I thank You Lord that it will be accomplished according to Your time.

Lord, I present this prayer before You in the heavenly court as the prayer of my heart. I ask You to appropriate this prayer to my own personal life. Lord, I ask for Your justice. I ask that You will render this prayer into Your courts as a legal document. Jesus, as my advocate, I ask that You go before the Father, and ask the Father to declare this a "done deal" in my life and in my generational line.

Prayer Breaking Ungodly Ties Between a Person and the Dimensions

I repent on behalf of myself and my generational line for connecting or entering into any realm, dimension or location in order to gain information and power from the enemy. In the name of Jesus Christ, I now reject any ungodly inheritance of power or information. Lord, please take any part of me out of those locations and close and seal all ungodly doors, gates or portals.

Lord Jesus, please stop all ungodly dimensional shifting as it relates to me and my family line.

Lord please remove me from any black holes, vortexes, or out of any voids between dimensions.

Lord, please remove me from being trapped in infinity and from any ungodly constant or unending cycles.

Lord, please remove from me any ungodly repeating patterns, any ungodly device, deposit, attachment, agreement, or entities from those dimensions, black holes, vortexes, or from any voids between dimensions.

In the name of Jesus Christ, on behalf of myself and my family line, I repent and renounce and break all ungodly ties between me and my family line and the first dimension,
…between me and my family line and the second dimension,
…between me and my family line and the third dimension.

I break all ungodly ties between me and my family line and the fourth dimension.
Lord please put me and my family line and time and space back in right alignment.

I break all ungodly ties between me and my family line and the fifth dimension,
the sixth dimension, the seventh dimension, the eighth dimension, the ninth dimension, the tenth dimension, the eleventh dimension, and…twelfth, etc. and all dimensions through eternity.

Lord, where it affects me and my family line, please break all ungodly agreements between dimensions and all ungodly linkages between dimensions. Please remove any evil spirits energizing these ungodly connections and agreements.

Lord please return anything good that was stolen or given away and close and seal all ungodly doors.

Lord Jesus please open up the godly dimensions that lead to You and the revelation of Your purposes in my life.

Prayer of Renunciation for the Misogynistic Spirit

Heavenly Father, on behalf of myself and my generational line, I repent for and renounce all hatred and dishonor of women.

For myself and my family line I repent for and renounce engaging in forced marriages, prostitution, and the treating women as objects, to be bought and sold without regard to their safety or calling for the purpose of sexual exploitation or financial gain. I repent for all who used women, particularly older or unattractive women, as slave labor. Lord, please break off all the consequences on my family line for those who were treated as burdens and rejected as worthless because of their feminine gender.

I repent for and renounce for myself and my family line for all who considered women a little better than animals, without spirit or genuine intelligence. I repent for all who enforced female genital mutilation to control and subdue women. I repent for all who believed the lie that women were created first and faulty.

For myself and my family line, I repent for and renounce all who accepted a practice that enabled the owners of feudal estates to deflower virgins on their wedding night. I repent for all who valued women based on proof, real or imagined, of their virginity. I repent for all who dehumanized women by romanticizing them as pure and untouchable, or demonized them by reducing them to only sexual roles. More specifically, I repent for all who were deceived by the manifestation of the misogynistic spirit known as the Madonna/whore complex.

For myself and my family line, I repent for and renounce the generational hatred of the female gender that led to infanticide of girls in many cultures. I repent for all who murdered women.

For myself and my family line, I repent for and renounce getting hysterectomies without medical cause to solve emotional distresses in women.

For myself and my family line, I repent for and renounce all participation in dishonorable legal practices regarding women, withholding from them the right to own property, to have custody of their own children, or to have a voice in their own lives.

For myself and my family line, I repent for and renounce all participation in legal violence against women. I repent for all who committed financial abuse against women, refusing to provide for them.

For myself and my family line, I repent for and renounce denying women access to education to subjugate them. I repent for all who have denied women access into various trades because of fear and greed which denied them a way for providing for themselves. I repent for all who devalued the equal physical labor of a woman by seeing it as less than equal.

For myself and my family line, I repent for and renounce committing violence against women during the days when women peaceably demonstrated for the right to vote.

For myself and my family line, I repent for all who engaged in abortion, forced or voluntary and renounce this act. I repent for all who participated in corrupt medical practices, such as the outlawing of forceps, because of a belief that women were to suffer during childbirth.

For myself and my family line, I repent for all who participated in medical practices that administered drugs, not to relieve pain, but to disorder a woman's mind so that she would not remember giving birth and then removed the baby forcibly while the mother was trapped in restraints.

For myself and my family line, I repent for all who have participated in medical practices that ignored the needs of the mother and gave preference to the doctor, practices such as giving unnecessary cesareans, episiotomies, and all other procedures that treat pregnancy as an illness.

For myself and my family line, I repent for all who valued women solely on the basis of their ability to bear children, particularly male children. I particularly repent for all those who blamed their wives for the failure to produce children.

For myself and my family line, I repent and renounce for all who have objectified women by valuing them solely on the basis of their beauty. I repent for all who have debased women by participating in pornography and prostitution.

For myself and my family line, I repent for and renounce any rejection of women based on flaws in comparison with the beauty standard of the time. I repent for all who fixated on female beauty and missed the genuine beauty that God placed within woman.

For myself and my family line, I repent for all who have twisted the original intent of the submission of women in marriage, dishonoring the knowledge that women are co-heirs with Christ and I renounce their error. I repent for all who have used their authority to humiliate abuse and control women.

For myself and my family line, I repent on behalf of all of the mothers in my generational line who failed to bond with and support their children and passed on a distrust and hatred of women and I renounce this failure to love. I repent on behalf of the children in my generational line who held bitter root judgments against their mothers and sisters and opened a door to misogyny.

For myself and my family line, I repent for all who have been deceived by the feminist mindset which views God, marriage, and motherhood as the primary avenues of violence against women and I renounce this mindset. I repent for all who rejected their roles as women. I repent for all who have dishonored women by this rejection.

In the name of Jesus of Nazareth, I forgive everyone who has hurt me and my family by agreeing with and acting in a misogynist spirit.

Father God, please cleanse all misogyny from my generational line and restore to the women in my family line the place you originally intended for them. I ask you to bless them with the knowledge of Your love and a desire to claim their inheritance and an acceptance of their calling in You.

For women to pray: I repent for and renounce my personal agreement with the woman-hating spirit. I now break every curse I have spoken over myself, including my body and its functions, in the name of Jesus. I repent for and renounce any spiritual rebellion or anger over the choice of my Heavenly Father to create me as woman. I accept my female gender and bless it, in the name of Jesus.

Prayer to Restore Me into Proper Time and Amend My Body Clock

Father, on behalf of myself and my family line, I renounce and repent for rejecting Your timing and taking timing into our own hands. I repent for all those who used devices as a method of time control including stop watches, charms, amulets, talismans, clothing or any other ungodly device.

On behalf of myself and my family line, I renounce and repent for worshipping time instead of worshipping the God most high who holds time in His hands.

Lord, on behalf of myself and my generational line, I renounce and repent for all who attempted to control, bend, or warp time, for all who tried to control time for their own purposes and for all who attempted to travel through time to change and manipulate their own lives or the lives of others.

Lord, please disconnect my family line from any ungodly clocks. Please disconnect me from the magnetic field of the land that seeks to control my body clock, and please disconnect me from any ungodly time. Please remove any ungodly connection to Greenwich.

Lord, please break any connection between me and any ungodly priest of time. Please break all soul ties between me and any false or ungodly fathers or mothers, grandfathers or grandmothers of time. Lord, please break any connection between me and any time lords. Lord, I renounce and repent on behalf of myself and those in my generational line for any agreements that were made with the grim reaper who we believed came when it was time to die.

Lord, please remove any connection between the ungodly clock-face and my physical and spiritual senses. Please break, shatter, cut off, and destroy the connectors between the ungodly clock face and my eyes, ears, mouth, nose, and hands. Please remove the ungodly pendulum so that I may be correctly balanced in Your time.

Lord please remove the ungodly clock face and replace it with Your righteous clock face. Please cause the hands of the clock to move according to Your time and bring my body clock back into your control and nobody else's. Please establish the correct time, so that confusion, lack of self-awareness, and loss of time will not occur.

Lord please stop the deceleration of my body clock and restore me to godly acceleration.

Lord, I renounce and repent on behalf of myself and those in my generational line who spoke word curses to do with time against themselves and others. Lord, I repent for lies about time to myself and to others: I repent for believing or saying that we were 'living on borrowed time,' 'out of time,' or 'walking on the sands of time.' I repent of saying of myself and anyone else that our 'time is or was running out.' Lord please remove from above my head the ungodly hourglass.

I renounce the power of kronos to slow down time and work through fallen thrones to cause decay in my body with the elemental spirits. I declare I will not have a premature death, and there will not be a slowing down in my bodily functions or brain functions. I declare that I will reach the potential of the birthright you have given to me in my scroll. Remove any evil associated with this and all ungodly spiritual beings associated with this. Lord, please disconnect me, my family line, and my descendants from all ungodly time keeping. Lord, please synchronize me to your time. Please cancel all ungodly multiplications or dividing of time. Lord, please remove all ungodly fractals of time. Please restore the elemental spirits to your correct creative design. Lord, remove all distortions and decaying and fractures of time. Remove death from the equation. Lord, please restore all telomeres to your intended length.

I declare the truth that as a believer in Christ my time is not up and will never be up. I am seated in heavenly places and will live for eternity. I choose to believe that whoever believes in you shall not die but have eternal life. I declare my eternal timeline and nature in Christ who lives forever and ever.

Father, please restore eternity to my heart and readjust it to beat with your Kairos. Lord, please make Your timing my timing and your seasons my seasons. Lord, I ask that You give me a heart that is able to discern both time and Judgment.

Lord I declare the truth that You are the alpha and omega. You are the one who places eternity in the hearts of man. You are the creator and controller of time. Lord You are the one who has written all the days of my life in your book. You knew them before even one came into being. You are the one who has seen the beginning and the end, and I now chose to place my time into Your hands. I chose now to believe and trust that Your timing in my life is better than my timing.

Lord, please apply Your blood to the mechanisms, gears, and springs of my body so that they will work as You have ordained and planned them to work. Please now anoint with oil all the parts of my body clock. I choose now to step into Your time for me and Your excellent glory.

Lord please replace the ungodly clock parts with godly clock parts so that the body clock that You have given me will click and move, synchronized with You in glory from now onwards.

Lord, please unite my body clock to You and the Body of Christ, so that we will be synchronized and not go ahead of one another or ahead of You. Please bring us collectively into right time. Restore me now fully to correct time with a righteous body clock.

Prayer to Release Us into Emotional Healing

I repent for all those in my generational line, beginning with Adam and Eve, who, in their desire to know good and evil, opened a door of fear and shame. Lord, please close the portal and cleanse the neutral pathways of the brain to reestablish your joy.

I repent for myself and for all those in my family line who have hidden themselves from their own emotions and from the Lord when He has come to help. I choose to remove all fig leaves of self-protection and to come into the place of intimacy that the Lord Jesus provided by His redemption.

I repent for all those in my generational line who exchanged the glory of the Lord for the fruit of the knowledge of good and evil. Lord I declare that all wisdom and knowledge are hidden in Christ; and I choose to set my mind on things above.

I repent for all those in my generational line who denied their emotions and projected their fear and shame onto those around them. Lord, please repair the attachment patterns in our brains and restore them to the perfection that existed when Adam and Eve walked with You in the Garden.

I repent for all those in my generational line who refused to rejoice in the Lord, who allowed their countenances to fall, thus allowing sin to enter their doors.

Lord, please remove the iniquity and pattern in my family line that flowed from Cain's choice to remain in pain and not return to joy. I choose to count all joy, believing that endurance and maturity are gifts from above.

I repent for myself and all those in my generational line who did not acknowledge You as the I AM. I repent for all those who, not seeing your LOVE, turned to false attachments to comfort themselves. Lord, please cleanse the attachment center of my brain and wash over the DNA in my family with Your precious blood.

I repent for those who rejected You as Loving Father, Provider, and Sustainer of all life.

I repent for those who gave their hearts to idols, worshipping and serving them in place of the Lord.

I repent for everyone in my family line who rebelled against parents and authority figures in an effort to escape shameful emotions.

I repent for my generational line who became thieves and refused to see You, Lord, as the source of all provisions. I repent for all those who lied and deceived out of fear or greed.

I repent for all those in my generational line who coveted things and for all who attached themselves to the belongings of others.

I repent for all those in my generational line who became drunk with alcohol, seeking to escape painful emotions rather than seeking your Face.

I repent for all those in my family line who used or provided others with drugs to exit from this world and enter into ungodly places. Lord, please clean and call back any parts of my spirit or my generational inheritance from ungodly places and seal the door with Your blood.

I repent for those in my generational line who did not forgive the sins against them and who held onto anger as a protection. Lord, please release all debts and debtors that have been held by my generational line and please remove the tormentors that have come against my life.

I repent for all those who boasted in chariots, horses, and the might of men for their deliverance and protection.

I repent for all in my generational line who demanded life for life, eye for eye, tooth for tooth, hand for hand, foot for foot, burn for burn, wound for wound, bruise for bruise, and who did not love and pray for their enemies.

I repent for myself and all those in my family line who, not mastering their emotions, turned to their flesh, committing sins of immorality, impurity, sensuality, idolatry, sorcery, enmities, strife, jealousy, outbursts of anger, disputes and dissensions, factions, envying, drunkenness, and carousing.

I repent for myself and all those in my generational line who have refused to crucify the flesh with its passions and desires. Lord, I ask that you would release your holy fire and burn off the iniquity that has passed through the generations.

I repent for all those in my generational line who devised man-made rules, legalistic guidelines and spiritual laws to control emotions and behavior. Lord I choose to live and walk by Your Spirit relying on Your voice to direct my path.

I repent for all those in my generational line who have tried to live and breathe alone. Lord, please interrupt the pathway to the pleasure center in my brain and form new connections to your heart.

I declare that I am a new creature in Christ and that old things have passed away. I believe that when I walk by the Spirit I will not gratify the desires of my Flesh.

Lord, please strengthen the pathway of the Spirit in my mind so that I might enter Your gates with thanksgiving and Your courts with praise. Lord, please remind my spirit that it is seated with You in heavenly places far above all powers, rulers, and authorities. Lord, please judge every spiritual force connected to this iniquity and restore everything that has been stolen from my generational line.

Renunciations for Babylon

Heavenly Father, I ask you to forgive me and all members of my ancestral line for the spirit of rebellion that was in Nimrod who set himself to oppose you and revolted against you. I repent for the tyranny, despotism and ungodly dominion that Nimrod practiced. I repent for all participation in building ungodly empires, cities and world systems. I repent for all trapping and hunting of the souls of men. I repent for the trading of the souls of men.

We repent for the arrogance and presumption that holds that men could by themselves build the gateway to God. We repent for misusing the power of religion to share the glory of God, to make a name for ourselves like the Nephilim, and to try to control our lives and our futures. We repent for all agreement with the spirit of Babylon, which uses religious authority to gain earthly power and prestige. We repent for our rebellion, pride, and self-will—the arrogance that makes us believe that we can accomplish anything we want on our own without you.

Lord, we repent for being aligned with Babylon, the City of Man. Please help us to be citizens of and aligned with the City of God, the New Jerusalem. Lord, help us to enter into Your inheritance for us by faith, looking for a city which has foundations, whose builder and maker is You.

Lord, we repent for all worship of Nimrod and all emperor worship. I repent for all participation in advancement of the ungodly one world system, New World Order and reptilian agenda against You.

We repent for the worship of and covenants made with Nimrod as the Sumerian Enmer, Mesopotamian Ninurta, Greek Ninus, Greek Zeus, Greek Hercules, Greek Atlas, Babylonian Marduk and his planet Mars, biblical Merodach or Bel of Baal, Assyrian Ashur, Egyptian Osiris, Late Sumerian Dumuzi, Roman Chronos or Saturn, Chaldean Zoroaster. Please disconnect us from Nimrod, Enmer, Ninurta, Zeus, Hercules, Atlas, Marduk, Mars, Merodach, Bel, Ashur, Osiris, Dumuzi, Chronos, Saturn and Zoroaster.

We repent for the worship of and covenants made with Marduk as the Bull of Utu, as Moloch in Canaan, as the Bull of Heaven, as the Golden Calf in the wilderness, as Nandi in India, as Apis in Egypt, as the 'Bull of Crete,' the Minotaur and the constellation of Taurus. Please disconnect us from the Bull of Utu, Moloch, the Bull of Heaven, the Golden Calf, Nandi, Apis, the Minotaur and Taurus.

We repent for the worship of and covenants made with Semiramis, wife of Nimrod, queen of Babylon, also known as Queen of Heaven, as Ammas, Mother of the gods, as Ge or Gaia, the earth goddess; Isis in Egypt the Madonna in Italy, as Juno, Cybele or Rhea in Rome, as Athena, Minerva or Hera in Greece, as Shing Moo or Ma Tsoopo in China, Parvati in India, as Astarte or Ashtoreth in Phoenicia, Aphrodite of Greece, Venus of Rome, and Vesta or Terra of Rome. Please disconnect us from the Queen of Heaven, Ammas, Ge, Gaia, Isis, Madonna, Juno, Cybele, Rhea, Athena, Minerva, Hera, Shing Moo, Ma Tsoopo, Parvati, Astarte, Ashtoreth, Aphrodite, Venus, Vesta, Terra.

We repent for the worship of the unholy trinity in the Babylonian mysteries—Nimrod, his consort Semiramis and their posthumous son, Tammuz, who was proclaimed as the reincarnation of

Nimrod. We repent for all the paganism and idol worship that had their roots in the legends having to do with Nimrod, Semiramis, and Tammuz.

We repent for the system of mysteries of Babylon that was set up when this false worship went underground in Babylon at the time Nimrod was killed. We repent for the intended purpose— glorifying the dead Nimrod. We repent for the sacrifices to the dead and for the use of seals of secrecies, oaths, initiation ceremonies, and magic used to continue this idolatry in secret. We repent for spreading this secret mystery religion through the earth.

On behalf of myself and my family line, I repent for the practice of Freemasonry, the mysteries of the Egyptian Isis, the goddess-mother, wife of Osiris. I repent for practice of Satanism, Luciferianism, Illuminati, Gnosticism, the Knights Templar, Rosicrucianism, the Theosophical Society, the New World Order, New Age and Lucid Trust. Lord, please disconnect me from these cults.

Lord, on behalf of myself and my family line I repent for calling evil good and good evil. I repent for all ungodly mixing of light and darkness, for the shifting of Your ordained boundaries between light and darkness. I repent for substitution of darkness for light and light for darkness, for substitution of bitter for sweet and sweet for bitter. I repent for participation in mixing of the waters under the firmament with the waters above the firmament. Please restore Your godly boundaries between light and darkness, bitter and sweet. Please restore Your boundaries between the waters under the firmament and the waters above the firmament.

Lord, on behalf of myself and my ancestors, I repent for the worship of Tammuz, posthumous son of Semiramis, who was claimed to be Nimrod resurrected, the promised 'seed of the woman' who would deliver mankind.

I repent for the worship of Tammuz as the Sun God, as Horus in Egypt, Bacchus in Rome, Adonis and Eros in Greece, Dionysius in Greece, Cupid in Rome, Deoius in Asia, Baal-berith or Lord of the Covenant, and as Vishnu and Ishwara in India. Please disconnect me from Tammuz, Horus, Bacchus, Adonis, Eros, Dionysius, Cupid, Deoius, Baal-berith, Vishnu, Ishwara.

Please forgive me and my family line for the worship of the Moon God as Sin in Syria and as Allah in Arabia. Lord, please deliver me and my family line from all curses of insanity that have come upon us as a result of the worship of the moon. Forgive me for all ungodly rituals and practices associated with the different cycles of the moon, including rituals done at new moon, full moon, and all shape-shifting. Please cleanse the night, time and the lunar cycles.

On behalf of myself and my family line I repent for all worship of the sun and sun deities as Helios or Titan and Apollo in Greece, Shamash or Tammuz in Mesopotamia, the Germanic Sol, the Vedantic Surya and Adityas, the Incan Inti and Aztec Huitzilopochtli, the Egyptian Ra, Amaterasu in Japan, and the Slavic Dazhbog. Lord, please disconnect me from Helios, Titan, Apollo, Shamash, Sol, Surya, Adityas, Inti, Huitzilopochthli, Ra, Amaterasu, Dazhbog.

On behalf of myself and my ancestors I repent for the ungodly use of the caduceus or Rod of Asclepius in the practice of medicine based upon the astrological principles of using the planets and stars to heal the sick. I repent for all worship of Asclepius, Chiron, Hermes and all association of these false deities with the practice of medicine. I repent for the use of magic and hermetic arts in the practice of medicine. Please disconnect me from Hermes, Asclepius, Chiron.

Please forgive me and my family line for worship of and covenants made with the wisdom gods Anzu in Sumer, Thoth in Egypt, Hermes in Greece. Please disconnect me from Anzu, Thoth and Hermes.

On behalf my myself and my family line I repent for the worship of and covenants made with ungodly seraphim, serpent deities and dragons including Poseidon, Hydra and Triton, Gorgons and Medusa, Shiva, Naga, Auslavis in Lithuania, the Rainbow Serpent of the Aboriginal People of Australia, the Minoan Snake Goddess, Zombi in West Africa and Haiti, Degei in Fiji, the Mayan-Aztec Quetzlcoatl, the Incan Viracocha. Lord, please disconnect us from Poseidon, Hydra, Triton, the Gorgons, Medusa, Shiva, Naga, Auslavis, the Rainbow Serpent, the Minoan Snake Goddess, Zombi, Degei, Quetzlcotl, Viracocha. Lord, please disconnect us from Leviathan, the sea monster, from the ancient serpent, the dragon.

I also repent for the worship of and covenants made with the following Babylonian entities: Eridu or Ea, the god of wisdom, magic and waters; Enlil or Elil, god of air, land, earth and men's fates and Jupiter his planet; Nanna or Sin, god of the moon; Ninurta, An or Anu, the god of heaven; Ninlil or Nillina, the goddess of the air, wife of Enlil; Ishtar or Inanna, the goddess of love and war and her planet Venus; Nergal, god of death, and his planet Mars; Enki the god of water and fertile earth and his planet Mercury; Ki or Nirhursag, the mother-goddess representing the earth; Tiamat, the mother goddess and goddess of the salt waters. Lord, please disconnect us from Eridu, Ea, Enlil, Eli, Jupiter, Nanna, Sin, Ninurta, An, Anu, Ninlil, Nilina, Ishtar, Inanna, Venus, Nerga, Mars, Enki, Mercury, Ki, Nirhursag, Tiamat.

Lord, on behalf of myself and my generational line I repent for all ungodly participation in cosmic wars of rebellion with the Watchers and the sons of God against You. I repent for all alliances and covenants made with the ungodly sons of God in these wars. I repent in participation in stealing the jewels of the cherub and stones of fire and Tablets of Destinies which belong to You. Please remove the effects and consequences of us stealing and owning these stones and Tablets of Destinies. On behalf of myself and my family I repent for all participation in ungodly use of weapons of power, of planetary weapons.

Lord, please pronounce judgment against the ungodly Sons of God and set free the nations that they have authority over. Lord, these nations are Your inheritance. Please release the inheritance of the nations. Please restore the jewels to the ephod of the High Priest. Please restore the Tribes of Israel and their inheritance.

Please remove ungodly connections between me and the jewels of the cherub, the stones of fire and Stones and Tablets of Destinies. Please remove all ungodly inscriptions from the jewels and stones and cleanse them of all defilement. Please restore the stones and the jewels. Please disconnect me from false birthrights, destinies and inheritances, from ungodly stones, jewels and Tablets of Destiny. Please restore my birthright, my destiny and my inheritance.

Please remove the defilement of the stars, the stones, the Eyes of the Lord. Please cleanse all the connectors between the eyes of the Lord, the stars and the stones. On behalf of myself and my family line, I repent for all covenants and associations with the ungodly Seven Spirits. Please disconnect us from these and restore our connections to the godly Seven Spirits – Wisdom, Understanding, Counsel, Might, Knowledge, Fear of the Lord and the Spirit of the Lord.

Lord I repent for myself and for my generational line for all worship of, ungodly association and partnership with the ungodly Sons of God, the sun, the moon, the stars and constellations, especially the ones listed below. I declare that the Blood Covenant that I have with the Lord Jesus Christ supersedes all covenants made with these. Lord please declare all these covenants null and void.

Lord I repent for myself and my generational line for co-creating ungodly worlds and fantasy worlds with the ungodly Sons of God for escapism and other purposes. I ask you to destroy these worlds and remove all connections to the ungodly Sons of God through these worlds. Please bring me into the world where Jesus is the Beginning and the End.

Lord please remove all ungodly ties between me and Andromeda, Antlia, Apus, Aquarius, Aquila, Ara, Aries, Auriga, Boötes, Caelum, Camelopardalis, Cancer, Canes Venatici, Canis Major, Canis Minor, Capricornus, Carina, Cassiopeia, Centaurus, Cepheus, Cetus, Chamaeleon, Circinus, Columba, Coma Berenices, Corona Austrina, Corona Borealis, Corvus, Crater, Crux, Cygnus, Delphinus, Dorado, Draco, Equuleus, Eridanus, Fornax, Gemini, Grus, Hercules, Horologium, Hydra, Hydrus, Indus, Lacerta, Leo, Leo Minor, Lepus, Libra, Lupus, Lynx, Lyra, Mensa, Microscopium, Monoceros, Musca, Norma, Octans, Ophiuchus, Orion, Pavo, Pegasus, Perseus, Phoenix, Pictor, Pisces, Piscis Austrinus, Puppis, Pyxis, Reticulum, Sagitta, Sagittarius, Scorpius, Sculptor, Scutum, Serpens, Sextans, Taurus, Telescopium, Triangulum, Triangulum Australe, Tucana, Ursa Major, Ursa Minor, Vela, Virgo, Volans, Vulpecula.

"Rise up, O LORD! Let Your enemies be scattered, and let those who hate You flee before You."

I repent for trying to discover the will of the gods for man and his affairs from the stars, and in decisions about when to plant and harvest, when and whom to marry.

Lord, on behalf of myself and my ancestors, I repent for ungodly manipulation of light, electromagnetism, gravity and strong and weak nuclear forces, plasma torsions, scalar resonances and particle spins to alter geometries of space and time, to create weapons of mass destruction and bloodshed, to create natural disasters and for weather control.

On behalf of myself and my family I repent for ungodly control of mind, will and emotions through electromagnetism. Please cleanse all light, color, images, sounds, frequency entrainment, microwaves, radiations, numbers, electromagnetic and radio waves. I repent for all ungodly manipulation of the properties of matter and the aetheric medium for destructive purposes, for ungodly manipulation of weather, of matter and of time. Lord, please cleanse matter, the aetheric medium, weather and time and restore me to harmony with You.

On behalf of myself and my ancestors I repent for the use of drugs, hypnosis, pain and pleasure conditioning, programming trance states, cults, sensory deprivation, dehumanization, psychoelectronics, implants, surgery, torture and torment for the purposes of witchcraft, delusion, behavior control, brainwashing and propaganda. I repent for all ungodly erasing of memory, history and time. Lord, please remove all ungodly programming and conditioning. Please cleanse my brain, body, emotions from all evil. Please cleanse and restore my memory, will, time and history and all my connections to You.

Lord on behalf of myself and my ancestors, I repent for all ungodly breeding and engineering of genetic lines of man and creatures. I repent for participation in ungodly seed donation and the mixing of my bloodline with the Watchers, the Sons of God, Annunaki, Reptilians, angels, strange flesh.

On behalf of myself and my family I repent for creation of chimeras, for ungodly mixing of DNA from animals, reptiles, birds and man to create new creatures. I repent for all worship of and covenants made with these chimeras including griffins, sphinxes, mermaids, centaurs. Please disconnect me from the griffin, sphinx, mermaid and centaur. Please remove these from my DNA and from my generational line.

On behalf of myself and my family line I repent for all worship of and covenants made with the following creatures. I repent for shape-shifting into these creatures to acquire their abilities. I repent for mixing my blood and DNA with the following creatures. Please cleanse my blood and DNA from the snake, dragon, crocodile, behemoth, lizard, tortoise, turtle, viper, rat, bull, cow, ram, goat, horse, buffalo, bison, deer, sheep, eagle, owl, pigeon, crane, phoenix, wolf, fox, coyote, beaver, badger, bear, tiger, lion, leopard, monkey, donkey, elephant, cougar, rabbit, pig, cat, dog, fish, scorpion, locust, lice, cockroach, cricket, worm, fly, bug, beetle, moth, spider, wasp, bee, butterfly, crab, frog, clam, mussel, oyster, octopus, slug, snail, squid, dolphin, shark and whale. Please remove these totems from my generational line.

On behalf of myself and my generational line, I repent for mixing the seed of Man and the seed of Satan. I repent for ungodly mixing of my generational line and machines, for ungodly regeneration of my body, for displacing souls to possess their bodies. I repent for all ungodly displacement of time locks established at conception. Please set my time reference and my time lock to You. Lord please disconnect me, my blood and my DNA from the ungodly Sons of God, the Watchers, the ungodly seraphim, from the reptilians and their seed. Please remove ungodly machines and biological entities from my blood and DNA.

Lord please separate my Y-chromosomes, my mitochondrial DNA and DNA from all Annunaki content, from animal, reptile and bird content. Lord please remove corruption, the pit and the worm from my generational line. Lord please restore the integrity of my bloodline and the inheritance and treasures of my generational line.

Lord on behalf of myself and my ancestors I repent for ungodly monetary policies and banking systems, for the private monopoly issuance of debt as money that has enslaved nations and peoples. I repent for worship of money, for control of money, for being ungodly priests who have sold out to Mammon.

On behalf of myself and my ancestors, I repent for using ungodly weights and measures of value. I repent for ungodly trading of gold, silver, precious metals and slaves. I repent for the operation of false monetary systems using slave labor. I repent for ungodly accumulation of riches in my generational line as defined by the world system. I repent for participation in the ungodly control of the flow of money, enterprise, trade and industry.

On behalf of myself and my ancestors I repent for control of money by the issuance of false money receipts with no backing store of value, thereby changing the value of money. I repent for participating in false credit and debt systems. I repent for financial alchemy – for creation of money and value from nothing.

I repent for being ungodly moneychangers in ungodly alliance with the temples. I repent for participation in establishment of ungodly temple financial systems and all dedication of these systems and money to ungodly sons of God.

Lord, I declare that all that I have and all that I am belong to you. Please remove ungodly ties between me and gold, silver, precious metals, money, debt, credit, banks, temple systems. Please cleanse gold, silver and all precious metals. Please set the nations free from debt slavery and from the Babylonian trade system.

Lord, I ask that you will free me and my family from the Babylonian false monetary system. Please grant to us the seven-year release from debt, debt-slavery and wage-slavery. Please grant to us the Jubilee restoration of the properties that belong to my generational line.

Heavenly Father, on behalf of my ancestors and myself, I repent for coveting the things of Babylon or the world system and being seduced by the things of the world into disobeying Your commandments and going against Your ways. On behalf of myself and my ancestors who were part of the Babylonian system, I repent for agreeing with the seductive spirit of Babylon and for all that we did to seduce Your people away from You.

We repent for trying to find our legitimacy by displaying to the world the power, wealth, influence, gifts, talents, and treasures that You gave us and for using them in the world when they were meant to be dedicated to You and be used in Your service. We repent that we found our legitimacy in looking for admiration and favor from the world instead of deriving our legitimacy from our relationship with You. Lord, we repent for being found wanting when You tried us to know what was in our hearts. Please connect and align our hearts with Your heart.

On behalf of our ancestors, we repent for trading generational blessings and treasures from our generational lines and selling them to the Babylonian system. Lord, please restore to us these generational treasures.

Forgive us for not listening to or obeying the words of Your servants, the true prophets, for not turning from our evil ways and living in the land and inheritance that You have given to us. Forgive us for going after other gods to serve them and worship them and for provoking You to anger with the ungodly works of our hands.

Lord, please set Your eyes upon us for good, bring us into our land and into our inheritance, build us up and plant us. Give us a heart to know you—to know that you are our God and that we are Your people. We return to You with our whole hearts.

Renunciations for Hinduism

Note: Some of the prayers may not be fully Hindu in origin, but could reflect an overlap between Hinduism and Buddhism. We include them to cover as much ground as possible.

Heavenly Father, I ask you to forgive me and all members of my ancestral line for all ungodly beliefs in Hinduism and its philosophies, for all Hindu idolatry, and for all ungodly practice of Hinduism and its disguised offshoots: forgive us for obtaining knowledge illegally through ungodly Hindu sources, for practicing sorcery and witchcraft, and for making ungodly sacrifices to the false gods of Hinduism.

Heavenly Father I repent for and renounce the worship of and all covenants that my ancestors or I made with the ungodly trinity—Brahma the Creator, Vishnu the Preserver, and Shiva the Destroyer.

On behalf of myself and my family line I repent for believing or saying,

"I have no qualities, I am without activity and destitute of option,
Changeless, eternal, formless, without taint, forever free, forever without stain.
I, like the boundless ether, permeate the universe within, the universe without,
Abiding always, forever similar in all - perfect, immovable,
Without affection, existence, knowledge, undivided bliss,
Without a Second
The Supreme Eternal, That am I."

On behalf of myself and my family line, I repent for believing or saying,

"Brahma, primal motive force is my womb;
in that I place the seed;
Thence, O Arjuna, is the birth of all beings!
Whatever forms are produced, in all the wombs,
the great Brahma is their womb
and I am the seed-giving father."

Lord, please disconnect me from the heart and womb of Brahma, and from ungodly seed and seed-giving entities. I repent for all who allowed ungodly incarnations of gods within the human consciousness, within me. Lord please disconnect me from all ungodly avatars.

On behalf of myself and my family line, I repent for believing or saying,

"The knower catches in the ecstasy of his heart
the full light of that Brahman (that Divine Essence)
which is indescribable—all pure bliss, incomparable,
transcending time, ever free, beyond desire."

Lord please disconnect us from the light of Brahman and from all ungodly light sources.

On behalf of myself and my family line I repent for using the Hindu sacred texts as our source and direction. I renounce all ungodly invitations from, guidance by, and connections to the ungodly spiritual realities behind these texts.

On behalf of myself and my family line, I repent for all believing or saying,

"Oh mind, the greatest bird,
Play in the cage of the two lotus feet of Sankara,
In the tree with the Vedas as branches,
With the Upanishads as the top,
With fruits which destroy pain and whose juice is nectar."

Lord please remove us and our minds from ungodly trees, birds, fruits and cages. Please disconnect us from the Vedas, Upanishads, Puranas and from Sankara.

On behalf of myself and my family line, I repent for and renounce all beliefs in the repeated cycles of creation, preservation and destruction of this universe. I renounce the ungodly cyclic world view represented by the ungodly wheel of time or kalachakra.

Please forgive us for believing that

"This wheel of life is associated with pairs of opposites and devoid of consciousness;
That man who always understands accurately the motion and stoppage of this wheel of life,
Is never seen to be deluded, among all creatures.
Freed from all impressions, divested of all pairs of opposites, released from all sins,
He attains to the highest goal."

On behalf of myself and my family, I repent for believing or saying,

"Know the Self who alone is to be known,
He in whom these sixteen parts rest,
- the spokes of the hub of the wheel of life,
Lest death should hurt you !"

I renounce the belief that the supreme self is at the center of the wheel of life and that achieving this self is the goal that goes beyond death. Lord please disconnect me and my family from the kalachakra, the ungodly wheel of time and its cycles.

I repent for and renounce all beliefs in karma, the law of cause and effect by which each individual creates his own destiny by his thoughts, words, and deeds.

I repent for and renounce all false beliefs in karma as the deeds related to the cycle of cause and effect, action and reaction, that my future and my destiny is determined by all my actions in this life and my previous lives. I repent for striving through self-effort to free myself of negative Karma and trying to make my destiny better through mantra, meditation and positive deeds.

On behalf of myself and my family line I repent for believing or saying,

"As blazing fire reduces wood to ashes, O Arjuna,
So does the fire of self-knowledge reduce all Karma to ashes."

Lord please forgive us for believing that shaping ourselves to circumstances according to our karma is the only way to acquire happiness.

On behalf of myself and my generational line, I repent for and renounce all false beliefs in the principle of reincarnation or samsara, that after death, my soul transmigrates into a new body and I come back to earth.

I renounce the belief that through our individual choices, we can resolve karma, attain moshka or liberation, and realize God, thus ending this cycle of death and rebirth. I renounce the belief that my soul is on a cosmic journey meant for its purification and that it manifests a body again and again 8.4 million times until it is purified.

I repent for everyone in my family line who said or believed that our desires for earthly objects chained us to rounds of births and deaths and that moksha, or freedom from this cycle, comes from renunciation of desires.

On behalf of myself and my family I repent for all who believed and said,

"As man casts off worn-out garments and puts on other which are new,
Similarly the embodied soul, casting off worn-out bodies,
Enters into others which are new."

I repent for myself and all in my family line who accepted the cycle of death and rebirth as inevitable for us.

I repent for and renounce all beliefs in, worship of, service to and covenants made with the Hindu celestial beings - the devas, the ungodly sons of God, the mahadevas and the evil trinity or Trimurti. Lord please disconnect me from these.

I repent for believing that an enlightened master or satguru is essential to guide my soul to self-realization.

On behalf of myself and my family, I renounce,

"[Bowing] before the sacred footwear of my teacher,
Who taught me the meaning of "OM".

I repent for and renounce any ungodly practices of non-injury to all creatures - ahimsa - that reveres creation above the true Creator.

I repent for and renounce the belief that there is not a single way to salvation and that all spiritual paths are acceptable.

I repent for and renounce the belief that dharma is the aim of existence and that observing dharma will lead to attainment of jnana, or higher religious knowledge and to bhakthi, or union with God through devotion.

I repent for and renounce the belief that moksha is achieved by the observation of dharma, fulfilling one's assigned duty and moral obligation to society according to one's position in life. I renounce all belief that I am obliged by duty to accept my current place in society without hope for reward or change. I renounce all belief that men attain salvation by faithfully following predetermined paths of duty. Lord please remove the effects that these constraints had on me that I may enter into my birthright and inheritance in You.

I repent for and renounce all the practices of bhakti, or devotion to god and the gods of Hinduism, so that the atman, or individual soul and spirit can merge with Brahman or universal consciousness and allow the realization of moksha.

On behalf of myself and my family line, I repent for believing or saying,

"One who serves Me with unwavering devotion, at once
transcends the three-strand cord of creation, preservation and destruction
and becomes fit to attain oneness with Brahman."

Lord, please forgive me and my ancestors for all practices of the four main denominations associated with Hinduism: for Saivism and the worship of Siva; for Shaktism and the worship of Shakti; for Vaishnavism and the worship of Vishnu; and for Smartism and the worship of one of the six deities, Ganapati, Surya, Vishnu, Siva, Shakti, and Kumara. Lord please disconnect me from these entities.

Saivism

I renounce and repent for all worship of and covenants made with Shiva as the highest Supreme Self or Brahman, the All and in All, the Destroyer and Transformer of the Trinity and as Father God, who causes the continuous cyclic process of creation, preservation, dissolution and recreation of the universe. I repent for worship of Shiva and the phallic Shiva Lingam as the source of the universe, as static, unmanifested consciousness in the transcendental plane. I repent for believing that Siva is within and for all striving to be one with the Siva within.

Lord I repent for all worship of and covenants made with Shiva in any and all manifestations including the following: Nataraja, Lord of the Dance; Dakshinamurthy, Shiva facing south and teacher of yoga, music and wisdom; Sadashiva, Eternal Shiva; Parameswara, Shiva on Mount Kailash; Paramasiva, the highest, Maheswara, Lord of the manifest universe; Saguna Brahman, Cosmic Lord of Creation, Maintenance, Destruction; Iswara or Rudra, the Destroyer; Shankara, the doer of good; Nilakantha, blue necked; Bholenath, innocent God; Hanuman, monkey god; Dakshinamurthy, guru; Pasupati, Lord of the Animals; Indra, regent of the East; Vishveshwara, Lord of the Universe; Sarveshwara, Shiva Lingam; Prajapati, lord of creatures. Lord please disconnect me and my family from all these entities.

Lord I repent for all worship of and covenants made with Siva in his various tantric manifestations such as Bhairava, the wrathful, the fierce manifestation of Shiva, the embodiment of fear; Virabhadra, the wrath of Shiva; Mahakaleswar, Lord of Time and Death; Tripurantaka, the archer; Vastospati, the guardian of the dwelling; Agni, the fire god; Vayu, the wind god;

Ardhnarishwara, half Shiva and half Shakti; Ganesha, lord of obstacles; Murugan, god of war; Subramaniam, the god of war. Lord please declare these covenants broken and disconnect me and my family from all these forms of Shiva. Lord please annul any marriage covenants between my family line and Shiva.

On behalf of myself and my family I repent for believing or saying,

The lord of all, hidden in all beings,
In him are united the gods and knowers of Brahman alike.
He who knows him cuts the fetters of death asunder.
He who knows Siva, the blessed, "He alone at the proper time, is the guardian of this world, hidden in all beings
Like the subtle film that rises from out the clarified butter,
Alone enveloping everything,
He who knows the god is freed from all fetters.

On behalf of myself and my family, I repent for believing or saying,

"Lord Shiva is seated on Mount Kailash;
His forehead is adorned with the moon and the king of serpents as a crown.
The lord is the ocean of mercy and the remover of illusion.
Shiva is the only protector.
I surrender myself to such great Lord Shiv-Shankar."

I repent for and renounce the mantra Aum Namah Sivaya, Sadyojata, Vamadeva, Aghora, Tatpurusa, Isana. Lord please disconnect me from its sounds.

Shaktism

Heavenly Father, on behalf of myself and my family line I repent for and renounce all false worship of and covenants made with the entity Shakti - the Supreme Energy of Shiva, the ungodly feminine, creative and dynamic energy in the physical plane and all other planes. Lord I repent for those who tapped into the matrix of energy, the Goddess Power. Lord please disconnect me from ungodly matrices.

Lord, I repent for and renounce all worship of and covenants made with Shakti in her various manifestations: Divine Mother, Goddess, Supreme Mother of the Universe; Adi Parashakti, Original Source of the Universe; Devi, goddess; Lalitha, goddess of bliss; Tripura Sundari, goddess who is beautiful in three realms; Parvathi or Uma, divine Shakti, consort of Shiva; Saraswati, goddess of knowledge; Lakshmi, goddess of wealth; Gayatri, Mother of Mantras; Ganga, goddess as Divine River; Sita, Rama's consort and goddess of marital relations; Radha, Krishna's consort; Sati ; Meenakshi, avatar of Parvati; Bhuvaneshwari, world mother; Kumari, virgin; Bagalamukhi, hypnotic power of the goddess who paralyzes enemies; Kamala the lotus goddess. Lord, please disconnect me from all these.

Lord, for myself and my family line, I repent for and renounce all worship of and covenants made with Shakti in her various tantric manifestations such as Shakias Kali, goddess of cosmic destruction and eternal night; Badrakali, auspicious Kali; Bhavani, source of creative energy; Chinnamasta, goddess who cuts off her own head; Durga or Ambika, the invincible; Bhairavi, fierce goddess of decay; Dhumavati, who widows herself; Matangi, the outcast goddess, the goddess of pollution; Tara, the protector and guide.

Lord, please disconnect us from Kali as mother-goddess, Black Time, devourer of time, personification of manifest time and the color black. Lord please disconnect me from the ten forms of Kali known as Mahavidyas. Lord please disconnect time from Kali. Lord please remove all ungodly connections between Kali and my timeline, between me and Kali Yuga or Age of Kali. Lord please remove all dakinis and other tantric consorts from me and my family line. Lord please destroy all ungodly Kali time rifts connected to me and my generational line. Lord please annul any marriage covenants between my family line and Kali.

I repent for all agreement with goddess power, for saying that the feminine is the dominant power of the universe and for all goddess focused spiritual practices, mantras, yantras, nyasa, mudra and yogas.

Lord in the name of Jesus of Nazareth, on behalf of me and my family I renounce the aspect of Shakti called Kundalini, serpent power, and ungodly mystic fire. I repent for all ungodly contact with this spirit. I repent for and renounce all practices that would awaken, invite or allow the presence or activity of the sleeping goddess Kundalini in any way. I renounce and repent for accepting the ungodly blessing of a Siddha-guru, for all tantric sexual rites and for all tantric practices of Shakta yoga and Kundalini yoga that awaken this serpent power and make it ascend through the psychic centers, the chakras that lie along the axis of the spine as consciousness centers.

Lord please disconnect me from union of Shakti and Shiva above the crown or sahasrara chakra of my head. I repent for everything to do with any fusion of the ungodly absolute, attempting a union of the individual with the universe. Lord please remove from me all ungodly cosmic vibrations and radiant energies. Lord please restore godly chemistry and righteous elements of my body. Lord please separate me from Kundalini and from all ungodly coiled serpents.

Lord on behalf of myself and my family line I repent for practicing kundalini as a translocal vibration allowing Shakti to change the space-time continuum of my body-mind. I repent for bartering for and seeking the vibration to change our body-minds, to create a cinmaya or light body endowed with transcendent and supernatural powers. Lord please remove all abilities from my family line which came to us through ungodly sources.

Father, for myself and my family line, I renounce all declarations, affirmations, proclamations and beliefs about Shakti as divinity. I repent for identifying Shakti in any pantheistic way with any aspect of Your creation. Please forgive us for confusing Creator with creation and thinking that Shakti could ever encompass any aspect, good and evil of Your creation. Please cleanse us of her influence.

Lord on behalf of myself and my family, I repent for and renounce for believing or saying,

"This whole universe is interwoven in me.
I am the Supreme Controller in causal bodies,
The Stream of Consciousness and the Golden Womb in subtle bodies,
The Universal Soul in external bodies.
I am Brahma, Vishnu and Shiva,

I am the Brahma, Vaisnavi and Raudri Saktis.
I am the Sun, I am the Moon, I am the Stars.
I am the Beasts, Birds, Outcasts,
And I am the thief, I am the cruel hunter;
I am the virtuous, high-souled persons.
I am Female, I am Male, and I am Hermaphrodite."

Lord, I repent for use of the occult Shaktism symbol Shri Chakra Yantra, the tantric symbol of cosmic unity as the junction point between the physical universe and its unmanifest source.

Lord please disconnect me and my family from the Shri Chakra Yantra and all its mantras, rituals and sounds; disconnect us from all metaphysical and geometrical constructs that correspond to the psychic centers of the subtle body. Lord please disconnect us from ungodly lotus flowers, instruments, machines, geometries, swastikas, from ungodly circles as the energy of water, ungodly squares and the energy of earth, ungodly triangles and the energy of fire, ungodly lines, and the energies of air, water, fire, and all ungodly points and ungodly energy of ether. I repent for and renounce all Shamanic Shaktism and the use of magic, trance, mediumship, fire-walking and animal sacrifice for healing, fertility, prophecy and power.

Lord please disconnect me from ungodly positioning of planets, precious stones, metals, alloys. Lord please remove anything in me born of Shakti and any ungodly union of Shiva and Shakti in me or in anything godly connected to me. Lord, please cleanse all the connectors in my body.

For myself and my family I repent for believing or saying,

"Only when united with Shakti
has Lord Shiva the power
To create the universe
Without her, he cannot move."

On behalf of myself and my family I repent for all who believed or said,

"At the dissolution of things, it is Kala Who will devour all,
And by reason of this He is called Mahakala,
And since Thou devourest Mahakala Himself,
It is Thou who art the Supreme Primordial Kalika.
Because Thou devourest Kala, Thou art Kali, the original form of all things,
And because Thou art the Origin of and devourest all things Thou art called the Adya.
Resuming after Dissolution Thine own form, dark and formless,
Thou alone remainest as One ineffable and inconceivable.
Though having a form, yet art Thou formless;
Though Thyself without beginning, multiform by the power of Maya,
Thou art the Beginning of all, Creatrix, Protectress, and Destructress that Thou art."
For myself and my family I repent for and renounce the mantra Aum Chandikayai Namah. Lord please disconnect us from its sounds."

Vaishnavism

On behalf of myself and all in my family line I repent for and renounce all worship of and covenants made with Vishnu and his various manifestations: Vishnu as the Supreme God, Preserver of the Universe, All-Pervading essence of all beings, the master of—and beyond—the past, present and future, the creator and destroyer of all existences, one who supports, sustains and governs the Universe and originates and develops all elements within.

Father, I ask you to forgive us—for You alone are God, our Creator, and You alone uphold the universe by the word of Your power. Father, I repent for attributing to Vishnu anything of Your character or attributes and anything of the person, purpose, and authority of Your only son, Jesus Christ.

On behalf of myself and my family I repent for all who believed that in each age, whenever evil prevails over good, Vishnu comes down to earth in some mortal form to save righteousness. I repent for all practice of prapatti, single-pointed surrender to Vishnu or His ten or more incarnations, called avatars. Lord I repent for all worship of the avatars: Matsya the fish, Kurma the tortoise, Varaha the boar; Narasimha, half-lion, half-man, Vamana the dwarf, Parashurama or Rama with the axe, Rama the perfect man, Krishna the lover, Balarama the broker of Krishna and the coming avatar, Kalki as Eternity or Time.

On behalf of myself and my family I repent for believing or saying,

"I am the Goal, the Sustainer, the Lord, the Witness, the Abode,
the Refuge, the Friend, the Origin, the Dissolution,
the Resting-Place, the Storehouse and the Eternal Seed."

On behalf of myself and my family I repent for believing or saying,
"I bow to Lord Vishnu, the Master and Controller of the Universe,
Identical with the sun, Destroyer of all-destroying Time itself;
He that upholds the earth in space;
He is the food which supports the life of living creatures;
He that has incarnated on earth a hundred times,
To rescue the good, destroy the wicked and establish righteousness
He that leads us safely across the ocean of life;"

Lord please disconnect us from Vishnu, Seshnaga, Narayana, Matsya, Kurma, Varaha, Narasimha, Vamana, Parashurama, Rama, Krishna, Balarama, Kalki, Adinath, Hrishikesh, Badrinath.

I repent for and renounce the mantra Aum Namo Narayanaya. Lord please disconnect me from its sounds. Father, I renounce all beliefs and practices regarding the saints, scriptures, and temple worship connected to Vishnu and his incarnations. Father, cleanse me completely of Vaishnavism.

Smartism

Father, on behalf or myself and my familyI repent for all worship of Adi Shankara. I repent for belief in and practice of the philosophies of Advaita Vedanta

On behalf of myself and my family I repent for believing or saying

-Brahman is the One, the only reality, that this universe is unreal; and that the individual soul is the same as Brahman.

- The Atman or soul is self-evident and cannot be denied because it is the very essence of the one who denies it.

-Brahman is not an object, as it is beyond the reach of senses or intellect. It is infinite, imperishable, impersonal, self-existent, self-delight, self-knowledge, self-bliss and essence—the essence of the knower. It is the silent witness, always the witnessing subject, never an object as it is beyond the reach of the senses. Brahman is non-dual and has no other beside it.

- Brahman has neither form nor attributes. The essence of Brahman is existence, consciousness and bliss or Sat-Chit-Ananda.

-The world is not absolutely false but is relatively false compared to Brahman who is absolutely real. The world is a superimposition of non-Self or objects on Self or Brahman.

- The individual soul is only relatively real. There are not several atmans or souls. The one soul appears as multiple souls in our bodies because of illusion.

-Samsara or duality exists due to ignorance, knowledge alone can make an individual realize his true nature.

- Knowledge of Brahman is not about acquiring external knowledge as Brahman cannot be known, but about removing the ignorance and illusion. When these are removed there is no difference between soul and Brahman.

I repent for the belief that to be saved I have to be able to discern between the real substance (Brahman) and the substance that is unreal.

I repent for the belief that to be saved I have to renounce enjoyments of objects in this world and the other worlds.

I repent for the belief that to be saved I have to have the six-fold qualities of tranquility of the mind, control of external sense organs, focusing on meditation and refraining from actions, endurance of suffering, faith in Guru and Vedas, the concentration of the mind.

I repent for the belief that to be saved I have to have the firm conviction that the nature of the temporary world is misery and have an intense longing to be liberated from the cycle of births and deaths.

I repent for myself and my family for believing or saying

"A particle of Its bliss
supplies the bliss of the whole universe.
Everything becomes enlightened in Its light.

All else appears worthless after a sight of that essence.
I am indeed of this Supreme Eternal Self"

Lord please remove me from all that is not me and reestablish my godly boundaries. Lord please remove me from the ungodly depths and seat me with Jesus Christ in Your heavenly places.

In the name of Jesus Christ, I renounce and repent for all belief in and connections to ungodly Vedic cosmology. Lord please remove all parts of me that are trapped in the seven lower lokas or worlds and please disconnect me from Sutala, Vitala, Talatala, Mahatala, Rasatala, Atala, and Patala – Deepest Hell and the serpents or Nagas and demons there.

On behalf of myself and my generational line, I repent for believing or saying,

"The four chakra triangles of Shiva,
The five chakra triangles of Shakti
Are the nine of the primal energy of the universe
All apart from the circle center
With a lotus of eight petals, one of sixteen petals,
The three circles and three lines,
Remain a total of forty four -
The angles of Your sacred abode of the wheel"

Lord please disconnect us from all the ungodly wheels, petals, circles, lines and angles of the Sri Chakra Yantra. Please disconnect us from ungodly Mount Meru. Please disconnect us from the ungodly union of the Masculine and Feminine Divine and all ungodly webs of the universes and wombs of creation. Lord please disconnect us from ungodly geometries and portals.

Lord please disconnect us from the cosmic dance of Shiva, the tandava that is the source of the cycles of creation, preservation and dissolution, salvation and illusion and the rhythm of birth and death. Lord please remove us from the rhythms, violence, grief and anger associated with these ungodly cycles.

On behalf of myself and my family I repent for those who meditated on the goddess Kalika in the trikona, in the six petals the six limbs, in the navel the Shaktis of the directions, in the heart the twelve suns, in the throat the sixteen kalas of the moon, in the two-petalled lotus Kala and Kali together. Lord, please disconnect us from ungodly trikonas, suns, phases of the moon, lotuses.

On behalf of myself and my family I repent for worshipping the Hindu deities of time and for believing or saying,

"I worship you Shani – you are the essence of time!
The universe and time itself dissolves in you!
You are the body of time, the self, the Source of Happiness,
the Soul that regulates time, the planetary guardians!"

Lord please disconnect us from the ungodly Shani and its cycles. Please remove the destruction associated with Shani. Lord please restore godly time, space, and the dimensions. Lord, please remove ungodly time locks and time references. Please restore my timeline and restore my origin to You.

In the name of Jesus of Nazareth I forgive anyone who released curses connected to Hinduism against me or my family. Lord please remove all curses, backup curses, time curses, re-empowerment of curses and negative consequences that may come against me or my family line for breaking covenant with Hindu entities.

On behalf of myself and my family line, I repent for and renounce all beliefs in and participation of the ungodly division of society into four social classes and castes. I repent for and renounce the historical exclusion from the caste system of the untouchables or dalits.

On behalf of myself and my family line, I deeply repent for and renounce all discrimination, oppression, and abuse that we have practiced on our fellow men because of the caste system.

I repent for and renounce the belief every person is born into and must marry, live, and die within their caste. Lord please remove the effects in my life of the rigid limitations of the caste rules in determining my food, occupation, marriage and association with people in other castes. Lord please remove all ungodly boundaries, barriers and ceilings in my life.

On behalf of any ancestors who were oppressed because of the caste system, I forgive those who discriminated against us and oppressed us because of the color of our skin and our caste.

I repent for and renounce all practices of child-marriage, dowry, sati or self-immolation of a woman on her husband's funeral pyre.

Lord, for myself and my family, I renounce and repent for all ungodly gender inequalities we have agreed with. I repent for those in my generational line who have degraded, oppressed, suppressed, humiliated, murdered, and raped women. Father, will you please break off the ungodly consequences of domination and victimization and restore the women in my family to their equal status in the family of God. Please restore the inheritance, property, position, status, and gifting of all the women in my generational line.

Lord, please disconnect us from all victim spirits related to discrimination due to caste or gender.

On behalf of myself and my family line I repent for believing or saying,

"The syllable AUM is both the higher and the lower Brahma
He who meditates on the highest Person with the three elements of the syllable AUM,
is united with brilliance in the Sun
As a snake is freed from its skin, even so, is he freed from sin
And led to the world of Brahma."

On behalf of myself and my family line, I repent for and renounce all ungodly uses of our bodies in and during false worship, including all forms of idol worship: dedication to idols, bowing to idols, icon worship, daily darshan or viewing of idols, eating food sacrificed to idols as well as eating prasada or food offered to idols. I repent for maintaining home shrines for idols, visiting and worshipping in temples of idols, participating in festivals, making temple offerings, viewing or participating in ungodly processions, pilgrimages, dramas, and story-telling associated with idols. I also repent of ungodly fasting, self-mutilation, whipping, singing, dancing, wearing special clothing, and chanting that is linked to idolatry.

On behalf of myself and my family line, I repent for and renounce other ungodly uses of our bodies during false worship including temple prostitution yoga, fornication, ritual sex, sex with animals, sex with demons, with the dead, ungodly masturbation, pedophilia, same-sex relations, and viewing of sexual imagery in sculptures, books, dance, or movies.

On behalf of myself and my family line, I repent for and renounce all ungodly uses of my soul during false worship including being in ecstatic states, reading and studying the false scriptures, and false meditation.

On behalf of myself and my family line, I repent for and renounce all ungodly use of my spirit during false worship including astral travel, inhabiting the bodies of other people, all shamanic practices, shape-shifting and forming ungodly communications and ties with the ungodly places and with false deities, false priests, and other people.

I repent for and renounce all ungodly openings of the eye of my spirit, my pineal gland, my third eye. I pray that you will shut down any ungodly opening of my third eye and seal it with your Holy Spirit.

On behalf of myself and my family line, I repent for and renounce all false worship of the elements including stone, wood, water, fire, air, and ether. I repent for and renounce all ungodly worship of the sun, moon, and any other heavenly bodies. I repent for all witchcraft, animal sacrifices, people and child sacrifices, all necromancy, blood covenants, drinking of blood, eating of flesh, mingling of blood, and communication with the dead.

I repent for and renounce ungodly use of ungodly Vedic calendars, based upon illegal mystical knowledge of equinoxes and solstices. I repent for and renounce the use of Vedic astrology to determine decisions and propitious times for public and personal ceremonies and events.

On behalf of myself and my family line, I repent for and renounce all ungodly vegetarianism, celibacy, monasticism, and asceticism practiced as Hindu religious acts. I repent for and renounce the use of all herbal medicines in the ayur-vedic tradition that have been made by knowledge gained from the enemy.

Lord Jesus, please cleanse all pathways of my mind, my will and my emotions. Align my body, soul and spirit to You and You alone. Lord, please restore all parts of me that were lost to other dimensions. Lord, please unite all parts of me in You. Lord, please join me to You and to Your body which is the Church. Lord, I ask that You will fill me with Your Holy Spirit and guide me as I continue to walk in the healing that You have provided for me.

Prayer of Restoration and Regeneration

I renounce and repent for myself and for all those in my family generational line and also as a current member of the body of Christ for:

- Not interceding for justice.
- Rebellion, treachery, falsehood, muttering wicked things, disunity, mockery, and not valuing truth.
- Those who cursed or crushed the children of God who were weaker, injured, or immature. I bless them and pray that they will come into the full knowledge of Christ.
- All participation that I have had in causing the shredding the Body of Christ.
- Resisting the Kingdom of the Lord, driving out the priests of the Lord, the sons of Aaron and the Levites, and making our own people priests as other lands do.
- Removing the Ark of the Covenant from its rightful place, subjecting it to defilement and birthing the name Ichabod, "The Glory has departed."
- Those who stole the manna and Aaron's rod out of the Ark of God, thus cursing our provision and our authority.
- Giving the enemy legal access to the ark and its contents and causing the defilement of the ark.
- All my sins against the sanctuary, the sin of abomination that leads to desolation.
- Defiling my body as the Temple of the Holy Spirit.
- Ungodly worship and for despising and disdaining godly worship.
- Attempting to connect God's worship with ungodly worship.
- Worshipping heavenly bodies and any forms of ungodly light.
- Any generational worship of any counterfeit deity that established itself against the true priestly order of Melchizedek.
- Profaning the covenant of our fathers by breaking faith with one another.
- Teaching false doctrine that does not agree with the sound instruction of our Lord Jesus Christ and with godly teaching. I repent for an unhealthy interest in controversy and for quarrels about words that result in envy, strife, malicious talk, evil suspicion, and constant friction.
- Ungodly sacrifices and sexual perversion that defiled the holy places of the Lord.
- All unholy alliances that mingle the seed of God with the seed of Satan.
- Cooperating with the perversion of our DNA and all genetic and spiritual components of DNA, including the cellular and sub-cellular levels.
- Believing I have the right to create life, alter life, or destroy life.
- The sin of passivity and for not standing or speaking out against the sin of trying to create life, manipulate life, or destroy life.
- Sacrificing our children and unborn children on the fires of Molech and for all shedding of innocent blood.
- Exchanging Your true divine light for the counterfeit light of Satan.
- Not being in my position or sphere of influence as a watchman over the creation of God and therefore relinquishing my position of stewardship of the creation by not subduing it in accord with godly principles.
- Speaking against the Most High, oppressing His saints, and trying to change the set times and the laws.

Lord, please reconnect us to You, our Head and true source, and cut any ungodly connections that would cause any ungodly electrical impulses. Lord, please balance all electro-magnetic fields that would deceive, defile, corrupt, and contaminate our spirits, souls and bodies.

Please disconnect me from all ungodly heavenly places.

Please complete our regeneration.

Please cleanse and reconnect the DNA of our bloodlines and of the Body of Christ and weld the fragments together with the fire and glory of God.

Please give me discernment of my memories in my brain and in my cells. Please allow me to know if they are true or false, if they are past or present, ancestral or my own. Please give me your wisdom and direction to know what to do with your answer.

Oh Lord, the great and awesome God who keeps His covenant of love with all who love Him and obey His commands, we have sinned and done wrong. We have committed iniquity. We have done wickedly and rebelled and even by departing from Your precepts and judgments. Neither have we heeded Your servants, the prophets, who spoke in Your name, to our kings and to our princes, to our fathers and all of the people of the land.

I declare that You are the head and establisher of the true priestly line of Melchizedek.

I declare that You are the One who establishes us as living stones who are being built into a spiritual house, a holy priesthood, to offer spiritual sacrifices acceptable to You Father, through Jesus Christ.

I declare that I am part of a chosen people, a royal priesthood, a holy nation, a people belonging to God and that we will reign on earth with You.

Now therefore, O God, hear the prayer of Your servants, and our supplications, and for the Lord's sake cause Your face to shine on Your sanctuary, which is desolate. O Lord God, incline Your ear and hear; open Your eyes and see our desolations, and the city which is called by Your name; for we do not present our supplications before You because of our righteous deeds, but because of Your great mercies. O Lord, hear! O Lord, forgive! O Lord, listen and act! Do not delay for Your own sake, O God, for Your city and Your people are called by Your name.

Prayer to Activate and Release Creativity

Lord Jesus, I acknowledge you as the Son of the only true Creator God. I declare the Most High God to be the only true intelligent designer. On behalf of myself and my generational line, I repent for all who used their creative skills, abilities and knowledge for idolatrous works.

I repent for all generational intellectualism and for those who did not use their mental abilities for creative works and who denied wisdom as a creative attribute. I repent for all those who took part in human sacrifices and sexual immorality and for those who made images that gave recognition to the gods and goddesses of men.

Lord, I renounce all allegiance with Artemis. I repent for all in my generational line who relied on the goddesses Muse for divine creativity and grieved the Holy Spirit in Divine inspiration.

Lord, I repent and renounce for myself and my ancestors who used their senses and presented their bodies in an unholy way to the other gods and goddesses in dance and orgies.

Lord I repent for those who used the visual arts for generational pornography. Father, forgive us for making idols of fertility. Lord we have sinned and have not taken responsibility for causing others to walk away from You, their gifts and their callings. Lord, please remove all lust and immorality off the creative gifting.

Lord, I ask You to forgive me and my ancestors for grieving you and ignoring wisdom, understanding and knowledge in creativity. Lord in Your mercy, will You remove Your anger and the consequences of this evil and restore integrity to the giftings, callings and inheritance of this generational line.

Lord, I repent for all those who were called to be caretakers and artisans for the temple and did not protect the sacred articles in Your tabernacle. I repent for those who allowed Your holy temple to be defiled.

Lord, I repent for all those who used their creative abilities and made defiled works in covenant with sheol, death, Hades, the underworld or hell. Lord will you now break off all alliance with death.

Lord, please forgive me and my ancestors for generational shamanism and for attaching evil spirits to works of art. Lord, please remove all ungodly healing and ungodly anointing from all future artistic designs and creative expressions. Lord, please remove all connections to any ungodly realms or dimensions. Please shut and lock all ungodly doors, portals and gates.

Lord, please restore godly healing and deliverance to the creative works. Lord, I ask You to forgive us for using our creative gifts and prostituted them for wealth or selfish gain.

Lord, I repent for my ancestors and myself for using sound and speech in ungodly ways and agreeing with Satan to defile creation. Lord, please remove the defilement off of creation. Father I want to be a co-creator in Christ as a son of God so creation itself will be healed from its depravity.

Lord, please sanctify and restore creative ideas and inventions for Your Kingdom purpose in the marketplace.

Lord, forgive me and my generations for shutting down and holding back the children of God in creativity in art, dance, music and teaching. Lord, please restore the reverential and obedient fear of God.

Forgive me for not passing on and nurturing our gifts, abilities and talents to the next generation. Father, please sanctify the creative arts for Your Glory in our generations to come.

Father, please make us scribes who manifest and instruct in Your kingdom design and who bring out the secrets of Your treasury both new and old. Lord, restore revelation to the arts.

Ruling and Reigning with Christ

Lord Jesus I repent for any decision that I may have made with the enemy before conception because of fear or doubt about your goodness and plan for my life. I understand that this decision may have resulted in the right for the enemy to negatively affect my DNA and RNA and the living water that was to flow out of me. I now exercise my authority in Christ based on the finished work of the cross and the blood of Christ over the contamination of the fiery stones and the living water. I now ask you Lord to remove the influence of wormwood over the living water and purify that water. Lord please remove me from any ungodly orbs, trapezoids, and geospheres in all dimensions and from the ungodly depth.

Please release into me the fullness of your living water and assign to me all righteous lights. I now ask Lord that you will come against all assignments made against me and heal all of my diseases. Please remove from me any ungodly coating and all ungodly garments. Please remove me from any ungodly constellations and all ungodly zodiacs.

Please close all ungodly gates and doors that give the enemy access to me especially through any ungodly triangles, tetrahedrons, and trapezoids. Lord, please purify all the living water assigned to me. Please remove all ungodly water spirits and seducing spirits.

I repent and renounce for all ungodly baptisms and water rituals. Please remove me from Wormwood and from all ungodly places in the depth, height, length, and width associated with wormwood. Please disconnect me from all ungodly stars. Please reconnect me according to your original design to the length, width, height and depth. Bring all godly dimensions and quadrants into perfect equality.

I repent for all generation bestiality. Please bring all uncontaminated fiery stones through Your blood back to me. Lord please remove all animal, fish, bird, and Nephilim DNA and RNA from my DNA and RNA. Lord, please remove all reptilian scales from my eyes and the seven spiritual eyes you have given to me.

In the name of Jesus Christ, I repent for anytime I may have said that I did not want You to make me and that I was angry about how You made me and I decided that I would remake myself. I repent for any time I was unwilling to yield to You as the clay yields to the potter. I repent for any time I chose the enemy's plan rather than Your plan.

I understand that any decisions I may have made before conception may have given right for the enemy to take the jewels of my spirit into the void and the darkness. I also understand that this may have affected my spiritual authority and my ability to rule and reign. I understand that this may have also sealed up the treasures in darkness that you intend me to have.

I acknowledge that in my generational line this may have resulted in phallic worship and the lust of the eyes, declaring that I would produce my own seed without you and that I would save myself through prostitutional idolatry trying to reproduce without You, Lord. I acknowledge that my generational line and I may have tried to multiply and fill the earth without You, Lord, by trying to find secret knowledge. I repent for discontentment with Your ways and Your design of Me. I repent for my discontentment and the discontentment of my family line with how you made me and what you gave to me. I repent for my discontentment and the discontentment of my family line with the authority, position, and place you have assigned me.

I acknowledge that this may have affected the spiritual eyes You have given me and may have resulted in all kinds of barrenness. I ask Lord that You will return through Your blood to me any parts of my spirit that may be scattered in the void. Lord please resurrect all parts of my spirit.

I now declare that I will rule and reign with the scepter that You have given to me. Lord please correctly align the scepter You have given to me with the stone in my hand and the seven eyes of the Lamb.

I now repent for trying to be my own sacrifice rather than acknowledging that you are the only sacrifice. I remove myself from the ungodly altar and I declare that I am seated with Christ in heavenly places and that I will rule and reign with My God. Lord please remove any dragons from me that are seated on any thrones.

Lord Jesus, I take my position as a revealed son of God and I stand against the spirit of Shebna[5] who has taken the key of David in my family line and restricted the access that You desire me to have to the house of wisdom and the godly height and I acknowledge that this spirit has hewn a grave and placed itself in the ungodly height and has placed himself into the ungodly rock, perverting the rock who is Jesus. I now ask, Lord, that You will throw him away violently, this one who is the leader of the ungodly mighty men. Lord please seize him and turn violently against him and toss him like a ball into a large country where this spirit will die with all of his ungodly chariots. Lord please cause him to bring shame to his master's house and drive him out of his office and from his position so that he will be pulled down. I do not allow the spirit of Shebna to cause me to dwell in his ungodly tabernacle.

I now ask Lord Jesus that You will take the key of David and place it on Your shoulder and I declare that You are the rightful authority over the Father's house because the Father has delegated the house to You. I acknowledge Lord that You are clothed with a robe and You are strengthened with a belt and that all in my household is now Your responsibility.

Lord, I now declare that you are in the role of Eliakim and I declare Lord that You are fastened in a secure place and that You occupy a glorious throne in Your Father's house and Lord I acknowledge all of the glory of Your Father's house is hung on You and on all Your sons and daughters. I declare that Your glory now fills all the vessels from the smallest to the greatest. Lord please remove Shebna's peg and the burden that was on it. We cut it off because the Lord has spoken.

I declare that all the gates and doors that Jesus opens will remain open and all the gates and doors that Jesus closes will remain closed. I declare my family and I will no longer be contained by the religious system and by false houses and that my tent pegs will be extended and I will operate in the sphere of authority that the Lord has given to me and I will no longer be contained by mere men. I break the power of all those words of containment off of me and all words of jealousy and envy and gossip I break off of me. Lord shut these ungodly gates and doors that encircles me and open up the righteous gates and doors that You are knocking on that give me the ability to come and go as the Holy Spirit directs.

---

[5] Isaiah 22:15-25

I break off the power of limitations, of pastor's words and leader's words and the ungodly words of the body of Christ. I declare Jesus will be my God and I will be His person and I choose to submit myself unto others even as they submit themselves unto me. I declare that I and those in the Body of Christ will now make up the one new man in Christ in which every joint will supply and everyone will do his part.

I am no longer the audience. I am the participant. I ask Lord that you will remove the ungodly rock and I declare that the Lord Jesus Christ is my rock and He will destroy the systems of the world and fill the Earth as a great mountain.

Renunciations for Egypt

Lord, on behalf of myself and all ancestors in all branches of my family line, I repent for all who said, "Homage to you, Osiris, Lord of eternity, King of the gods, whose names are manifold, whose forms are holy, being of hidden form in the temples, whose Ka is holy."

I repent for those who said, "You are the governor of Tattu, Busiris, and also the mighty one in Sekhem of Letopolis. I repent for those who said you are the Lord to whom praises are ascribed in the Nome of Ati, and are the Prince of divine food in Anu."

Lord, I repent for all worship of Osiris. Lord, please disconnect me from Osiris, Tattu, Sekhem, Ati and Anu.

I repent for all who said, "You are the Lord who is commemorated in Maati, the Hidden Soul, the Lord of Qerrt, the Ruler supreme in White Wall. I repent for those who said you are the Soul of Ra, his own body, and have your place of rest in Nekhen.

I repent for those who said you are the beneficent one, and are praised in Nart, and that you make your soul to be raised up. I repent for those who said you are the Lord of the Great House in Khemenu, the mighty one of victories in Shas-hetep, the Lord of eternity, the Governor of Abydos.

Lord, I repent for all worship of Ra. Lord, please disconnect me from Maati, Qerrt, Memphis, Ra, Nart, Khemenu, Shas-hetep, Abydos, Ta-tcheser.

I repent for all who said, "Your name is established in the mouths of men, you are the substance of two lands, your are Tem, the feeder of Kau, the governor of the companies of the gods, you are the beneficent spirit among the spirits, the god of the Celestial Ocean who draws from yourself the waters.

I repent for those who said you send forth the north wind at evening, and breath from your nostrils to the satisfaction of your own heart and that your heart renews itself into youth."

Lord I repent for all worship of Nu. Please disconnect me from Tem, Kau, and Nu.

I repent for all who said, "The stars in the celestial heights are obedient to you, and the great doors of the sky open themselves before you. I repent for all who said you are the one to whom praises are ascribed in the southern heaven, and thanks are given for you in the northern heaven. I repent for those who said the imperishable stars are under your supervision, and the stars which never set are your thrones, and that offerings appear before you at the decree of Keb."

I repent for all who said, "The companies of the gods praise you, and the gods of the Tuat smell the earth in paying homage to you. I repent for those who said the uttermost parts of the earth bow before you, the limits of the skies offer you supplications when they see you, the holy ones are overcome before you, and all Egypt offers thanksgiving to you when they meet your majesty."

Lord please disconnect me from Keb and Tuat.

I repent for all who said,

- You are a shining spirit body, the governor of Spirit-Bodies and permanent is your rank, established is your rule.
- You are the well-doing Sekhem of the company of the gods, gracious is you face, and beloved by him that sees it.
- Your fear is set in all the lands by reason of your perfect love, and you cry out to your name making it the first of names, and all people make offerings to you.
- You are the lord who is commemorated in heaven and upon earth. Many are the cries which are made to you at the Uak Festival, and with one heart and voice Egypt raises cries of joy to you. You are the great chief, the first among your brethren, the prince of the company of the gods, the establisher of right and truth throughout the world, the son who was set on the great throne of his father Keb.
- You are the beloved of your mother, Nut, the mighty one of valor, who overthrew the Sebau-fiend.
- You did stand up and destroy your enemy, and set your fear in your adversary.
- You did bring the boundaries of the mountains and your heart is fixed, your legs are set firm.

Lord I repent for all worship of Keb and Nut. Please disconnect me from the Uak Festival, Keb, Nut, and the Sebau-fiend.

I repent for all who said,

- You are the heir of Keb and of the sovereignty of the two lands of Egypt and Keb has seen your splendors and he has decreed for himself the guidance of the world by your hand as long as times endure.
- You have made this earth with your hand, and the waters, and the winds, and the vegetation, and all the cattle, and all the feathered fowl, and all the fish, and all the creeping things, and all the wild animals.
- The desert is the lawful possession of the son of Nut and the two lands of Egypt are content to crown you upon the throne of your father Ra.
- You roll up into the horizon and have set light over the darkness.
- You send forth air from your plumes, and you flood the two lands of Egypt like the disk at daybreak.
- Your crown penetrates the height of heaven.
- You are the companion of the stars, and the guide of every god.
- You are beneficent in decree and speech, the favored one of the great company of the gods, and the beloved of the little company of the gods.

I repent for all who said,

- His sister, Isis, has protected him, has repulsed the fiends and turned aside calamities of evil.
- She uttered the spell with the magical power of her mouth.
- Her tongue was perfect and it never halted at a word.
- The beneficent in command and word was Isis, the woman of magical spells, the advocate of her brother.
- She sought him untiringly, she wandered round and round about this earth in sorrow, and she did not stop until finding him.

Lord I repent for all worship of Isis. Please disconnect me from Isis.

I repent for all who said,
- Isis made light with her feathers.
- She created air with her wings and she uttered the death wail for her brother.
- She raised up the inactive members of one whose heart was still and she drew from him his essence.
- She made an heir, reared the child in loneliness in the place where he was not known and he grew in strength and stature, and his hand was mighty in the House of Keb.
- The company of the gods rejoiced at the coming of Horus, the son of Osiris, whose heart was firm, the triumphant, the son of Isis, the heir of Osiris.

I repent for all who said,
- Homage to you, you who has come as Khepera, Khepera the creator of the gods.
- You who are seated on your throne who rises up in the sky, illumining your mother Nut.
- You who are seated on your throne as the king of the gods.
- Your mother Nut stretches out her hands and performs an act of homage to you.
- The domain of Manu receives you with satisfaction.
- The goddess Maat embraces you at the two seasons of the day.

Lord, I repent for all worship of Khepera and Maat. Please disconnect me from Khepera, Man, and Maat.

I repent for all who said,
- May Ra give glory, and power, and truth-speaking, and the appearance of a living soul so that he may gaze upon Heru-khuti, to the Ka of the Osiris, the Scribe Ani, who speaks truth before Osiris.
- Hail, O all ye gods of the "house of the soul," who weighs heaven and earth in a balance, and who gives celestial food to the dead and who says hail, Tatun, who is the one, the creator of mortals and of the companies of the gods of the south and of the north, of the west and of the east.

Lord, I repent for all worship of Ra, Heru-khuti, Ani, and Tatun. Please disconnect me from these gods.

I repent for all who said,
- Give thanks to him in his beneficent form which is enthroned in the Atett boat.
- Thoth and the goddess Maat mark out your course day by day and every day.
- Your enemy, the serpent, has been given over to the fire. The serpent- fiend, Sebau, has fallen headlong, his forelegs are bound in chains, and his hind legs has Ra carried away from him.

Lord, I repent for all worship of Thoth. Please disconnect me from Atett, Thott, and Sebau.

I repent for all who said,
- The sons of revolt will never more rise up.
- The house of the aged one who keeps a festival and the voices of those who make merry are in the "great place." The gods rejoice when they see Ra crowned upon his throne, when his beams flood the world with light.

- The majesty of this holy god, Ra, sets out on his journey, and he goes onwards until he reaches the land of Manu.
- The earth becomes light at Ra's birth each day.
- He proceeds until he reaches the place where he was yesterday.

I repent for all who said, "Let me gaze upon your beauties. Let me journey above the earth. Let me smite the ass. Let me slit apart the serpent-fiend Sebau. Let me destroy Aepep at the moment of his greatest power. Let me behold the Abtu fish at his season and the ant fish with the ant boat as it pilots it in its lake. Let me behold Horus when he is in charge of the rudder of the boat of Ra with Thoth and the goddess Thoth on each side of him."

Lord, I repent for all worship of the Abtu fish, the ant fish, and Horus. Please disconnect me from Aepep, the Abtu fish, the ant fish, and Horus.

I repent for all who said, "Let me lay hold of the tow-rope of the Sektet boat, and the rope at the stern of the Matett boat. Let Ra grant to me a view of the disk, the Sun, and a sight of Ah, the Moon, each day. Let my Ba-soul come forth to walk about hither and thither and wherever it pleases. Let my name be called out. Let it be found inscribed on the tablet which records the names of those who are to receive offerings. Let meals from the sepulchral offerings be given to me in the presence of Osiris as to those who are in the following of Horus. Let there be prepared for me a seat in the boat of the Sun on the day when the god sails. Let me be received in the presence of Osiris in the land of truth-speaking, the Ka of Osiris Ani."
Lord please disconnect me from the Sektet boat, the Matett boat, and the Ka of Osiris Ani.

I repent for all who said,
- Homage to thee, O thou glorious being, you who are covered with all sovereignty.
- Tem-Heru-Khuti, Tem-Harmakhis, when thou rise in the horizon of heaven a cry of joy goes forth to you from all people.
- thou beautiful being, you did renew yourself in your season in the form of the disk within your mother Hathor and therefore in every place every heart swells with joy at thy rising forever.

Lord, I repent for all worship of Tem-Heru-Khuti and Hathor. Please disconnect me from these gods.

I repent for all who said,
- The regions of the south and the north come to you with homage and send forth acclamations at your rising on the horizon of heaven.
- You light the two lands with rays of turquoise coloured light.
- Ra, you are Heru-Khuti, the divine man-child, the heir of eternity, self-begotten and self-born, king of the earth, prince of the Tuat, the other world, and the governor of Aukert.
- You did come from the water-god.
- You did spring from the sky-god Nu who does cherish you and order your members.

Lord, I repent for all worship of Heru-Khuti. Please disconnect me from Heru-Khuti, Tutat, and Hukert.

I repent for all who said,

- god of life, you lord of love, all men live when thou shine.
- You are crowned king of the gods.
- The goddess Nut embraces you and the goddess Mut enfolds you in all seasons.
- Those who are in your following sing to you with joy and they bow down their foreheads to the earth when they meet you, the lord of heaven, the lord of the earth, the king of truth, the lord of eternity, the prince of everlastingness, sovereign of all the gods.
- You are a god of life, you, the creator of eternity, maker of heaven where you are firmly established.

Lord, I repent for all worship of Mut. Please disconnect me from Mut.

I repent for all who said,
- The company of the gods rejoices at your rising, the earth is glad when it beholds your rays.
- The people who have been long dead come forth with cries of joy to behold your beauty every day.
- You go forth each day over heaven and earth and you are made strong each day by your mother Nut.
- You pass over the heights of heaven.
- Your heart swells with joy and the lake of Testes, the great Oasis, is content there.
- The serpent-fiend has fallen, his arms are broken off, and the knife has severed his joints.

I repent for all who said,
- Ra lives by Maat, the law, the beautiful.
- The Sektet boat advances and comes into port. The south, the north, the west and east turn to praise you.
- You are first, great god, Pauta, who came into being of your own accord.
- Isis and Nephthys salute you, they sing to you songs of joy at your rising in the boat and they stretch out their hands to you.
- The souls of the east follow thee and the souls of the west praise you.
- You are the ruler of all the gods.
- You who are in your shrine has joy for the serpent-fiend Nak has been judged by the fire and your heart will rejoice forever.
- Your mother Nut is esteemed by your father Nu.

Lord please break all ungodly connections to the south, north, west, and east. I repent for all worship of Nepthys. Please disconnect me from Nephthys, Nak, and Nu.

I repent for all who said,
- A hymn of praise to Osiris Un-Nefer, the great god who dwells in Abtu, the king of eternity, the lord of everlastingness, who travels millions of years in his existence.
- You are the eldest son of the womb of Nut.
- You were born of Keb,the Erpat.
- You are the lord of the Urrt crown.
- You are he whose white crown is lofty.
- You are the King, Ati, of gods and men.

- You have gained possession of the scepter of rule, the whip, the rank, and dignity of divine fathers.
- Thy heart is expanded with joy, you who are in the kingdom of the dead.

I repent for all who said,
- Your son Horus is firmly placed on your throne.
- You have ascended your throne as the lord of Tetu and as the Heq who dwells in Abydos.
- You make the two lands to exist through truth-speaking in the presence of him who is the lord to the uttermost limit.
- You draw on that which has not yet come into being in your name of "Ta-her-sta-nef."

Lord, I repent for all worship of the Lord of Tetu, Heq and Ta-her-sta-nef. Please disconnect me from these gods.

I repent for all who said,
- You govern the two lands by Maat in your name of Seker.
- Your power is wide-spread.
- You are he who the fear is great of in your names of Usar and Asa.
- Your existence endures for an infinite number of double henti periods in your name of Un-Nefer.
- Homage to you, king of kings, lord of lords, and prince of princes.
- You have ruled the two lands from the womb of the goddess Nut.
- You have governed the lands of Akert.

Lord, I repent for all worship of Seker, Usar, Asar, and Un-nefer. Please disconnect me from these gods.

I repent for all who said,
- Your members are of silver-gold, your head is of lapis-lazuli, and the crown of your head is of turquoise.
- You are of millions of years.
- Your body is all pervading, o beautiful face in Ta-tchesert.
- Grant to me glory in heaven, power upon earth, truth-speaking in the divine underworld, and power to sail down the river to Tetu in the form of a living Ba-soul.
- Grant to me the power to sail up the river to Abydos in the form of a Benu bird and the power to pass through and pass out from, without obstruction, the doors of the lords of the Tuat.
- Let there be given to me bread-cakes in the House of refreshing, and sepulchral offerings of cakes and ale, and propitiatory offerings in Anu, and a permanent homestead in Sekhet-Aaru, with wheat and barley therein—to the double of the Osiris.

Lord, I repent for all worship of the lords of the Tuat. Please disconnect me from these gods and from Abydos and Sekhet-Aaru.
Lord, I repent for all worship of the gods whom you judged by sending the plagues against Egypt—Anuket, goddess of the Nile, Khnum, the guardian of the Nile, Hapi, the spirit of the Nile, Osiris, who had the Nile as his bloodstream, Heqt, the frog-goddess of fertility, Geb, god of the earth, Hathor, a cow-like mother goddess, Qadshu, goddess of sexuality, Imhotep, the god

of medicine, Serapis, protector from locusts, Shu, god of the air, Nut, the sky goddess, and Set, god of the desert, storms, darkness and Chaos.

Please disconnect me from these gods.

Prayer to Establish us as
Kings and Priests in His Kingdom

I exercise my position in Christ and I break all agreements with laws, codes and regulations made with the ungodly sons of god in all realms, dimensions, and depths.

I exercise my position in Christ and I break all agreements, covenants and contracts with rebellion that were embedded in those codes, acts, regulations and laws.

I exercise my position in Christ and I cancel the agreement that my ancestors made that gave the enemy the right to make demands on future generations, especially for the purpose of serving darkness and eliminating the light, life and love of Jesus Christ.

I exercise my position in Christ and I cancel the written code with all its regulations that were against me and stood opposed to me and I declare that they were nailed to the cross and that Christ has triumphed over the enemy to the intent that He might expose the rulers and principalities and powers to His amazing grace and power.

Lord Jesus I ask that you reformat our spiritual DNA and RNA, our physical DNA and RNA and soul DNA and RNA and that you will do a reinstall of the nature and mind of Christ and restore our original design.

Lord, please disconnect me from any ungodly control over the physical elements in my body and rightly connect me to the physical laws you have established for me.

I exercise my position in Christ and cancel all agreement with all laws and constitutions that were made so that ungodly spiritual stars could have authority.

I repent for my generational line that entered into ungodly governments by writing, endorsing unrighteous laws and governments that established laws that attempt to redefine what life was, is and will be. Lord we declare you are the only creator.

We renounce and repent for all human laws that intended to change times and seasons that gave the enemy permission and access to change times and seasons. We renounce and repent for all laws that gave the enemy the right to redefine life.

We repent for the Supreme Court of the US that made laws that redefined life and for any unjust laws that violated the Laws of Almighty God. I renounce and repent for any of my ancestors in my generational line that were involved in any superior courts decisions that made agreement with evil in order to change the laws and rules of heaven and earth.

I renounce and repent for my family line who initiated new laws and by line upon line, precept upon precept added layer upon layer of evil laws and practices. Lord please destroy that system and remove any portion of my spirit or soul that have been trapped in these layers.

I renounce and repent for anyone in my generational line who traded future generations for their own protection, power, knowledge and wealth and entered into ungodly dimensions to make agreements with fallen sons of god and the fallen stars. Lord please break curses off future generations and restore their original purpose and design.

Lord please remove the ungodly turban, all the blasphemous writings, the ungodly ephod, all ungodly priestly garments, ungodly prayers, declarations and rituals.

Lord Jesus I repent for all of my ancestors that refused to draw close to the thunder and lightning of the Living God and refrained from entering the holy fear of the Lord. I repent for all those in my generational line who forsook the Lord and who built their own cisterns choosing mediators of priests and kings rather than intimacy with the Lord.

I declare that I give up the kingdoms of this world for the kingdoms of my Christ. Lord extract any parts of my spirit out of any ungodly star systems, constellations, and zodiacs out of outer darkness, out of utter darkness and pull me out of any black holes.

I declare that I will be seated in heavenly places with Christ and my enemies will become my footstool and I will rule and reign with Christ, and He will be my God and my Lord. I will not give up my position of ruling and reigning with Christ to the enemy. I will not give up any kingdom, any dimension, any place in time, any place in earth under the earth or above the earth that the Lord has given to me as my sphere of influence.

Lord please remove the bronze gates and iron bars over my sphere of influence and I say lift up your heads oh you gates that the King of Glory will come in. Lord please make the crooked places straight and Lord open every door that should be opened and close every door that should be closed so that the gates will never be shut again.

Lord please rightly connect my sphere of influence over the multidimensional worlds that you have given to me, to the other spheres of influence and Lord allow your power to flow in unity through those spheres.

I declare the kingdoms of this world have become the kingdoms of our Lord and of His Christ, and He shall reign forever and ever! We give You thanks, O Lord God Almighty, the One Who is and Who was and Who is to come because You have taken Your great power and reigned.

I declare that salvation and strength, and the kingdom of our God, and the power of His Christ have come, for the accuser of our brethren, who accused us before our God day and night, has been cast down. I declare that we have overcome him by the blood of the Lamb and by the word of our testimony, and that we do not love our lives to the death.

I take my position in Christ and I declare before all the universes, realms and all spiritual beings that I reject the ungodly codes and regulations that have been written on my DNA and RNA that contain ungodly precepts, laws, rules, writings, decisions, agreements, contracts, covenants and agree with the decision in the throne room of heaven that they be expelled from my body.

I now reject any past claims that my generational line made to these codes and regulations and I appropriate the blood of Jesus Christ over those codes and regulations and I exchange those codes and regulations for my life in Christ. I choose my rightful inheritance for my life in Christ and my position as a son and heir of my Heavenly Father.

I declare that I am seated with Christ in Heavenly places and I will choose to live my life according the blueprints of love that He has written for me before the foundation of the earth.

I declare that I come into alignment with Your Kairos time, Father, and I reject Saturn and Kronos time. Lord, I ask if I have been compressed back in time or put in the wrong time line, I agree and declare that I will be in the right time line and ask that I be released from any imprisonment so that I am established in the correct time. I demand that I be released as I am under the Lordship of Jesus Christ and not under any other gods or goddesses.

I declare that I am not bound by the speed of light but am only bound by the laws of the Kingdom of God.
I declare and agree that I am released to operate in unity with those heavenly laws that are under the Lordship of Jesus Christ and those Kingdoms now belong to HIM.

O Lord, the great and awesome God, who keeps his covenant of love with all who love him and obey his commands, we have sinned and done wrong. We have been wicked and have rebelled. We have turned away from your commands and laws. We have not listened to your servants the prophets, who spoke in your name to our kings, our princes and our fathers. The Lord our God is merciful and forgiving, even though we have rebelled against him. We have not obeyed the Lord our God or kept the laws he gave us through his servants the prophets. Lord please break the effects of the curses, iniquities, and sworn judgments written in the law of Moses that have been poured out on us and our generational line because we have sinned against you.

Lord, please change all evil addresses that have been installed in the seven eyes of the Lord and please restore them to the original locations that the Almighty God chooses.

Prayer for Breaking Christian Curses

Heavenly Father, I come representing and speaking on behalf of my generational line and myself. I thank You for your promise *that no weapon formed against me will prosper and every tongue which rises against me in judgment, I shall condemn.* I understand Your promise that if we wrongly judge or condemn without a view of mercy, we will also be judged or condemned. Therefore, I ask You Holy Spirit to help examine my own heart so I may see and remember my judgments and condemnations towards other Christians. Help me make a list of those I know I wounded, as well as those who were unaware of my criticism or condemnation. Father, help me find and remove all bitter thoughts and judgments, hurtful proclamations, and every curse I've spoken, including all associated prayers not in line with Your will.

Father, I repent for those of us who cursed and murdered members of the Body of Christ with our words by speaking vengeance, slander, gossip, and ungodly judgments; including declarations of lack, zero prosperity, and doom over other Christians, and especially against members of our own family. I also specifically repent for such judgments from our positions of leadership within Your Body as pastors, teachers, apostles, prophets, and evangelists; justifying ourselves because of offense, jealousy, differences in theology, and misunderstandings. Lord, we have sinned with our words and thoughts, thus invoking curses and consequences over others as well as ourselves. Please forgive us.

Father, I confess that with most of these judgments we have kept our lists of offenses or dislike, justifying our wrong responses with willful, stubborn rationalizations that were amplified by our unhealed hurts. I acknowledge that we have not been merciful, and we judged outwardly, neither remembering the goodness You see in others' hearts nor how much You love them. Even worse, these we judged were in Christ, so we have invoked curses and condemnation upon Him and His Body. Because I am also in Christ, I confess that as we have judged others, we have been judged. Father, I repent for all this and ask Your forgiveness. Please forgive us. Please forgive us for all the damage we caused to Your family—especially Your leaders, their families and followers, as well as all of our brothers and sisters in Christ. Lord Jesus, please bear these curses that we invoked, whether knowingly or unknowingly, and remove them from us.

Father, please cause Your Kingdom to come near, and disconnect both those we have offended and us from all curses and the associated consequences of bitterness, un-forgiveness, mistrust, strife, hate, jealousy, manipulation and estrangement. Father, please disconnect us.

Father, in Jesus' Name I partner with You to break all ungodly spiritual ties between the offended and ourselves. I renounce, ask, and choose to be disconnected from all unhealthy associations, co-dependencies, and alignments that were made between individuals and family lines. I release them into Your Hands and ask Your blessings over them and their family lines. Please heal every wound we have caused, and cause Your Kingdom to destroy every demon we have loosed. Please release to the offended and their family lines every blessing that has been hindered or stopped because of our verbal sins and iniquity.

Father, please help me speak blessings over those in His Body that we cursed or injured through ungodly words and actions. Help me to reverse these curses by speaking blessings over those on my list. (Insert and repeat as needed: <Name> , I bless you in Jesus' Name with blessing , blessing, and blessing .) In Jesus' Name, I bless and speak life to heal the wounds we created in their spirits, souls and bodies. I ask Holy Spirit to help us restore godly unity, walk in love, bless, do good, and pray for these individuals and their families.

Father, You see every Christian curse, judgment, and condemnation released toward my family line and me. Please forgive those members of Your Body who invoked these curses and murderous words upon us, including all prayers not in line with Your will. Please forgive them for partnering with the evil thoughts that came to their mind disguised as their own. Please forgive them for all vengeance, envy, jealously, control, pride and religious manipulation, as well as all subsequent sin including slander, gossip and back biting. Father, please forgive them? I also choose to forgive and ask You to disconnect us from the resultant ungodly ties, connections, alignments, and associations. Please disconnect, heal and restore us from every evil weapon stabbed in our back or hurting us in any dimension; heal our offenders from the effects of every weapon that came upon them for judging and cursing us; and heal us with Your breath and life in every dimension of our spirits, souls, and bodies.

Father, these curses have an effect of holding both the offenders' hearts and ours away from You; estranging us from one another and from You, and leaving us feeling like distant servants or orphans who relate to You only from afar. We are kept from resting in our identities as those seated next to You in Christ in heavenly places, and from our ability to experience Christ abiding in us here on earth through the ministry of the Holy Spirit. We are prevented from the realization of our true identities as beloved sons and daughters, and blocked from drawing near to You in our spirit. Father, please release now the fullness of the Kingdom to restore us as beloved sons and daughters in Christ who abide with You in heaven, even as You do with us on earth.

In Jesus' name, I choose not to wrestle with flesh and blood, meaning those speaking and praying against me; but to walk in love, bless, do good, and pray for these individuals and their families. Holy Spirit, please bring to mind each person, family or family line to which I need to speak out a blessing. (Insert, and repeat and declare as prompted by the Spirit:<u>Name></u>, I bless you in Jesus Name with <u>blessing</u>, <u>blessing</u>, and <u>blessing</u>.) Father, please restore us from all resultant separation and distance from one another to a place of abiding in Christ in love and unity. Please restore all of the offenders' blessings, prosperity, health, giftings, callings and relationships; and release them into their full destinies.

Father, thank you for restoring me to my abiding role as Your son or daughter as I partner with You to break the curses that were invoked. I take my authority in Jesus' Name and, seated next to You, declare that the Kingdom of Heaven has come near to dismantle, break, cast off, and annihilate every curse that we have sent, as well as those that were directed toward us. I also declare that no weapon formed against me will prosper, and every enemy that rises against me in judgment is now condemned and cast down.

Father, You see all these curses, and know how evil has instigated and maintained them, never wanting the finger to be pointed at themselves. In Jesus' Name, I partner with You to take authority over every evil spirit or force that was empowered by all ungodly words and actions noted above and, I declare that:

- The violent advancement of the Kingdom of God is released to divide, conquer, and consume you.

- The Kingdom of God has come near to you to bind, capture, silence, plunder, imprison, and bring judgment upon you.

- It's your time to stand in judgment before King Jesus.

- Your greatest fear has now come upon you and that you are receiving His righteous justice and judgment before your time.

- What you have stolen in every dimension will be paid back seven fold.

Vengeance is from our Father and that He is now repaying you and your associates completely for what you have done to His children and to Christ's Body.

Prayer for Healing of Depression and Anxiety

Lord Jesus, I know that somewhere in the past my family's DNA was damaged so that depression has been passed down through the generations. I also know that Satan has taken advantage of this vulnerability to torment my family line.

I acknowledge and confess that my ancestors have sinned, and as a result my DNA has been damaged and I have become vulnerable to Satan's attack on my mind.

Jesus, as the current representative of my family, I repent on behalf of my ancestors for their sin that brought depression as a curse or iniquity into my family line and damaged our DNA.

Specifically, I repent for any involvement by my ancestors in witchcraft or occult practices such as séances, fortune telling or divination. I repent for their memberships in associations that required oaths and promised curses for breaking those oaths. I repent for any unholy vows they have made. I repent for my actions that have allowed these curses or iniquity to continue.

I forgive my ancestors for their sin and for how they have brought depression and other curses and iniquity into my family. I now renounce all unholy agreements that have been made by my ancestors or me. I renounce any agreements I have made with this curse and iniquity.

I now break off any and all generational curses and iniquity that may have come down to me. I break all generational ties to the occult and witchcraft, and sever its influence over my family and me. I place the cross of Christ between me and the sin and genetic damage that has been running through my family.

Lord Jesus, I take back the ground and authority that has been given to the enemy. I cancel all assignments and bondages the enemy has against my generational line and me. I take back all authority and control of my life and turn it over to You.

Lord Jesus, please wash each generation with your blood, and I call forth the blessings that have been blocked to come down through all the generations; past, present and future.

I acknowledge that our family DNA may have been damaged as a result of traumatic events in the lives of my ancestors.

I forgive the people who caused the trauma. I forgive my ancestors for agreeing with the fear caused by the trauma and for believing the lie that their minds were permanently damaged. I forgive myself for believing that I cannot escape from the curse or iniquity of depression. I repent for everything my ancestors did in response to this trauma that has brought depression into my generations.

Use the following Section as an example of how to pray every day
I repent for basing my identity on the diagnosis that I have depression. I choose to forgive anyone including myself who has convinced me to believe the lie that my identity is my diagnosis and that I will have this for life.

Through the blood of Jesus, I renounce agreement with the lie that has attached my identity to something other than who Jesus says I am. I break your power in Jesus' name.

I receive the truth that you, Jesus, have made me in your image, totally accepted, fully loved, and created with a destiny and a purpose.

I choose to forgive my mind for failing to work correctly so that I have not been able to control my thoughts.

I repent for believing lies that you won't heal me, that I will always be depressed, and it will always be in my family. I repent for agreeing with the expectations that my illness is a life sentence. I repent for any vows I have made or curses I have spoken to myself in response to this illness. Jesus, forgive me for believing the lies and agreeing with them, thereby empowering them in my life. I instruct my soul and my spirit to embrace the truth that I will not always be sick.

I repent for everything I have done, said or thought based on those lies. I repent for using depression as an excuse for sinful behavior. I repent for every time I have hurt someone physically or emotionally, including myself because of depression.

I renounce every agreement I have made with the spirits of depression and I command them to be loosed from me and go to the foot of the Cross in the name of the Lord Jesus Christ. I hand to you, Jesus, the identity I assumed as a depressed person.

Lord Jesus I take back the ground and the authority that I gave to the enemy. I cancel all assignments and bondages the enemy has against any in my generational line and me in the past, present and future. I take back all control and authority of my life and return it to you, Lord Jesus.

In the name of Jesus, in the power of the Holy Spirit, and in the authority of the blood of Christ, I command all spirits attached to depression and to the lies that I have believed to leave me now in Jesus' name. Specifically, I command the spirits of depression, fear, insanity, death, suicide, addictions, torment, self-mutilation, self-hatred, shame, humiliation, inferiority, low self-esteem, discouragement, rejection and self-pity to leave me now.

I speak now to my DNA, "Be healed in Jesus name." I speak to the nerve cells in my brain, "Be healed in Jesus name." I declare that I have the mind of Christ.

Jesus, I now receive your healing into my body, soul and spirit.

Prayer for Healing and Freedom
from the Trauma of Others

Note from Brian P. Cox: I was led to assemble the following prayer based on my work with those in the fire service and the field of medicine. However, this is a useful prayer example for "daily cleaning" regardless of the occupation. As always, the prayers we provide should not be prayed in repetition, but should be considered starting points as you follow God's lead.

In the name of Jesus Christ, I break all ungodly ties between any co-workers and myself. I also break all ungodly ties between myself and any person I've encountered in my work or ministry.

In Jesus' name, I cancel any curses, gossip or slander spoken against my family or me. I declare that I forgive those people and give them over to you, Lord.

Lord, I please break all ungodly territorial ties between all locations and me. Please cancel any plans of retaliation against my family or me.

Lord, I surrender to you the memories of all traumatic and stressful situations I've encountered. Please cover these memories with Your blood. Help me to never internalize stress, trauma or death; but to always give it over to you. Please heal me from any infirmity that has already been caused by internalizing stress, trauma or death.

Lord, please remove any hardening or callousness from my heart. Cause me to see the people I help the way you want me to see them.

I repent for anytime I accepted the criticism of others as true, which may have caused parts of me to be trapped in ungodly or contaminated locations. Lord, please clean up and return all parts of me and restore me to my position of ruling and reigning with Christ.

Lord, I pray that Your Kingdom come and Your will be done in my workplace and all the locations I visit during my job. Please equip me to advance your Kingdom.

Prayer of Restitution

Lord, I renounce and repent for those in my family line who broke marriage covenants and mated with the fallen sons of God.

I also renounce and repent for all Moloch and Baal worship in my generational line. On behalf of both sides of the family, please forgive us for choosing to fashion the golden calf at the foot of Mount Sinai when we were too afraid to draw near to You because we feared Your might and power. Forgive us for not waiting for the return of Your servant, Moses, and for breaking covenant with You by worshiping the golden calf through sacrificial burnt and peace offerings.

Forgive us for holding a festival to the golden calf and indulging ourselves in pagan revelry and sexual sin. Most of all Lord, I renounce and repent for first believing, and then declaring, "These are your gods, O Israel, who brought you out of Egypt"; when it was You who set us free from 430 years of Egyptian captivity. Lord, please forgive us for this wanton display of pride, self-deception, stubbornness and unbelief.

Forgive us Father, for not only worshiping the golden calf and sacrificing our children to it, but also for worshiping the star god Rephan, or Saturn, while wandering in the wilderness for 40 years.

On behalf of every ancestor in my family line who entered the land of Canaan after wandering 40 years in the wilderness, I renounce and repent for our refusal to obey Your explicit command not to engage in the pagan sexual practices of incest, adultery, homosexuality and bestiality that were intertwined with the worship of Moloch. Forgive us for sacrificing our sons and daughters in the fires of Moloch in exchange for favor and prosperity. I know this idolatry was a great offense to You, and I now repent and apologize.

On behalf of every ancestor who was involved with Baal or Moloch worship throughout the history of Israel; from the generation who succeeded Joshua, to the reign of Jeroboam, to Ahab and Jezebel, to Manasseh and beyond; I renounce and repent for every evil connected to this false lord-ruler including child sacrifice, sorcery, witchcraft and the worship of the stars of heaven.

Lord, I now ask You to open every bronze door that has been shut in my generational line because of Baal and Moloch worship so that the righteous gates the enemy has closed and contaminated can no longer be shut. Come now King of Glory, flood the heavenly places in my generational line with Your cleansing power and unseal what the enemy has sealed in the heavenly places, making straight every crooked path and smoothing out every rough place. Smash the bronze doors Lord, and sever the iron bars of my captivity. I now declare that what You have opened will remain open and what You have shut will remain shut. Prepare the way of the Lord.

Lord, I repent for and renounce all worship of the rulers of darkness in my town, city and state. I ask you to forgive me, my family line and the citizens of this region for worshiping false gods at false altars, sacrificing our children to Moloch, and breaking the covenant of marriage through incest, adultery, homosexuality and bestiality. On behalf of the church, I repent for not fearing Your name, not obeying Your Word, not obeying the leading of Your Spirit; and for presuming upon your grace that we can sin sexually, defy spiritual authority, and not suffer the consequences. Please forgive us for slandering the glorious ones and disconnecting ourselves from Your Glory.

Lord, please disconnect me from the ungodly Mazzaroth and cleanse my spirit, soul and body down to the cellular and sub cellular levels from all ungodly influence, defilement and power.

Please remove all parts of my trifold being from the lowest regions of the ungodly depths by disconnecting me from the Nephilim and Rephaim and removing any witchcraft bands from around my arms.

Please transfer me from Mount Horeb to Mount Zion and reconnect me back to You, Lord so Your light will shine through me to others as I proclaim the Gospel in power to Jerusalem, Samaria and to the ends of the earth.

Please disconnect me from the mountains of Esau and move me to Mt. Zion.

I declare to my spirit that you will be under and submissive to the Holy Spirit; and I declare to my body and soul that you will be submissive to my spirit, even as my spirit is submissive to the Holy Spirit.

Lord, please balance correctly the male and female portions of my human spirit.

Please remove all fractal imaging in my family line and remove all mirrors. I declare I will only reflect the image and nature of the Lord Jesus Christ.

Please remove me from the ungodly council and establish me on Mt. Zion and in your heavenly council.

Lord, I repent for those in my family line who turned our family line over to the enemy, thus giving authority for the removal of righteous elders and permission for establishing unrighteous elders over us. I acknowledge that these unrighteous elders caused the family to veer off course, moving out of the right time sequence into other time sequences. I now declare, as a revealed son of God, that these unrighteous elders must leave my family line. Father, please establish the righteous elders over my family line and put us back on the right course and into the right time, removing us from Chronos time and placing us into Your Kairos time.

On behalf of the entire church, forgive me Lord, for syncing my life according to Chronos time and my plans and agendas, instead of Your Kairos time and agenda. Please forgive me Lord for not inquiring of You to see what You want, where You are moving and what You are doing.

Forgive me for believing the lie that Your Second Coming is so close that I need not reach out to the lost and fulfill Your Great Commission. I decree and declare Lord, that it is time to align my life with Yours.

Please remove me from Chronos time and sync me with Kairos time. Open every bronze door so that the gates are no longer shut. Open all the righteous doors and flood my life with Your Glory.

Please remove me from any ungodly place in the depth where parts of me are trapped by sonar, and release your righteous sound that will neutralize that ungodly sonar. Please free all of my trapped parts and fragments.

Please break all ungodly ties and connections between myself and the Rephaim or any other person's soul parts, and remove those connectors.

I renounce and repent for those in my family line who traded their souls for favors from the enemy. Please, through the Blood of Jesus, return all scattered soul parts back to my family line and me. I command Beelzebub to leave.

I ask, Lord Jesus, that you will come as the Son of Man and remove all fallen sons of God from my family line and me.

Please disconnect me from Abaddon and remove any parts of me from the bottomless pit.

Please unlock the ciphers and the ungodly algorithms established by the enemy.

I renounce and repent for those in my family line who gave over the family line to the enemy in order to be able to rule and control others for their own advantage and financial gain. I now understand that this gave the enemy the right to cause me to be knit in the ungodly depth; placing me in a position of servitude rather than one of ruling and reigning over creation, which is my God given right. Please take me back in time to the origin, to your womb of the dawn, and please knit me together in the godly depth. Please remove from me all DNA and RNA contamination that took place during the ungodly knitting.

I declare that I will not be in subjection to others by means of their control and abuse. Lord, please remove the desolation of generations and take me out of any ungodly places in the depth or the height, disconnecting me from those regions and placing me in the godly depth and in the godly height. I reject the discord that has imprisoned me because of my agreement with the ungodly position in which I found myself. I repent for believing the lie that I was to be in submission to others without having any voice, and that this position was normal and was ordained by God.

Please release the righteous sound and vibrations that will align me with the heavenly sounds and vibrations.

Please disconnect me from the dark angels and other unrighteous beings that rule in the ungodly height.

I recognize that my mindset of being a victim has inhibited my ability to fulfill the call on my life to rule and reign under the Lordship of Jesus Christ. I also declare that the wealth that I am to gain for the purposes of the Kingdom of God has been stopped up by my ancestors' sin of wanting personal wealth to use for their own purposes. I now declare that I will receive all the wealth that the Lord wants me to have to fulfill my Kingdom mandate of ruling and reigning. Lord, please release all restrictions against the resources that you originally intended for me to have.

I declare that I will rule and reign in the godly height under the Lordship of Jesus Christ, and I will use all created resources for His Kingdom.

I renounce and repent for my family line and myself for all who entered into sexual activity outside of marriage. Please break the consequences of those who were molested and became victims of sexual abuse. I also repent for all of us who have used pornography for sexual satisfaction. I understand that all this sexual activity resulted in our joining to someone other than our spouses. Lord, as an adult, I ask that You remove me from my parent's sphere of influence and place me in my own sphere of influence. Please remove me from the ungodly length and place me into your godly length.

Heavenly Father, I come in the name of your Son, Jesus; Your only begotten Son; the only Son of God who became a son of man who takes His place upon us, His body. I come into agreement with a common passion to see heaven's intention that was built and established before the foundation of the earth. I ask you, Heavenly Father, Righteous Judge of heaven and earth, to issue a decree against the fallen sons. I call our bloodlines back. Please remove us from the ungodly womb of the dawn. I take back our households in the name of Jesus of Nazareth. I surrender them through the blood of Jesus Christ to be sanctified, glorified, and to come into alignment with their place in the kingdom of Melchizedek. I will no longer drink the wine of the fallen sons of God. I renounce and denounce the spirit of religion, the spirit of debate, the spirit of legalism, the spirit of opinion, the spirit of criticism and the spirit of high-minded intellect. I renounce the mind of the old Adamic way, as well as any mindsets that have been born of the doctrines of the fallen sons of man and the fallen sons of God. I ask for a divorce decree between the fallen sons of God and us. I choose to no longer put faith in the defeated enemy but in the victorious Son of God, Jesus Christ.

Lord, I ask you to reverse the polarity of any ungodly device and extract us from the ungodly collective; removing all microchips, transmitters, and receivers. Extract from my mind all voices and communication from others. Remove me from the ungodly width and the ungodly cloud. I choose to no longer to be affected by the ungodly thoughts of others.

Please correct all molecules, atomic, and subatomic particles corrupted by the fallen sons of God.

Please destroy any dimensions, kingdoms or spheres that the fallen sons of God created due to the agreement of my ancestors or myself.

On behalf of my family line I repent for all blood that was shed on the land and for all idolatry and sexual sin committed on any land area. Please break all ungodly ties between my ancestors and myself with any land area.

Please remove ungodly words of the fallen sons of God that were added to my original design when I was knit together in the deep.

Please activate any righteous words that were covered up by the fallen sons of God on my scroll when I was knit together in the deep.

Please remove any mismatch and misaligning that took place when I was knit together in the deep; remove all ungodly elders, rulers and powers that were involved when I was knit together in the deep; and remove all stones from the fallen sons of God that were knit into me in the deep.

Please break all ungodly agreement between the ungodly deep and the ungodly height, and disconnect me from all fallen stars, star systems, galaxies, and constellations that were involved in contaminating my original design.

Please remove off of me all contamination from the fallen sons of God that affected the light, sound, frequencies, vibrations and colors that made up my being.

Please remove any genes added by the fallen sons of God. Please repair any genes damaged by the fallen sons of God and return to my DNA any genes that were taken away by the fallen sons of God.

Please destroy any ungodly cloning of my genes and chromosomes. Please undo any ungodly fusion with evil that took place with me.

Lord, I ask that You will come with your measuring rod and linen cord and measure the temple in me, removing all generational ungodly temples, kingdoms, spheres, doors, gates, altars, pillars, priestly garments, worship tools and sacrifices.

[Women] Lord Jesus, I understand that as a child I may have accepted the lie that a female was not to become more than a male would permit. I understand that this may have crushed my spirit and caused parts of my spirit to be trapped in the ungodly width. I now reject that lie and I declare that I will be all that the Lord Jesus has created me to be. Please remove all parts of my spirit that have been trapped in the ungodly width and in the ungodly stars, star systems, constellations and zodiacs. I no longer allow the enemy to project around me that I am worthless and that I am always a victim and powerless. I will take my position in Christ and rule and reign equally with males. Please disconnect me from all fallen sons of God who have perpetuated this lie in my family line.

Father, I recognize that the fallen sons of God did not want to be your sons, and so disconnected themselves from you as Father and established themselves as father. I also acknowledge that this may have resulted in generational parts and parts of me to have been trapped in Saturn, the fallen stars, star systems, ungodly galaxies, constellations and zodiacs and in the ungodly length, width, height, and depth.

I renounce and repent for those in my family line who did the same thing with their fathers, and were so distraught about their fathers that they disconnected themselves from them and declared that they would be fathers without being a child. I understand that this established a disconnection generationally between father and child, resulting in generational blessings not being passed down the family line. I also acknowledge that this may have prohibited me from taking my place as a revealed son of God. I acknowledge that this ungodly fractal patterning may have caused a disconnection between father and child resulting in bitterness and anger in my family line and in my life. I now ask, Lord, that You would remove me from Saturn, the fallen stars, star systems, ungodly galaxies, constellations and zodiacs and in the ungodly length, width, height, and depth.

I now forgive my father and all fathers in my family line for not fathering correctly. I also forgive all sons and daughters in my family line that, because of the cruelty of their fathers, disconnected themselves from their fathers and broke the God-intended linkage between generations, thus also breaking the free flow of generational blessings.

Lord, please connect my generational line and me correctly to the godly length, width, height and depth so that I can take my place as a revealed son of God and rule and reign with Christ. I also ask that You will correctly connect me to my generational line so that the generational blessings that were to come down the family line will now be completely restored to the family line and to myself. I reclaim and receive your spiritual blessings that were intended for my family line and me. I now ask that what has happened in the heavenly places will now be done on earth in the physical realm. I now claim all physical, emotional, and spiritual health that you intend me to have. I also claim all physical inheritance that is my right as a revealed son of God.

Lord Jesus, by your life sacrificed on the cross and by your life-blood, please dismantle and remove all structures that have been built from these sins and from unclean spirits, including ungodly habits, curses, devices, conduits, attachments, lies, "gifts" or deposits. Free us from ungodly structures, from distortions in my life and family line, and even from any distortions of our DNA and RNA. God Almighty, please close any doors or openings that these sins and ungodly structures created. Open any godly doors to you and your blessings that these sins and ungodly structures had closed. Holy Spirit, please empower righteous choices in my family line and myself. I choose to honor You, growing godly habits while enthroning Your name in our lives, relationships, and land.

Prayer to Replace Ungodly Alignment with godly Alignment

Lord, I come before you on behalf of my family line and myself in regard to the all of the issues that have placed us into ungodly alignment.

I repent and renounce for:
- Allowing enticements to draw us away from your original plan for our lives
- Allowing the land to be contaminated by those who met during certain seasonal and astronomical times in order to perform rituals and sacrifices that empowered curses on the unsuspecting, and set traps for the theft of inheritances and birthrights
- Luring people into ungodly alignment through deception or shape shifting
- Making decisions out of fear or panic rather than fighting the battle from the rest and giving our burdens to You to deal with
- Business men and women who traded inheritances willingly in order to become more successful and gain power
- Performing ungodly ceremonies and dedications for corporations and land territories, thus opening doors for the enemy's access

Lord, I reject all of that evil. Please disconnect me as well as my land, ministry, relationships, and finances from all ungodly land territories, ceremonies, alignment with stars or constellations, and astrological signs or symbols. I declare that you are higher than all the stars, constellations, and any man-made signs or symbols.

I repent and renounce for:
- Abusing the resources and elements that You gave us and exploiting them for financial gain
- Contaminating and manipulating those resources and elements by adding unnecessary additives in an effort to win friends or influence people, without regard for the damage that could be caused
- Using witchcraft spells or incantations, and calling on demonic influences to pervert or take control over the elements of creation in an effort to use them against us.

Lord, please return all portions of the elements that are part of our inheritance and healing, washing and cleansing them first in the blood of Jesus.

I repent and renounce for:
- Perverting the waters and deceiving others into drinking that perverted water
- Worshiping and/or performing rituals in exaltation to any water spirits
- Calling up any demonic influences through water rituals
- Aligning with the New World Order and disregarding all of Your written laws and guidelines found in the Word of God
- Twisting Your words in order to justify our behavior or deceive others
- Setting up counterfeit temples and places of worship
- Performing ungodly water baptisms
- Operating in a false gift of healing
- Offering blood sacrifices on the land in an effort to establish ungodly territory and bring curses on any that would come upon that land

- Being so stuck on looking good to others that we had an appearance of godliness but denied Your power
- Setting up false pillars of lust, deception, enticement, and religion
- Establishing ungodly centers for worship and using the Lord's name to attract people
- Establishing ungodly offices and positions of power, worshiping ungodly thrones, and seeking after positions in ungodly places rather than the positions of authority You had for us

Lord, please rescue our inheritance, transfer our wealth from any ungodly tabernacles, and bring restoration to our finances and land. Please cancel all assignments on our land and finances, and help us to keep our finances in your godly institutions.

I repent and renounce for:
- Taking liberties that were not allowed and going into a holy place without washing first or feeling a sense of obligation to honor Your holy tabernacle
- Encroaching upon the true Holy of Holies as a spy in order to gain secret knowledge to take back to our camp to further our own purposes.

Lord, please escort the encroachers out of Your tabernacle, and help me to honor Your holy places and be a watchman on the wall for your tabernacle.

I repent and renounce for:
- Worshiping money and/or using money to sow seeds and finance ungodly organizations and projects
- Finding our worth in wealth, instead of realizing that our wealth and identity that is in You
- Paying tithes into churches or places of worship where You didn't want us to sow into from the beginning
- Refusing to bring important decisions about finances to You for approval and guidance
- Purchasing memberships and entering into agreements with ungodly places of business, resulting in financial curses
- Intermingling with the enemies' camp or associating with those of evil intent

Please Lord, disconnect our land and us from all this evil and release a blessing.

I confess that we have gone away from your laws and compromised our beliefs and our finances for instant gratification, and I repent and renounce for:
- Intermarriage with those worshiping the gods and goddesses of men, thus becoming unequally yoked
- Becoming parasites who sucked godly people of their resources, energy, identity, healing and gifts
- Allowing ourselves to be used as a part of the ungodly web through gossip or slander
- Deliberately trying to connect to others in order to weave the ungodly web
- Suspending others in the ungodly web; or forcing them to be stuck in an ungodly place, unable to move forward, break free, or be stuck in time

Lord, please disconnect us from the ungodly web and set us free. Please remove all cobwebs and any predators that have been assigned to trap or overtake us. Please help us to refrain from evil and avoid the traps set up by enticement and temptation.

I repent and renounce for:
- Bringing distractions and isolation to those operating in discernment

- Setting up assignments to keep them from connecting to other believers in order to correctly discern the battle.

Lord, please help us to remember to assemble together, and to fellowship with like-minded people.

I repent and renounce for:
- Ignoring our discernment or allowing ourselves to be deceived or desensitized to the enemy's tactics and plans to destroy
- Not exercising self-discipline in setting aside time to pray, dig into Your Word and connect with You daily, in order to plan our day and make good decisions
- Not seeking you first, and trusting you to prosper us, but trying to prosper ourselves
- Following ungodly prophecies, or taking your true prophecies into our own hands and trying to figure out or manipulate them through our own abilities
- Putting too much emphasis on others' prophecies instead of submitting them to You and/or the body of Christ for testing and confirmation
- Surrendering our discernment because we trusted the leadership, or authority figures, to be hearing correctly
- Putting too much stalk in family and making decisions based on pleasing family members more than You
- Listening to those with their own agendas and motivations for speaking prophecy, and for those in leadership who allowed wolves in sheep's clothing to hold places of authority
- Exalting the spiritual gift instead of exalting You, and assuming that gifted people were godly
- Abusing our gifts, and using them to further our own purposes or the purposes of the false signs and wonders connected to the ungodly network

Please disconnect us from all false prophecies, and help us follow the true way of the Lord. Please dismantle all assignments of the enemy to bring division that is intended to destroy the unity of the family and the church.

Lord, please help us to guard our hearts, both coming and going; help us to not act out of desperation; help us to discern where we should go and what we should participate in; and help us not to align with any ungodly network because of lust, deception, enticement, or religion. Please release to us the godly Alignment You have for us.

I repent for any time we opened up ungodly portals, gates, cracks, and seams; and I ask You now to close all them. Please open up your heavens and connect us to your plumb line. I give you permission to come and go in my life as you please.

Land Repentance Prayer

Lord, I come before you on behalf of my family line and myself in regard to the all of the issues that have cursed or otherwise tainted our land.

Lord, I repent and renounce for:
- Those who dedicated land to the works of freemasonry, religion, ungodly organizations or Satanism
- Knowingly or unknowingly bringing curses on the land through sacrifices or rituals
- Husbands and wives that were not in unity about their land
- Wives that tilled the land thinking it was dedicated to God, but it was not
- Those whose hands were defiled because they tilled the land until it became fruitless
- Women that reaped the consequences of a bent back because of tilling ungodly land; thinking they were doing a righteous thing, but actually taking on burdens their husband should have carried; resulting in empty works because the land was dedicated for ungodly purposes
- Husbands that would not till their own land and let their wives do it, bringing disunity to the family
- Husbands that traded the land and went against godly principles for tilling the land
- Those that purchased land and allowed defilement to come upon it through ungodly agreements with unrighteous authorities, especially their city of residence
- Going to places in the city for meetings that may have been dedicated to ungodly purposes, thus bringing home defilement on our feet that allowed evil hitchhikers to accompany us
- Letting any secret tunnels or underground networks to be attached to our property, or allowing unrighteous access through water rights or ungodly waterways

Lord, please disconnect our elemental inheritance, especially any water or mineral rights, on our land from all ungodly governmental authorities.

I repent and renounce for any who took our properties' resources and squandered them away, or used them in an ungodly way. Lord, please protect our resources from any ungodly governmental authorities.

I renounce ungodly governmental authorities that mapped out our properties location and tracked it in order to pursue ownership, or to steal our inheritance or the resources on the land. Lord, please remove our property from the enemy's radar.

I repent and renounce for those that connected to a death spirit through suicidal thoughts and/or hopelessness, valuing property and finances more than life; and for those that committed suicide on land, enabling a curse of death. Lord, please disconnect my land from all spirits of death and suicide.

I repent and renounce for
- Those of freemasonry that built the aqueduct, as well as any rituals or sacrifices that took place during the building
- Those that ran into the city before it was a city in an effort to control all the resources of that land
- Those that stole land from the Native Americans and for all resulting bloodshed

Lord, please disconnect our land from the blood that cries out and from any relics that could have been buried on our land before we owned it.

Prayer of Repentance for Misandry
(The Hatred of Males)

This is intended to be prayed by women.

Heavenly Father, I come before You on behalf of myself, my family line, my gender and my culture to repent and renounce for all hatred and dishonoring of men who have been created in Your image.

I repent for and renounce:

- All unforgiveness, bitterness, hatred and retaliation towards men who have mistreated women with spiritual, mental, emotional, physical and/or sexual abuse, discrimination, injustice of any kind, rejection, abandonment, debasement and dehumanization through pornography, prostitution, violence, rape and/or slavery.
- Pride and rejecting God's design of the human race, of two genders, of marriage and family, His designation of men to be the spiritual leader in marriage and families and His creation of woman to be a helper[6] to man.
- Independence from men and denying our need of men.
- Believing the lie that the God-given role of being a helper to men means that women are inferior to men, and for reacting to that lie in rebellion to God and men's authority.
- Despising, disrespecting, dishonoring, dismissing, rejecting, and rebelling against my father and other male authority figures and their God-given authority as a result of their sin, imperfections and lack because God requires that we respect the position of authority not just the person.
- All use of witchcraft and curses against men to inflict death, suffering, pain and everything men have inflicted upon women.
- Rejection of men and God's design of men; and rejecting God's design in the difference between men and women by trying to create a unisex world or a feminized culture and/or trying to alter any male traits in men and boys, constantly trying to change them or demanding more or different from how God created them to be.
- All genital jealousy.
- Denying, degrading, disrespecting and not valuing the unique traits that men have of physical and inner strength, fortitude, and protection that differ from female tendencies toward caring, closeness and homemaking.
- Making fun of any guy interests.
- Any participation in jokes, ungodly fellowship, ungodly entertainment and/or ungodly media of any kind – romance novels, soap operas, magazines, books, TV shows and internet sources which make fun of, mock and/or belittle men, their character traits, sexuality and/or sexual organs and/or portray views of men, husbands, wives, women, marriage and children which are contrary to the truth, principles and design of God.
- The fear of men and reacting to the injustices towards women in fear and control, blaming men, retaliating against men and trying to right the injustices towards women in our own strength and not according to God's ways and principles.

---

[6] Genesis 2:20 states Adam did not find a helper <u>comparable</u> to him. Furthermore, Genesis 1:26&27 states that God made mankind in His image and gave mankind dominion over the earth. In other words, man and women were created to rule equally over creation.

- Usurping male authority either overtly or by coveting male authority, taking over, controlling situations, withholding information from male authorities, using deception, and/or going around male authorities instead of discussing and initiating change according to biblical principles.
- Using rebellion, whining, arguing, moods, complaining, crying, pouting, anger, yelling, berating, fussing, disappointment, shame, guilt, resentment, dissatisfactions, stubbornness, rejection, tantrums, domination, nagging, butting in, nitpicking every error, bringing up past errors, criticism, griping and/or manipulation to change men or a situation they have authority over.
- Seeing men as the enemy, oppressors, predators, insensitive, aggressors, violent and the source of pain instead of as partners in the Kingdom of God, fathers, brothers, friends, and co-laborers in Christ.
- All disrespectful, hostile, disdainful, dismissive, dominating, disappointed, belittling, mocking, and/or undermining attitudes and behavior towards men.
- The Jezebel spirit, spirits of manipulation and control, all witchcraft and witchcraft spirits, and every emasculating spirit.
- Using sexuality for selfish gain, to manipulate, control and/or to gain power.
- Using men or any relationship with men to gain legitimacy, financial stability or status.
- Any adherence to and/or propagation of the belief that woman does not need a man.
- Using any feminist agenda to create laws and social programs that are unfair to men in the guise of liberating women and righting past injustices.
- The feminist belief of having it all and the feminist thinking which wants to replace love, marriage, and family with personal power and success when God has called an individual to marriage instead of seeing marriage and raising a family as being the God ordained way.
- Denying the desire for marriage and rejecting marriage out of fear of rejection and shame.
- Rejecting the God-given roles, responsibilities, and joys of being a wife and mother because of the feminist belief system that women don't need men or don't need to raise children to be happy, that married woman at home with children are not real woman fulfilling their potential.
- Women's belief that everything male is evil, stupid, and oppressive.
- Any hostility towards and/or rejecting the responsibilities, obligations and roles a woman has as a wife and mother within the covenantal relationships of marriage and family and/or resenting having to do the domestic work of cooking, cleaning, laundry and child care in a marriage relationship. I acknowledge that both man and woman share domestic responsibilities.
- All selfishness and self-centeredness in relationships with men and all ingratitude for the qualities and blessings that men bring to relationships, family, culture and society.
- Elevating pride, selfishness, self-gratification and self-esteem over humility, sacrificial service and love in relationships with men.
- Being oblivious and insensitive to the destructive behavior of women to men and marriages, ungodly independence, the lack of concern about the needs or desires of husbands, withholding affection from men.
- Expecting men to be sensitive but withholding sensitivity from men.
- Looking to relationships with men, marriage and having children as the source of fulfillment and happiness in life rather than a personal relationship with God and taking responsibility for who I am.

- The sense of entitlement in relationships with men that comes from being impossible to please, demanding perfection, letting feelings of happiness dominate behavior rather than character.
- Replacing the love of a male with other activities so as to avoid relationships with men.
- Ignoring and not validating and appreciating the efforts of men in relationships.
- Neglecting the proper care of husbands and children because of overextending ourselves, wearing ourselves out by trying to do too much and not making the time for and not putting the priority on the relationships with husband and children in the order that God wants us to after our relationship with Him and above our obligations to work and ministry outside of the home.
- Reversing the order of God-given priorities by putting children ahead of spouses, being obsessed with domestic issues, not caring for our physical appearance, always giving command and forgetting to be a wife, a woman, a lover and a companion during private moments with my husband.
- Treating our husbands like children instead of the head of the household.
- Condemning men for not doing their share at home and not acknowledging that they do help.
- Being deceived by, and adhering to the feminist mindset, which views God, men, marriage, and motherhood, rather than the enemy, as avenues of violence against women.
- Rejecting the roles of men in God's Kingdom, marriage, family, and society because of this and dishonoring men by this rejection.

I repent for my own participation in the man-hating spirit. I now break every curse I have spoken over men, in the name of Jesus. I repent of any spiritual rebellion or anger over the choice and design of my Heavenly Father to create men and their God-given place of authority in His kingdom, marriage, family, and society. I accept the male gender and bless them to be all that God created them to be, in the name of Jesus.

I ask you, Father God, to cleanse all misandry for my generational line and restore to the men in my family line the place you originally intended for them. I ask you to bless them with the knowledge of Your design and love, a desire to claim their inheritance and an acceptance of their purpose in You. I forgive all in my family line and through the ages who have operated under the Misandrist spirit.

Heavenly Father, I ask for Your forgiveness for and cleansing in my generational line from everything repented for in this prayer and I ask that You would bring the cleansing forward to me and into the future to a thousand generations of my physical and spiritual seed.

In Jesus name, I accept the God given role of women in His Kingdom, marriage, family and society and I now declare that I, as a woman, will rule together with men over Creation and will walk in the fullness of my God-given birthright and purpose as a woman and as a fellow heir of the grace of life according to God's design.

Prayer for DNA

I repent for all ungodly beliefs held by my family line and me that have allowed ungodly inscriptions to be written, either on any of my genes or within the DNA base sequence.

Lord, will You please:

- Go into the enemy's library and destroy all books that contain the enemy's inscriptions upon my DNA, RNA and proteins
- Go into the righteous library and retrieve the original design of my DNA, RNA and proteins, and imprint it on my DNA, RNA and proteins
- Clean off all ungodly paths connected to my DNA, RNA and proteins and restore the original paths, correctly connecting each gene to the righteous lines
- Remove all ungodly inscriptions on the stones
- Remove my DNA, RNA and proteins from the ungodly length, width, height and depth
- Correct the sound, resonance, and frequency of each strand of DNA in each chromosome, and remove the enemy's resonance of evil
- Disconnect each base from any ungodly star, star system, zodiac, constellation and/or galaxy, and remove the stars from their ungodly courses
- Redesign the inscription on my genes to the original blueprint and intent
- Cancel all blood, salt, and threshold covenants in my family line that have corrupted each DNA, RNA and protein
- Heal all of the mitochondria DNA
- Remove any gene out of any ungodly time lines
- Remove any animal, fish, plant, reptilian, and any spiritual being's DNA and RNA from any captured part that is still stuck in any ungodly dimension and the ungodly grid
- Remove any unholy sequencing in my DNA and RNA placed there by the fallen sons of God
- In the womb of the dawn, correctly sequence the ACGT coding of my original design in the conception replication of all my DNA and RNA
- Disconnect me from the ungodly rainbow angel and the ungodly little book

I shut each door that has been opened to allow evil to affect each base, base pair, gene, chromosome, and my entire DNA.

I ask You to open all doors that should be opened to each base, base pair, gene, chromosome, and my entire DNA so the righteous gates cannot be closed.

I declare the correction of each base, base pair, gene, chromosome, and my entire DNA is accomplished by the finished work of Jesus Christ on the cross.

I recognize You, Lord, as the Master Builder and the Maker of the original design of my DNA and RNA. I now agree to align as a co-creator to the new creation design that You established on the cross.

Lord, please restore the path to me. This day I choose Life and not Death.

(If praying over specific genes[7]) Lord, please clean each gene as I indicate it and then put it back in the correct location.

---

[7] See "Ministering to the DNA" located in this book

Ministering to the DNA and How to Locate a Problem on a Chromosome

1. There are 23 pairs of chromosomes – 22 pairs of autosomes or non-sex chromosomes and 1 pair of sex
2. Chromosome 23 is either X or Y, so the chromosome pair 23 is either XX (female) or XY (male).
3. Each human's chromosome has two arms that are separated by a centromere. The top, shorter arm is the "p arm" and the lower, longer arm is the "q arm"
4. In most cases, a known chromosomal abnormality may be searched using any internet search engine in order to find the location of the abnormality or problem on the chromosome(s). In the search bar, include the abnormality, disease or problem and the words, **"chromosome location".** The results should indicate the known locations of the issue being investigated
   1. Example: The problem of diabetes
   2. Type into a search engine, **"diabetes chromosome location".**
   3. A series of articles will be generated, which will require some scanning to find the information you are searching
   4. Below are two paragraphs from one article that will give an example of what to look for. The key information is highlighted:
      1. *Type 2 diabetes is a common multifactorial heterogeneous disease with both genetic and environmental determinants and an uncertain mode of inheritance. At least three groups have recently completed genome scans for type 2 diabetes and many are nearing completion. Hanis* et al *reported genome-wide significance on chromosome 2q31 on a combined data set of 440 Mexican-American affected sib pairs (ASPs). In a sample from Botnia, Western Finland, a small number of selected pedigrees with the lowest quartile for mean 30-min insulin levels after oral glucose tolerance tests showed significant evidence for linkage to type 2 diabetes on chromosome 12q. More recently, evidence for linkage was obtained on chromosome 11q for both diabetes and body mass index (BMI) in 264 Pima Indian families.*
      2. *In contrast, maturity-onset diabetes of the young (MODY) is a rare monogenic form of type 2 diabetes that has an autosomal dominant mode of inheritance. At least five different genes, located on chromosomes 20, 7, 12, 13, and 17, independently cause MODY within single pedigrees. MODY genes may also play a minor role in the common form of type 2 diabetes.*
   5. In the examples above, notice that more than one chromosome is implicated in diabetes. The first notation is "**2q31**" - in other words, **chromosome 2, (q) arm, region 3, band 1** and read "two Q three one." The second notation is **12q.** This would be **chromosome 12, (q) arm.** The third notation is **11q,** which would **chromosome 11, (q) arm**. Diabetes can also be found in **chromosomes 20 and**
5. Using the OMIM website is another way of finding problem, the gene address and the location of the gene on the chromosome. Go to the website www.omim.org
   1. In the search engine type in the problem/disorder/medial issue/psychological issue. The results will yield several gene addresses in the format described above. If you would like to see the gene location on the specific chromosome,

go to the list below the search engine and find *Advance Search* and click on *gene map*. At the bottom of that page you will see a list of the chromosomes. Using the example above for diabetes gene address – 2q31 – click on chromosome 2 and you will find the map for chromosome 2 and you can locate the specific gene. Using your finger as discernment you can ask the Lord if there is a problem with that gene.

2. Pray and ask the Lord to:
   1. Repair that gene
   2. Correct any mutations in this region
   3. Remove any additions to the chromosome that the enemy has made
   4. Retrieve any deletions to the chromosome that have been made by the enemy

Prayer for Release from Bigotry (Racism) and its Effects

Holy Father, I pray on behalf of my family line and myself and repent for:

- Participating in ethnic prejudice through slander, discrimination, inappropriate joking, oppression, abuse, or the denial of justice
- Not showing hospitality to strangers who were of a different ethnic group, and by so doing forsaking the blessing of entertaining angels
- Frustrating your will to join together as man and wife by rejecting or condemning a family member with a spouse of an ethnic group different from our own
- Participating in stereotypes
- Using hateful words or pejorative terms to refer to those of other ethnic groups
- Desiring salvation for ourselves but hypocritically withholding the Good News from other ethnic groups, thinking their problems to be intractable and just punishment

I declare that Jesus bore our punishment and I will freely help others as I have been helped, without arrogant condescension.

I declare that Your plan for blessing the Jews and choosing them to be a light for all ethnic groups is good, and I repent for the times when we have resented your blessing of the Jews and your plan for our salvation, discrimination against the Jews, or participation in robbery, rape or murder against them. I repent for any times we thought the King of the Jews had no relevance for our ethnic group, and I embrace Messiah Jesus as the Savior of the world.

I also repent for:

- All hatred, bitterness and failure to bless any ethnic group that mistreated us through genocide, colonization, slavery, exploitation, internment camps, concentration camps, forced moves to reservations, etc.
- Failing to love our enemies when they failed to do good to those who hate us
- Not blessing those who curse us, or praying for those who mistreat us
- Engaging in the genocide, colonization, slavery, exploitation, internment camps, concentration camps, forced moves to reservations, etc., of any ethnic groups
- Cowardice in failing to act for justice at times when we were complacent in our silence concerning these things, for Revelation 21:8 says the cowardly have no share with you
- Participation in justification of such things as segregation, apartheid and Jim Crow laws
- Any participation in groups such as the KKK

Father, I thank you for my ethnic heritage. All ethnic groups have strengths and weaknesses and I believe my ancestry descends through the first Adam. I believe Jesus Christ is the second man and the last Adam, who purchased our redemption through His blood so that all who belong to Him shall bear His image. (1 Cor. 15:49)

Thank you for releasing us from rejection and from the effects of rejecting others.

Prayer to Release Dreams

On behalf of my entire generational line and myself, I renounce and repent for all of us who ever discounted or ignored our God-given dreams.

I repent for all who have: believed or said, "I never dream," or "God doesn't speak through dreams"; discouraged, mocked and/or shut down the dreams of others in any way, especially those of children; received and believed false dreams and/or dream interpretations; become false prophets or teachers based on dreams.

I now break all self-curses that I have made in regard to dreams, and in the name of Jesus I command all dream-blocking spirits to leave and go to the feet of Jesus. I also command the fear of dreaming and all deception, including religious spirits and false prophecy, to leave and go to the feet of Jesus.

Lord Jesus, please close all of the unrighteous doors that have been opened against my dreams and open the doors of righteousness. I invite you to possess the gates of my dreams, come into them, live in them, and speak Your truth into my heart and mind. Please increase my discernment, grant me Your wisdom and knowledge, and teach me to understand my dreams. Your promise in John 14:26 states:

> *But the Helper, the Holy Spirit, whom the Father will send in My name, He will teach you all things, and bring to your remembrance all that I said to you.*

Lord, please fulfill that promise in my life in regard to dreams, visions, and twilight experiences.

Prayer to Re-establish God's
Original Creative Design

Father, I offer this prayer for myself and on behalf of the iniquities of my generational line back to the beginning of time.

I renounce and repent for:

- Agreeing with a mindset of poor judgement and so-called wisdom from man
- Rejecting the free gift of salvation and refusing to acknowledge the body and blood of Jesus
- Coming into agreement with the stupidity of others, rejecting godly knowledge and understanding
- Not inquiring of the Lord before making a decision
- Choosing man's pathways instead of God's righteous pathways
- Intentionally and unintentionally closing my senses to what is true
- Choosing injustice and unrighteousness and deception over wisdom, righteousness, justice and truth
- Fear of man rather than fear of God
- Desiring the approval of man instead of God
- Embracing the right hand of falsehood
- Being shrewd and wise hearted to do evil
- Intentionally choosing not to know God.
- Embracing the identity of a fallen son
- Not fearing God
- Being actively passive, and not standing up for what is right
- Choosing cowardice instead of godly boldness
- Compromise, and lack of righteous indignation about sin
- Not acknowledging the master workman, Wisdom, who was established for all creation
- Not praying for wisdom

Lord, please remove the spirit of stupidity and its seven ungodly pillars, and establish me with wisdom. I now intently choose Wisdom to lead in all my discussions for the restoration of the intent of the original creation.

I declare that our sons may be as plants grown up in their youth; that our daughters may be as pillars, sculptured in palace style; that our barns may be full, supplying all kinds of produce; that our sheep will increase by thousands and tens of thousands in our fields; that our oxen may be well laden; that there be no breaking in or going out; I declare that we will be part of a happy people because our God is the Lord.[8]

Father I recognize that I was with I AM in eternity as a created son of God, and I clearly knew your eternal attributes, your eternal laws, and the difference between right and wrong. I

---

[8] Psalms 144:12-15

understand that when I was conceived, I entered into sinful rebellion against you and that even though I knew you at some place in my heart—even though I remembered you—I turned against you. I confess my sin of rebellion against your law, your ways, and ask that you recalibrate my heart. Please also recalibrate the dimensions so that everything will be in alignment make all adjustments necessary so the roots of sickness and disease as well as all curses of iniquity and ungodly foundations will be completely destroyed.

Father, I repent for not only rebelling against your laws but also for then deciding to make our own laws in defiance of You. I confess our society is doing that today. Please remove all ramifications of those actions.

I renounce and repent for attempting to:

- Open the seven eyes of the Lord to other realities rather than trusting You to open my eyes according to Your reality
- Seek truth through self-effort and by asking the fallen sons of god or other ungodly beings
- Travel through the stars by self-effort, requesting the assistance of ungodly beings

Lord, please bring my eyes into alignment according to your design, and my perception into alignment with your truth. Please remove all deception. I choose to seek Your truth.

I repent for trying to activate the third eye, trying to see realities ahead of your timing and my expectations, while being unwilling to wait for Your timing. Please change my focus to see through the lens of Your eyes and cause my eyes to see correctly. Please correctly align the seven eyes of the Lord on the white stone.

I repent for all judgments I have made because of life situations that distorted my self-perception. Please correct the frequencies and tune me to godly wisdom.

I repent for not speaking of Your attributes and Your name, and for operating contrary to Your character, name and precepts. Please restore intimacy, both emotionally and intellectually, to Your perfect law; and remove all contamination that took place on the fiery stones because of disregard for You and Your law.

Lord, please remove all ungodly words that were written on my heart by the fallen sons of God and remove the words, etchings and all other contamination off every cell of my body, covering it with the blood of Jesus.

Please disconnect me from the ungodly height, width, length, depth and time, and correctly connect me to the godly height, width, length, depth and time as well as to all other righteous domains and dimensions.

I repent for all ungodly trading and for all agreement or acceptance of ordinances written against me by any spiritual beings, ancestors, or other humans. Further, I repent for any pride that initiated this rebellion. Please remove those ungodly ordinances from my heart and remove all books in the ungodly libraries that give any legal rights for the enemy to come against me.

Lord, please cause all things to become visible to me and expose every memory that has caused any part to become trapped between any windows and/or mirrors.

May Your Glorious Light remove all evil, and please expose all shame and pain, bringing health to all the parts dirtied by shame. Disconnect all parts of me from Kronos.

I renounce and repent for:

- Not understanding that my sin and the sin of my generational line has caused a negative effect on creation and on light, corrupting Your wonderful creation
- Not taking responsibility for Your creation laws
- Compromising Your creation laws, and then incorrectly teaching the truth about them
- Not take responsibility for caring for the earth, allowing the earth to become cursed through our disobedience, for I understand that this sin prevented the land from yielding its strength to us
- Participation in the corruption of creation in heavenly places and sowing disorder in the heavenly places, thus reaping back to the physical creation of that corruption
- Idolatrous worship of the cosmic entities
- Ignoring our responsibilities of sowing and reaping and not understanding and acknowledging that what is sown in corruption is reaped in corruption
- Trading away future generations' DNA and RNA to the fallen elemental principles of the world
- Contributing to all the ungodly libraries that are connected with the false mind of the fallen sons of God and the adversaries
- Using our creative abilities to exchange the glory of the incorruptible God for corrupted images
- Buying into false doctrines, false prophesies, false philosophies, and false teachings that have been stored in the ungodly libraries
- Being argumentative and legalistic, and for teaching such behaviors
- All false mathematical equations, corruption of the elements and the DNA and RNA and the false headship
- Use of intimidation or coercion to force others to believe a certain way, based on my opinion and not the word of God
- All ungodly sounds and vibrations connected to the ungodly libraries
- Hiding my lamp under a bushel, and not sowing a harvest
- Receiving and believing opinions that were false, which helped to form false clouds
- Not taking care of what I listen to, thus receiving by my own standards a greater measure of evil
- Allowing Your truth to become so diluted in my life that as Your salt on the earth I lost my flavor and became no longer good for anything other than to be thrown out and be trampled under people's feet
- Feeling the power of the ungodly libraries and placing my trust in that power instead of weighing it against Your word because of a lack of discernment
- The pride of life, and attempting to sit on the ungodly thrones
- Trying to rule based on false opinion and false knowledge
- Listening to and speaking gossip
- Growing weary of doing good and agreeing with a culture of deception and a luciferian mindset

- Cooperating to change God's original time and seasons, especially for naming the Sabbath day, Saturday, in honor of Saturn, Cronus, or Moloch

Lord, please break/remove/disperse/disconnect from:

- Connections that attach through the stars, windows, and libraries to create a false image,
- All false treasures of darkness
- All ungodly fruit that came from my judgments
- False clouds and ungodly words
- The opinion of all ungodly councils in my generational line which have collaborated together to speak falsehoods that are not based upon the word of God
- All ungodly thrones that have powered false and persuasive words
- All that has been recorded in the ungodly library
- The anti-Christ system that is documented in these libraries

I renounce and repent for declarations by the fallen sons of God that they created someone in their own image. I break the lie and the agreement that says that the sons of God can create in their own image and that all their descendants are made in their image. Please remove the imprint of that false image and false sound off my DNA and RNA. I declare that my image does not come from the stars, zodiac, hosts or Remphan[9], for my image comes only from Almighty God. Lord, please remove this ungodly imprinting from me, repair any version of false equations, false builders and imprints, and remove me from this ungodly system. Created in the image of God, both male and female, I break the lie of the false sons of God that there is no male or female.

Lord, please disconnect me from all ungodly thrones that are affecting and empowering the twelve signs of the zodiac, restore stability to each sign of the Mazzaroth[10], and unlock the treasures inherent in my family line. Please remove all instability, indecision and wavering of opinions so that I am no longer tossed to and fro.

Please disconnect me from the ungodly scales and ungodly gyroscope that twist Your direction for my life and connect me to Your compass so that I am correctly aligned to Kairos and the time of the fullness of the cross.

Please re-center me within the Holy of Holies in the Heavenly Tabernacle so that each set of three tribes is in the correct location. Please remove me from any land I should not be connected to.

I renounce and repent for agreements with Nimrod, participation in building the tower of Babel, and agreements with the fallen sons and fallen zodiac that have allowed their ungodly sounds and frequencies to vibrate through my DNA. Please disconnect me from the ungodly council of Nimrod, the tower of Babel and the ungodly stars in Jesus' name. Please clean my body, DNA

---

[9] Acts 7:43
[10] Job 38:32

and RNA, and align my DNA and RNA to the sound and frequency of your original creation design.

I renounce and repent for giving up, selling, sacrificing, trading, cursing and/or diminishing the lines of the Lord that lead to the pleasant places. I repent for any form of mockery of the pleasant places of the Lord through prayer, Christian talk, teaching, theology, and self-righteousness. Please remove the bitterness of my heart because I did not understand and acknowledge the lines that were to be connected to the pleasant places.

I repent for causing unrighteous alignment and folding of the dimensions, or of the height, width, length, depth and pleasant places. Forgive us for causing this by thought, word, and deed. Please undo all of this, break the consequences, and return any God-given laws of these places back into the God-given form. Please put all formulas, including $E=mc^2$ back into correct created order according to Your wisdom and remove any unrighteous mirroring, astral travel, and fractal patterning in the lines and the pleasant places. Please undo every damage and connection concerning fertility cults and the unrighteous sexual mating with the stars, sons of God, and the land. Please correctly connect me to the lines of the Lord and the pleasant places so that I may release the sound of Your love.

Father, I ask to be connected to the headship of Christ as a pure bride of Christ, dressed in the robes of righteousness and re-established according to Your original creative design.

Backdoor Prayer

Lord, please forgive my generational line and me for all unrighteous thought and for believing the lies of the enemy.[11] Please forgive me for not setting my mind on things above and for allowing fear, worry, and regret to dominate my thinking.[12]

Lord, You are my Creator/Designer/Programmer. Please access Your backdoor to my brain/mind, which is like an elaborate computer system. Close all doors that should be closed, and open all doors that should be opened so the gates of my mind may never be shut against You.

Please kill all viruses and erase all ungodly pathways. Please upgrade my speed, memory, and storage capacity so I can quickly process and recall all that You want me to know. Please reprogram me; upgrade my existing programs and install new ones that align with your latest designs for my life; and set my entire being for automatic updates and releases. Please build a firewall of Your truth through which deception cannot penetrate, and install the Word of God as my always up-to-date anti-virus program. Please cause all of my thoughts to be aligned with Yours so I can always understand what You are doing and know how to respond appropriately in the world. Conform me to Your image, Lord.

---

[11] In other words, live according to the flesh, Romans 8:5-8
[12] Philippians 4:8

Prayer to Renounce the Illegal Access of the Windows of Heaven

Lord, I lay claim to the world court case against the enemy that occurred on February 5, 2015 at Aslan's Place in Apple Valley, CA. I ask that You enforce the judgments made against the enemy on that day, and that you will close all windows that need to be closed and open all windows that need to be open. Lord, remove any ungodly branches and totally graft me into You as a branch in Your vine. I declare You are the true vine and I am a branch of You. Please remove all ungodly branches and burn them. I repent for establishing and nurturing these ungodly branches, and for not acknowledging you as My true vine and myself as a branch on Your vine. I submit this prayer on behalf of my family line as well as myself.

Father, in the name of Jesus, I ask You to forgive us for illegally accessing the windows of heaven for the purpose of personal financial gain. I repent for and renounce opening any heavenly windows through occult practice, idolatry, divination, witchcraft, covenant breaking, ungodly trading, the exploitation of others and false religions. I also repent for closing windows that should not be closed. Please close every window, gate and door that we opened illegally, and open every window, gate and door that should not have been closed.

Lord, please take me back to the womb of the dawn and recreate my DNA and RNA so that any influence of the fallen sons of God in my DNA and RNA is totally removed.

Lord, please remove all ungodly roots and branches.

Lord, I repent for not aligning to Your times and seasons to open and close windows. I repent for building my own times in reference to the windows. I repent for interrupting the flow of God's times. I repent for extending times when they should not be extended.

I repent for defiling and making the windows dirty. Please clean the windows in the generational line, and cleanse me now, Father, by the blood of Your Son, and set me free from the consequences of opening heavenly windows by illegal means. Lord, You stated in John 14:6 that You are the way, the truth and the life and that no one can access the heavenly realms except through You. Please close every window, every door and every gate that was opened illegally, and restore us to Your plumb line. From this day forward, I will enter the windows of heaven only though You, as Your Spirit leads.

Lord, take the ax to the ungodly root in the ungodly womb of the dawn and destroy all ungodly roots and branches. Rightly connect me to Your roots, branches, and vine so that I can function as a godly branch in the order of Melchizedek. Please give me a new heart.

I repent for any ungodly way in which we accessed windows. Please apply the scarlet thread, the hyssop, and the cedar to all ungodly covenants that opened windows that should not be open, and remove all access that ungodly stars gained because of those ungodly covenants in my family line. I repent for all ungodly covenants that affected any land area. Please disconnect us from those land areas.

Please break all ungodly ties to time, and to the windows of time and times. I repent for ungodly access to time and times and half of time, and ask You to apply Your blood to all markers in time. Please restore godly boundaries between space and time, and close all ungodly windows and doors between time and space. I repent for any way that we accessed time through space or space through time.

Please break off ungodly connections between stars and time. I repent for making all ungodly calendars based on the cycles of time and for changing times and seasons, and declare that all my days are written in Your book.

Lord please remove the abomination of desolation off of my family line, and remove all generational pages of the enemy that have been inserted into my book.

I repent for those who did not understand that the tithe was to go to Melchizedek; to Jesus, our High Priest. I repent for giving according to my own desires or due to the pressure of others, rather than asking Melchizedek, Jesus, our High Priest where I am to give my tithe.

As I am conceived in the womb of the dawn, do not allow any parts of me to be influenced by the fallen sons of God, or stars, or any other fallen spiritual beings. Please do not allow any animal, plant, fish, or spiritual DNA and RNA to be weaved into my DNA and RNA. Please remove any unholy sequencing in my DNA and RNA placed there by the fallen sons of God. In the womb of the dawn, please correctly sequence the ACGT coding of my original design in the conception replication of all my DNA and RNA.

At my birth from the womb of the dawn, do not allow me to be scattered, but establish the righteous pillars of wisdom. Melchizedek, the true Lord Jesus, do not allow me to be scattered in the stars and in other time periods. I do not agree with that. Please do not allow any parts of me to be scattered in the unholy height, depth, length and width, or in all unholy dimensions and kingdoms.

I repent for those in my family and tribe who, by majority, made agreements with the enemy that ended up entrapping me even though it was not my desire.

At conception, please establish the correct lightning strikes to fuse my spirit to my soul and body. Please breathe into me so I am a living soul according to Your original desire and not according to the plans of the enemy.

Lord, as my spirit is moving from Your throne, please guide me so that I go to the holy height, depth, length and width; and prohibit any effort of the enemy to capture me and place me or any parts of me in the unholy depth, length, width, and height. I lay claim to all repentance and renunciations that I have prayed, that the enemy may not be allowed to capture me.

Lord, please remove all unholy subscripts from my generational line that allowed unholy authorities to carry curses down my generational line. Please disconnect me from the ungodly library, ungodly scrolls, the ungodly librarian, and all ungodly knowledge.

In the name of Jesus Christ, I repent for nurturing humanistic mindsets. I repent for placing the standards of man at a higher priority than Your truth.

I repent for times I allowed personal decisions to override Your leadership and truth. Lord I ask that You now disassemble and clean off all false and ungodly branches.

Please clean all godly branches, close all windows that should be closed, and do the same for all gates and doors.

Please remove all influence from Chronos time, and bring me into Your full Kairos time.

Please burn and destroy all that You are cleaning off.

Lord, I ask You now to release Your power.

Elements Prayer

An explanation to this prayer is available at aslansplace.com[13]

Lord, I ask you to remove the ungodly thrones that have been manipulating the fiery stones, the essence of who I am. I no longer allow the basic equations of my spirit, soul and body to be affected by ungodly thrones. Please disconnect and sever me from the ungodly algorithms and equations affecting the elements of my body, and restore your righteous algorithms, correctly establishing the righteous throne. I no longer allow the enemy to constantly shift the elemental spirits through the dimensions and/or domains. Please stop the constant shifting of the ungodly pathways, windows, and thrones through the dimensions. I do not allow the enemy to undo Your righteous realignment.

Lord, please:

- Remove all ungodly bonding and covalent bonding of the elements
- Close all ungodly doors to the electrons, neutrons, protons and all sub-atomic particles of the elements on the periodic table, and open all doors that need to be open so the gates will not be shut again
- Remove any parts of me from the ungodly pathways and establish me on the righteous pathways so I will move on Your way
- Bring all these elements into correct creative order
- Correctly align the elements to each other
- Bring each element into balance and harmony with all other elements of the body
- Bring all pathways into alignment with the finish work of the cross

On behalf of my family line and myself back to the beginning of time, I repent and renounce for purposeful attempts to change the elements of creation and for unknowingly affecting them in any way, shape or form through ungodly means. I confess that these have been sinful actions taken against You. Forgive us, Lord.

I renounce all sin, iniquity, and transgression relating to the elements in my family line, and acknowledge that you, Jesus Christ, died on the cross and became sin for us that we might become the righteousness of God in Christ Jesus! Father, You are Lord of creation; You created all things and they are holy, good and right in You.

As I pray, please:

- Restore the elements to their proper levels so that they correctly affect my spirit, soul, and body
- Apply all corrections in the elements in my body to my children and grandchildren
- Cleanse each of the elements and remove any defilement, ungodly substance, ungodly entity as well as any attachments or unclean spirits throughout time, space, dimensions and any other way
- Apply your anointing and light cover, and saturate each of the elements in my life to the level that you desire so that I live a full life in the Lord Jesus Christ

---

[13] aslansplace.com/elements-introduction

- Adjust the electromagnetic fields of each element
- Break the power of all generational alchemy that has influenced the elements of my body
- Disconnect each element from all ungodly rulers, elders, powers, authorities, and thrones that bind me to each element in any ungodly way
- Bring the sounds, colors, and vibrations of each element back into your intended original creation design
- Disconnect each element from all ungodly stars, star systems, zodiacs, constellations and galaxies
- Correctly adjust the seven eyes of the Lord to each element and remove each element from any ungodly places in the length, width, height and depth, and from ungodly place in any time dimension

Lord, please:

- Bring each element that is supposed to be in my body to the correct created design, correctly balancing and stabilizing everything so that each element correctly affects my DNA, RNA, body, soul and spirit, and that of my children and grandchildren
- Remove any element on the Periodic Table that does not belong in my body
- Cause each element to bind correctly to itself and other elements; refine each element in Your fire, bringing each one to its proper level; and establish each element in me so that I am correctly established as a living stone from this day forward in the name and light of your name, Jesus Christ

Renunciation of Sins Associated with the Tree of Forgetfulness and the Release of godly Inheritance

In the name of Jesus Christ, as a representative of my family line. I repent for all those who sold others, including family members, into slavery. I repent for causing others to walk around the tree of forgetfulness[14] and for placing curses of amnesia on them. I repent for stealing freedom and inheritance from others for personal gain or profit. I declare on behalf of myself and my family line that we reject all profit gained by ungodly practices.

In the name of Jesus Christ, I break all curses associated with those acts, and I command all evil associated with those curses to leave and go to the place Jesus sends you. Also, Lord, please remove anything that is blocking your favor and blessings.

Lord God please restore all godly memories and inheritances to me and my family line. Lord, please release any blessings, favors, and gifting that has been blocked.

---

[14] http://www.museeouidah.org/VisitingOuidah.htm

Prayer For Release From the Iniquities of Conquering and Conquered Peoples

Territorial Conquest Times and Circumstances:
Father, I offer this prayer on behalf of my generational line and myself from before the beginning of time. I renounce and repent for:

- Having concubines and many wives at the same time; as authorities of a kingdom, city, or tribe having many women at our service for the purposes of our own pride, pleasure, and power

- Using women as spoils of war, having abducted and raped the concubines, women, daughters, mothers, and grandmothers of men that we defeated; using them as objects of our sexual lust and our lust for power; making them pregnant with our own children and then discarding them as the mothers of our own children as if they were inferior to us because we believed in a supposed superiority of the male conquerors; abusing local or native woman in physical, sexual, sentimental, economic, social, cultural and spiritual ways

- Seeking the death of men in power and authority in order to take their women as merchandise and violate and/or share them, and silence all who saw it, then not recognizing the children that we had with them

- Not bringing or allowing our wives from the land of our origin to accompany us on trips of conquest over new territories; seeking sexual and sentimental relations with native or local women while away from our families; starting irregular, parallel families

- Believing in the superiority of European men; allowing promiscuous lifestyles without respect for the marriage covenant; enjoying privileges that a woman did not have, believing that men could do whatever they wanted in their family regarding emotional and sexual areas

Church and Political Interests:
On behalf of my generational line and myself from before the beginning of time, I renounce and repent for:

- Taking on the form of Christianity without adhering to its moral standards and principles; preserving, defending, and affirming appearances, even though well-known circumstances clearly disproved them; hiding known family secrets that we were unwilling to confront, much less to heal; complicity in maintaining family unity by giving unwanted advice and engaging in sexual harassment; hiding information in order to control and manipulate and 'keep the peace' in marriage

- Mixing Christian faith with paganism; engaging in a faith that was defined by rituals, syncretism, idolatry, and impregnated with emotions without subjection to truth; absolutes in doctrine but permissiveness in practices that fostered emotions to the imaginary mother, ignoring the Father and His commandments; bringing another gospel that was incomplete, mixed, tainted, distorted, hidden, deceitful, heavy, false, malicious, opportunistic, and without power to save, heal and restore the spiritual and natural orphan-hood; preventing the manifestation of the fatherhood of God

- Pretending as a church to be impotent when it was not convenient, thus not limiting the sexual conduct of conquering men in new territories and intentionally ignoring the biblical teachings on the marriage covenant

- Not knowing or maintaining the personal covenant between the believer and God, wanting to channel that relationship through sacraments and rituals administered by the clergy

- Being and allowing a church with a militant character; conquering at the point of the sword; mixing all sorts of worldly interests of religious leaders with those of political leaders; being accomplices in the abuse of natives on the part of the conquerors; as a strategy of power, control, domination, business, sustainability, growth, vainglory and security, forcing the conversion of thousands and millions of natives/Indians to the teachings of the Spaniards, French, Portuguese, English, or Americans; not reading the Bible or to understand it, but to follow traditions, commandments, decrees and human promises that were perpetuated, distorted, changed and/or imposed by religious, priests, bishops and Catholic kings and European Kings.

Male Chauvinism:
On behalf of my generational line and myself from before the beginning of time, I renounce and repent for:

- Substituting the responsible commitment of a covenant for the falsity of a romantic love; treating the instruments and language of romance as a sport, using imaginative, symbolic and poetic games to access the hearts of young women, using words to gain the favor of improper concessions; pretending to be suffering and lost in love for a woman, using a romantic game to catch her heart; emotional blackmail; asking for concessions of reciprocity at the cost of moral integrity; losing all interest in women while achieving our hunting feat and taking them as prey and victims; luring minors as easy prey to relieve lust and lack of self-control

- Being lustful men who did not respect their wives, with compulsion to be faithful to our wives, consider them to be inferior and becoming unfaithful, deceitful liars and womanizers

- Actions of husbands or wives who did not respect the marriage covenant, consequently learning to disrespect other human covenants, whether contracts, constitutions or civil laws; teaching children through our violation of the marriage pact, the model for all other covenants, not to fulfill vows, promises, or covenants; not modeling mutual submission to the marriage pact

- Covering up our insecurity by exaggerating our courage, putting it to the test by conquering women and flaunting a false virility; letting men turn into sex addicts, driven to lust and insecurity; ignoring morality and making believe that sex was the only way to prove ourselves as males; confusing masculinity with being a womanizer; identifying sexuality as the only characteristic of manhood and love; being unable to genuinely love with self-surrender and confidence, reducing love to sex; being unwilling to take risks in love; being insecure, avoiding the humiliation of rejection and pretending to be invulnerable; hiding under a false and harmful inscrutability; holding onto distrust and fear of being hurt or discovered

- Lust and the desire to be valued, using methods of conquest such as flattery, the suggestion or proposal made indirectly as a joke in case it was rejected, in order to make a love conquest; intoxicating the victim, employing physical and emotional harassment and emotional blackmail

- Acting as remote parents, demanding husbands, despots, violent and cruel leaders; shouting, imposing threatening behavior, and showing a lack of authority; ruling with arrogance through threats or verbal, emotional and physical abuse

- Not being the spiritual head of our homes, refusing to govern our passions and serve our families, thus becoming the tail rather than the head of our homes; not exercising our priesthood at home

- Putting our mothers above our wives, the mothers of our children, often neglecting, mistreating and taking advantage of them

- Male chauvinism that led to a loss of authority and a state of loneliness away from our own family

Mothers:
On behalf of my generational line and myself from before the beginning of time, I renounce and repent for:

- Assuming our role as co-administrators of our marriage covenant to demand fidelity, due repentance and discipline of the unfaithful husband, paving the way for a moral and spiritual restoration; saying, "Men are like that," in a fatalistic way without heeding what the Bible says; responding to male chauvinism with resigned and servile subordination; allowing a system in which we lived in a frustrated, sad and abused state and only tolerated husbands, verbalizing obedience but holding resistance and scorn in our hearts

- Being mothers who taught our daughters to tolerate the infidelity of men; teaching daughters to submit, even to their younger brothers simply because they were male

- Raising daughters to attract the attention of men; allowing them to be satisfied with the compliments and extravagant lies of men

- Setting the example for children to grow up under male chauvinism, allowing them to become spoiled and irresponsible at home and causing them to learn through our bad behavior that they had a right to use and abuse their women

- Conforming to the sexual behavior of men so that we would not be ashamed publicly; demanding an appearance of decorum and decency rather than a moral, respectful view of the marriage covenant; accepting this double standard

Love and Emotions:
On behalf of my generational line and myself from before the beginning of time, I renounce and repent for:

- Not taking seriously the feelings of our wives because our sinful sense of superiority did not let us see it; replacing compassion with pity, thinking that our wives were inferior and believing they cried because they were weak, immature or capricious; despising the emotions of our women, considering them 'women's things' and denying our own emotions that resulted in anger, jealousy and rage

- Being emotionally incomprehensible, indifferent and unable to offer pure love; confusing the need of each other for weakness and considering it to be risk rather than love; repressing normal emotions, believing that we would become vulnerable to the abuse of others; seeking power and displacing love because of our own insecurity; trying to win love through conquest and imposition

Matriarchy:
On behalf of my generational line and myself from before the beginning of time, I renounce and repent for:

- Losing respect for men, and taking away their place of authority when we did not see them governing with justice; weakening men until they lost their position as leaders in the family; resorting to manipulation and dishonesty to compensate for male domination; preventing our husbands from fulfilling their priestly mission in the family

- Being emotionally needy as mothers and raising our children for our own benefit; emotionally governing our families in order to fulfill our desires; using our children as comfort, emotional support and best friends, thus preventing them from forming independent homes; using the maternal role to improperly influence, compromise and dominate our children and our husbands; giving petty affection in exchange for demanded loyalty, obedience, subjection, and sacrifice of one's own will

- Keeping our children as infants all of their life, childish, tied to their mothers and unable to undertake challenges alone; not allowing our children to assume responsibilities in the home; relying on other people to handle our problems and provide solutions; not being responsible ourselves; teaching our daughters to take authority from their husbands

- As mothers, controlling our daughters in their marriages; as daughters, sacrificing the happiness of our homes to please and pamper our mothers; flattering those who spoil us, and despising those we consider inferior

- In our homes, creating emotionally harmful relationships that are full of manipulation and dependence; sowing behaviors of injustice, impunity, corruption, infidelity, violence and instability as products of our deception, dissimulation, distrust and insecurity

Power:
On behalf of my generational line and myself from before the beginning of time, I renounce and repent for:

- Competing with our mothers-in-law for the love of our husbands; wanting to hold all power in the family as a result of our victim status under male chauvinism; perpetuating matriarchy; using seduction as a weapon; using secrets as an instrument of power and a currency of blackmail, such as the existence of children and half-siblings out of wedlock, or the degradation and sexual misadventures of relatives

- Taking advantage and dominating others in their weakness in order to feed our egos; desiring and seeking domination by means of our strong character through blackmail or seduction

- Teaching the superiority of men over women by misusing biblical passages; bringing misery and sadness to our homes through the unequal treatment of men and women

Government:
On behalf of my generational line and myself from before the beginning of time, I renounce and repent for:

- Creating many, distinct social hierarchies in an attempt to impose racism between foreigners and natives; arguing the superiority of some over others in order to remove individual rights with the aim or pretext of legitimizing legal, physical, social, cultural, economic and spiritual abuse

- Allowing civic service to be reduced to the use of power for profit; obtaining the illegitimate benefit of friends and allies from a culture with no sense adhering to covenants

- Refusing to provide education to our women that would allow them to model the healthy experiences of marriage; as a family, society and culture, affecting and damaging their dignity and identity; identifying with social and cultural expressions that celebrate and reinforce male chauvinism as acceptable and normal, including songs, sayings, compliments, jokes, phrases, and books; honoring and exalting with pride, remarkable men and women of letters who perpetuated their own histories of illicit loves; producing or enjoying music, art and literature that supports male chauvinism and matriarchy; allowing and promoting the debauchery of male chauvinism as it exists in our culture; not supporting our women to confront their husbands with the abuse of male chauvinism; not recognizing and denying our laws in the past that say infidelity by a man could be considered a just penalty toward a woman in marriage

Virginity:
On behalf of my generational line and myself from before the beginning of time, I renounce and repent for:

- Overemphasizing the virginity of women as their main virtue; punishing a woman victim more than the man who abused her in a sexual assault; exercising undue discretion or an exaggerated/skewed concept of the seriousness of sexual sin, with the consequence of causing sex to be viewed as shameful, unhealthy, harmful and taboo; exalting the virgin Mary as a model of a holy, abstinent family, and as a requirement to serve celibacy, forcefully marking sex as something dirty, suspicious, and a necessary evil; insisting that the virgin Mary persisted a lifelong virgin, offering a sacred family without sex; contradicting the apostle Paul's biblical teachings on marriage; the confusion of Catholicism that identifies sexual abstinence with holiness, subtly suggesting that sex disqualifies one from serving God; thinking that virtue was a renunciation of sex, not considering or obeying God and His commands

- Removing sex from the confines of marriage and promoting its pleasure outside of marriage; dividing women into two categories, the marriageable ones and the others; looking for marriage among women of respectable and educated families, but considering that sex was to be enjoyed with the non-marriageable women

- Marking Mary a semi-divine image, and using this image to conquer the colonies where women were filled with guilt over sex in circumstances of abuse; imposing at the same time, a false image of a woman who never had sex, but who had happiness; trying to make women believe that they could be happy without sex with an unfaithful and lustful husband; using the false image of Mary to subject women to passive behavior toward the infidelity of their husbands; perpetuating the idea that wives should be like the false image of Mary, without the need of pleasure; supporting the idea that having pleasure outside the marriage pact either in secret romances or in acts of prostitution was necessary to maintain the marriage covenant; believing that children came from illicit sex and could not come from a pure and righteous marriage.

Prayer for Releasing Burdens

In Jesus name, I repent for anytime I or those in my family line overstepped authority or took on burdens and responsibilities that you did not intend us to carry.

I repent for anytime I or those in my family line:
- Tried to be a savior to others
- Tried to act as a bridge between others and you, Lord
- Tried to act as a barrier between others and the enemy

In Jesus name, I reject all ungodly positions of authority. Lord please move me fully into the positions of authority that You have established for me.

I repent for allowing an imbalance in the carrying of one another's burdens. I repent for trying to take on other's burdens instead of helping to carry those burdens to you, Lord.

In Jesus name, I now surrender and give over to you, Lord, all burdens that are ungodly, worldly or inappropriate. Regardless of whether they were inherited, others placed them on me or I took them on myself.

Thank you, Jesus, that when I'm weary I can come to You. Thank you for your gentleness and humility. Thank you that what You want me to carry is easy and light. I surrender any remaining burdens over to You and I choose to carry only what You want me to carry. Please help me to continually surrender to you and to never try to take back what I have surrendered.

I repent for anyone in my family line who participated in ungodly trading. I repent for those who traded, cashed-in, or used as collateral the prosperity, well-being, health or inheritance of their descendants and stole it for themselves. Lord, please cancel all these ungodly trades.

I repent for those who were unforgiving, kept records of wrongs, held grudges and nurtured unforgiveness. I repent for those in my family line who established grudges, feuds and unforgiveness as an inheritance.

I declare that I forgive all those who have harmed or come against me or my family line.

Lord, please destroy all ungodly record books, including all records of wrongs.
I now reject all inheritance of unforgiveness and grudges. Lord I surrender all unforgiveness over to you.

I repent for anytime I or those in my family line considered your calling a burden or focused on works and deeds instead of making rest with You a priority. I repent for anytime I or those in my family line perceived your calling on our lives as a burden.

I repent for anytime I or those in my family line focused more on rules of religion or on the law rather than focusing on and nurturing a personal relationship with you. I repent for those in my family line who established religion, traditions and superstition as a burden. I repent for all participation in legalism, religiosity and superstition.

Lord, please cancel any remaining ungodly debt. Please clean up and return to me everything that has been lost, stolen or given away. Please remove from me anything that is not part of your design for me and my life.

Prayer to be Removed from the Ungodly Width

I repent for my generational line and myself back to before the beginning of time for all of us who did not trust the Lord.

Lord, please break the consequences of all those who were abandoned by parents because of religious activity and pull my spirit and heart out of any ungodly constellations, zodiacs, stars and star systems. Please remove every part of me from the ungodly width and establish me in the godly width; rightly align my spirit and heart so that I am at peace; stop all dimensional shifting and establish me in peace; and stop repetitive cycles of manic and depressive oscillations. Please remove all ungodly watchers, gatekeepers and doorkeepers on the grid and establish the righteous watchers, gatekeepers and doorkeepers.

I choose to seek after the Lord's wisdom and not after man's wisdom or intellectual understanding. I declare the fear of the Lord is the beginning of wisdom. Lord Jesus, I understand that as a child I may have accepted the lie that a female was not to be more than a male would permit, or that a male would be more than a female would permit. I understand that this has crushed my spirit and caused parts of my spirit to be trapped in the ungodly width. I now reject that lie, and I declare that I will be all that the Lord Jesus has created me to be. Please remove all parts of my spirit that have been trapped in the ungodly width and in the ungodly stars, star systems, constellations and zodiacs. I no longer allow the enemy to project around me that I am worthless and that I am always a victim and powerless. I will take my position in Christ and rule and reign equally with the opposite sex. Please disconnect me from all fallen sons of God who have perpetuated this lie in my family line.

Prayer to Realign the Pillars of Wisdom

Lord, I bring to Your remembrance all of the generational repentance that I have ever done, and ask that You will appropriate it to each of the seven pillars so that the seven aspects of my generational line that are tied to the seven pillars and the seven eyes are cleaned out. I also repent for and renounce the sin of:

- All of my ancestors who established ungodly sacred pillars on land areas, especially as defined by blood sacrifices and sexual immorality
- All negative perceptions that have resulted in a mindset that caused me to believe that I am not a legitimate child of God
- Entering into a belief that I lack, am in need, have unrealized wants, and that I must obtain what I expect
- Those in my family line who used the seven pillars to translocate to different places upon the earth

Lord, please:

- Correctly align the seven pillars so that they are in the correct order
- Return all aspects of the seven pillars to the correct pillars so that each one correctly contains the seven correct aspects
- Clean out each generational line in each pillar
- Remove all time distortions and time loops in each of the seven pillars
- Disconnect each pillar from all ungodly thrones
- Correctly allocate the four rivers that flowed out of Eden to each pillar
- Clean off all elemental spirits that are affected by the distortion of the seven pillars
- Correctly align each pillar to both the correct sound of the musical scale and the correct color according to Your original creative design
- Remove all ungodly whirlwinds in each pillar and establish the correct centripetal force in each pillar
- Correctly associate each pillar to every other pillar so that they are established in unity
- Please align the seven pillars dimensionally so that each pillar connects correctly to the right number of righteous dimensions
- Let each pillar be filled with only Your Glory and pureness of heart
- Strengthen each of the seven rods in each pillar and realign them to the original creative design
- Establish each pillar correctly on the foundations set aside for each of them
- Only allow what you have meant for these pillars to hold and support used only for Your original intent
- Please remove all walls that prohibit the correct alignment of the pillars
- Correctly align the DNA and RNA and clean off all contamination on the glorious ones and the fiery stones, which have been affected by the contamination of the seven pillars
- Restore the correct godly authority in each pillar

Holy Spirit, in Your function of Wisdom, please correctly build Your house in my life, retune each pillar so that it reflects the correct sound; clean off the seven eyes of the heart that are tied to the seven pillars of wisdom. Also, please:

- Correctly connect the seven pillars of wisdom to the seven spirits of God and the seven eyes
- Clean all contamination out of the seven spirits of the Lord, the seven pillars, and the seven eyes
- Close all doors that need to be closed, and open all doors that need to be opened
- Correctly position me so the perception of my heart is correct
- Bring all righteous beings and entities into correct synergy so that the seven pillars, seven spirits of God, glorious ones, elemental spirits, thrones, dominions, lines of inheritance, fiery stones and the pathways all function in correct unity

Lord, I declare that I want the eyes of my heart to be enlightened by Your truth so I may know that which is:

- The hope of Your calling
- The riches of the glory of Your inheritance in and for the saints
- The exceeding greatness of Your power toward us who believe

Please accomplish all of this according to the working of Your mighty power, which worked in Christ Jesus when He was raised from the dead and seated at Your right hand in the heavenly places.

Prayer for Cleansing the Contamination on the Living Stones

Lord Jesus, I renounce and repent on behalf my generational line back to before the beginning of time and myself for:

- Partnering with familiar spirits
- Refusing to invite in, require interest and profit from or enslave family[15]
- Agreeing with false messengers; listening and accepting lie(s) that were expressed as truth
- Contaminating, selling, or in any way compromising the anointing of God
- Allowing fear to overtake us
- Approving of and allowing false prophets and ungodly priests, thus causing astonishing and horrible things to happen in the land[16]
- Shedding blood and destroying lives to get dishonest gain like wolves tearing their prey[17]
- Entering into ungodly unity in religious churches
- Consulting the dead through spiritualists and other occult activities in order to transfer things from the kingdom of God to the kingdom of darkness
- Using the power of the harlot to gain wealth, fame and luxury, in an attempt to imitate the dunamis power of God
- Not trusting in the Lord
- Offering sacrifices that are corrupted and acceptable to the enemy instead of being built up like living stones into a spiritual house and offering spiritual sacrifices acceptable to God[18]
- Putting our offerings on false altars instead of listening to You for direction regarding our funds and our giving
- Giving out of obligation, or with the intent of receiving financial blessings in return
- Calling upon the stars and using astrology for guidance and direction
- Building false foundations[19]

---

[15] Leviticus 25:35-46
[16] Jeremiah 5:30-31
[17] Ezekiel 22:27
[18] 1 Peter 2:5
[19] Joshua 6:26

- Not standing up and saying no during the beginning stages when defilement was recognized; being complacent and not standing for righteousness either individually or as a culture

- Allowing and/or producing and distributing products of defilement for export from our land to other parts of the world

- Believing the lie that I don't matter and I'm not important, and not standing up in the face in unrighteousness

- The birthing of abortion[20]

- Maintaining the status quo, and praising wealth when the foundation may be corrupt

- Not speaking out against evil that is happening around us

- Accepting the counterfeit and rejecting the truth

- Choosing a darkened understanding that is separated from the life of God, and giving ourselves over to sensuality and greed[21]

- Practicing manipulation and control [witchcraft] over governing boards of churches

- Not taking responsibility for spiritual development, trusting false spiritual leaders and not being a Berean[22]

- Coming against each other instead of coming into unity

- Believing and perpetuating the lie that God does evil, and He causes or permits bad things to happen; blaming God

- Doing what is right in our own eyes, and thinking we can do good without His power and Spirit

- Anti-Semitism and all forms of racism

- Becoming desensitized and dumbed down to God's truth

- Relinquishing our full, God-given authority as men and women who co-rule together with Christ

- Creating communities within our churches that push toward image instead of authenticity

- Domination, intimidation and manipulation of women and men, which is witchcraft; and sexually taking advantage of anyone

- Despising our prophetic voice, and hindering the flow of God's Spirit

---

[20] Ezekiel 22:2
[21] Ephesians 4:17-19
[22] Acts 17:11 tells us that the people of Berea"…received the word with all eagerness, examining the Scriptures daily to see if these things were so." (ESV)

- Calling upon and making vows to gods and goddesses in exchange for power and/or provision

- Giving lip service to Holy Spirit while not fully believing, and being guilty of slackness in the work of the Lord[23]

- Pointing fingers at one another, thus joining with the accuser of the brethren[24]

- Conceiving and birthing righteous things in the wrong season, and birthing unrighteous things in any season

- Valuing comfort over calling

- Perpetuating disunity between the individual and God-given strengths of men and women

- All idolatry and adultery

- The sins of the harlot[25]

- The seven abominations: haughty eyes, lying tongues, hands that shed innocent blood, hearts that devise wicked plans, feet that run to evil, false witnesses who lie, and sowing discord[26]

- Not obeying God's commandments and statutes, and changing the form and design of food sources and vegetation in our land

- Not standing up for righteousness in our schools

- Incest, perversion, pornography and all spiritual defilement

- Seeking the help of physicians over seeking God's help[27]

- Establishing financial foundations based on love of money, greed, self-promotion and establishing an elite class

- Not believing and practicing the truth that what takes place spiritually in heavenly places really does come on earth

- Corrupting the heavenly places, which is then mirrored on earth in the physical, causing pain and suffering to God's people

- Partnering with death

- Dedications of products to false gods, and setting up perverted stones and foundations

- Giving up our influence over the seven mountains

---

[23] Jeremiah 48:10
[24] Isaiah 60
[25] Revelation 18:8
[26] Proverbs 6:16-19
[27] 2 Chronicles 16:12

- Not being involved in the election of a righteous government that supports the true foundation of the true nature of creation law
- Not standing up in government as righteous men and women to take our place

Father, I now declare:

- I will seek to speak the truth in love at all times
- The kingship of the Lord Jesus Christ, and that the one way to the Father is through Yeshua
- I will love the Lord my God with all my heart, and love one another as myself
- I am no longer a stranger and alien, but am a fellow citizen with the saints and members of the household of God, built on the foundation of the apostles and prophets, Christ Jesus himself being the cornerstone, in whom the whole structure being joined together, grows into a holy temple in the Lord. In Him I am also being built together into a dwelling place for God by the Spirit[28]
- I re-establish Christ as my foundation and chief cornerstone
- I see and ask for the ancient paths and choose to walk in them[29]
- I will support and teach the true foundation of a person's life rather that a false foundation in our educational system
- Unity over myself, and corporately over the Body of Christ, regarding Your original intent for our seed and food sources
- Jesus Christ is Lord over businesses and food
- Christian men and women will step into who God created us to be and walk in our identity on earth as we are in the heavens
- God is good and His loving-kindness endures forever
- Jesus is King over agriculture, food and medicine; and I will be a good steward of those, and take up the mandate God has given me
- The mountain of the Lord's temple will be established as chief among the mountains; it will be raised above the hills and peoples will stream to it[30]
- "In God We Trust" is my pledge
- A mantle of justice and righteousness is upon our land

---

[28] Ephesians 2:19-22
[29] Jeremiah 6:16
[30] Micah 4:1

- Our water is purified
- Whatever flows out of the land is holy and set apart for God
- The Lord has rendered a judgment in favor of the saints, and the time has arrived for us to possess the kingdom[31]
- Righteousness and justice are the foundation of Your throne; fire goes before You and burns up Your adversaries all around[32]

Lord, please:

- Remove all contamination of familiar spirits off of the living stones
- Establish yourself anew in my family line, in me, and in our lands
- Remove all contamination off of the food that came in because of wrong foundations in the food industry, businesses and universities
- Grant forgiveness for all of these sins, and remove altars and false stones that have been built
- Purify the multidimensional foundation of your creation that is tied to me and my generational line
- Restore Your truth in every aspect of my life where it has been compromised

---

[31] Daniel 7:22
[32] Psalm 97:2b-3

Prayer to Break Free From the Power of Critical Words and Remove the Ungodly Cloud

Lord, on behalf of my generational line and myself, I repent for and renounce the sins of pride and arrogance. Please forgive me for believing the lie that I am less sinful than others; and for thinking that since I am better than them, I can sit on Your judgment seat and criticize, slander and gossip about people who have also been created in Your image.

Forgive me for disobeying Your command in Matthew 7:1-3 not to judge others; help me to understand the difference between the sinful judgment of others out of pride and anger, versus righteous discernment between good and evil actions.

Forgive me for walking in hypocrisy as I praise Your name in worship, yet verbally tear others down by the unrighteous use of my tongue at other times.

Lord, please create in me a clean heart, and renew a right spirit within me. Be merciful, for I lack Your loving kindness and mercy when I condemn people for their attitudes and actions, yet do the same things without godly sorrow.

Father, I repent for judging other believers and church families. Please forgive me for:

- Judging their motives, beliefs and practices

- Angrily disrespecting politicians with whom I disagree (please remind me to lift them up at all times in prayer)

- Dishonoring my parents, spouse, other ethnic groups, and other denominations for falling short of my personal expectations

I forgive my parents for not speaking words of life over me; instead, wounding my heart and soul with harsh and hurtful words. Forgive me for speaking angry words towards my parents out of a heart of rebellion and ill will, for dishonoring them.

Father, I ask forgiveness for criticizing and cutting others down behind closed doors, spreading lies, sharing confidential information that I promised not to divulge, and ruining reputations through innuendo and gossip. I ask forgiveness for my divisive attitudes and actions, which have built walls between others and me.

Lord, on behalf of my generational lines and myself I come to Your cross and ask You to remove the legal rights that we have given the ungodly authorities to slime us with toxic spiritual waste, and to pollute all of the lands where we have lived, dividing our families, churches, states and nations. Disconnect me from the ungodly authorities and connect me to Your righteous authorities.

Lord, teach me to see others as people whom You have made in Your image. Train the eyes of my heart to see the treasures that You have deposited into other individuals so I can lead them to You.

I repent for harshly judging other believers who have chosen to sin or walk away from You. Teach me to meet with them face to face in Your Spirit of love and humility so that they may be restored to fellowship with You and Your family, the Church.

Finally, please remove me from the ungodly cloud, and cleanse me by the power of Your blood from the consequences of criticizing others, gossiping, unrighteous judgments and slander, which is character assassination.

Prayer to Break Free From
the Worship of Created Light

On behalf of myself and my entire family generational line, I repent for and renounce the belief systems, religions, exercise programs, martial arts and philosophies of the world that have led us to believe that the light God decreed into existence on the first day of creation was and is a god.

On behalf of every ancestor in my family line, I repent for and renounce every false belief system, philosophy and religion that teaches created or universal light is to be worshiped instead of the Light of the world.

Forgive us Father, for trying to gain wisdom by worshiping created light, deifying the light, and slandering the glorious ones.

Lord, on behalf of my entire family line I acknowledge that the vibrations and light You spoke into existence in Genesis 1:3 was the doxai, referred to in Scripture as the glorious ones, celestial beings or dignitaries[33]. Forgive us Lord, for worshiping Your created light instead of You, the Creator. Forgive us Holy Spirit, for not only slandering and defiling the glorious ones through the worship of the light but for contaminating them as well, through idolatry and unrighteous sexual practices.

Father, on behalf of all of my ancestors in my respective family lines, I repent for and renounce Gnosticism, New Age practices like the use of chakras, Reiki, Yoga, Transcendental Meditation, belief in the Yin (light) and the Yang (dark), Feng Sui, the Chi, the Gi, the Ki, Amida Buddha, Pure Land Buddhism, Shingon Buddhism, and participating in lantern ceremonies to honor and communicate with my ancestors.

Lord, please cleanse the heavenly places, including the grid, height, width, length and depth with Your shed blood; remove all contamination and defilement off of the glorious ones that have been empowered by worshiping the created light in my family line. And finally Lord, please release the righteous glorious ones so that the lava of Your love for the Lost may be poured out on our land.

---

[33] 2 Peter 2:10-12 and Jude 1:8

Prayer to Retrieve Scattered Parts

Father, please rescue me from every ungodly place to which I've been scattered in my lifetime and make me complete. Please retrieve every part of me that is entrapped in the ungodly width, length, depth and height, time, the stars, the zodiac or on the ungodly grid. Please disconnect me from all ungodly spiritual beings and return to me, through Your blood, every shattered part of my soul and spirit.

Lord, I desperately desire to have an undivided heart so that I may be united with myself, others, and with You. Lord, please release the sound of Your roar as the Lion of Judah to dislodge all scattered spirit and soul parts entrapped in every ungodly heavenly place. Please send the chariots of fire and horsemen of Israel[34] to retrieve every scattered part so they can be reunited and or integrated. I declare that I desire for Jesus to be at the center of my life and all that I am. Please unite my scattered parts with your centripetal force.[35] In Jesus name, I now give each scattered part permission to feel and express all the emotions bottled up inside of me.

---

[34] 2 Kings 2:12
[35] Centripetal force – a force that acts on a body moving in a circular path and is directed toward the center around which the body is moving.

Righteousness Prayer

Lord, please remove all generational and lifetime false grace and cheap grace, which is really lawlessness linked to an anti-Christ spirit. I understand that this false grace has resulted in an ungodly connection with the imposter who is the false I Am. I also understand that the false grace teaching has robbed me of an understanding of the sufferings of Christ that I am supposed to enter into.

Please remove all false pathways connected to false grace; and on behalf of my ancestors and myself, I repent for ungodly generational dedications, blood sacrifices and all other sacrifices to the enemy, including the ungodly sons of God. I repent for wickedness, participation in conspiracies, hatching of plots and agreements in high places, and trading of identities and birthrights with the enemy and the ungodly sons of God.

Lord of Hosts, please release Your armies to dismantle and burn all the root systems of false governance, including control and manipulation through wickedness and through the fantasies of the people of God. Please remove the false governance of institutionalism in the heart of religion that has produced spiritual wickedness and prevented me from breakthrough and from healing.

Please burn the soil, matrix, ungodly womb of the dawn, and all conceptions of spiritual wickedness in high places, as well as the ungodly structures in each of the seven eyes of the Lord. I understand that the enemy has sought after and planted the tree of knowledge of good and evil within the default seven eyes of the Lord. Please burn it all within the consuming fire of I AM so that Your original intent for the seven eyes of the Lord can be fulfilled. Please burn to the very center so the roots, ungodly soil, and all ungodly equations can be destroyed in the realms of darkness. Cause Your light and fire to consume it all in the ungodly height, depth, width, length and in the center of it all. Please remove me from the ungodly realm of the false I Am.

Lord, please close all the ungodly windows of darkness, deep darkness and outer darkness throughout all domains, dominions, kingdoms and all other dark places. I understand these windows were opened through ungodly trading and are connected to the trees of darkness and the tree of knowledge of good and evil.

Please destroy the ungodly hidden temple, which is the dwelling place of the false I Am, as well as the deep covenants of darkness that were intended to raise the sons of darkness. Also, destroy the ungodly seven layers of the heart and all libraries within them, which were formed because of specific covenants that were made to raise up the sons of darkness.

I confess that it is only Your shed blood that redeems us from evil, and I ask You to remove the ungodly conceptions, seeds of wickedness, unrighteous seeds, corrupted seeds, ungodly nests in high places, matrices, and wombs of the dawn that nurture and grow the wicked seed and all wickedness. Please do this throughout all domains, realms, spheres and dimensions in my life, including body, soul, spirit, time, space, family, workplace, birthright, ministry, career, finances and possessions. Then plant Your righteous seeds, establish Your righteousness and rightly align all domains, realms, spheres and dimensions in my life including body, soul, spirit, time, space, family, workplace, birthright, ministry, career, finances, possessions to You and Your throne. Please remove wickedness from the centrality of all things, and destroy the seven seats of the Antichrist that prevent me from entering into the Rest of the Lord; establish righteousness and justice as the foundation in all these areas so that Jesus Christ may be enthroned there and be the Precious Cornerstone, the Sure Foundation, and the Capstone of my life.

Lord, please release the armies of heaven to disconnect me from the ungodly host and stars of heaven, and break all ties to the ungodly host of heaven. I renounce all ungodly generational dedications, sacrifices, wickedness and trading that has empowered this evil. Please release all treasures of wisdom and understanding that are stuck in this realm, and destroy all ungodly hidden windows and doors of darkness so that the enemy can be plundered.

Lord, please:
- Remove all ungodly twins, replicas and clones
- Separate the good seed from the bad seed and the wheat from the tares
- Rightly divide the parts, inheritances and birthrights of commingled and twin seed in my life and reestablish the godly boundaries
- Send Your chariots to gather from the remotest parts of the heaven all that was scattered and bring back truth as the balance
- Release Your treasures of wisdom and understanding that are stuck in the realms
- Birth my identity in Your heart and make all things new
- Bring me to the center of the cross, which is the center of all righteousness
- Reestablish godly boundaries between Righteousness and Holiness and align these to You
- Let Your righteousness displace the ungodly governance
- Establish me back into Your right time and bring forth all those parts, including those that were lost in time, that have been stuck in wicked time and wicked dimensions. Cleanse my parts by Your blood and place them where they were originally meant to be in my life, establishing right standing in my inheritance

I declare that the waters will part so that I may go over onto dry ground, and when I reach the other side of the bridge of time, the waters close over and destroy my enemies. Thank You that I am coming into my inheritance.

Lord, please write on my stony heart so that it becomes flesh, and reestablish and align everything in my life to You. Please break off all things that the enemy uses to try to follow me. I pray that my mind will be stayed on You and on Your word, and that I will set my mind only on things above.

Lord, please cleanse the foundations of the seven eyes of the Lord, removing the defilement of the Holy Place and cleansing it. Holy Spirit, please pour out fresh oil, realign the lampstand and the seven eyes of the Lord, and restore the anointing flow of the Seven Eyes. Please bring true counsel, true might, true understanding to me in the realm of the Spirit, closing the ungodly windows and opening the godly ones. Please remove the ungodly mirror, all ungodly self-absorption and narcissism, and help me to rightly see my circumstances and to see You.

I repent for walking in the counsel of the ungodly. Please remove all ungodly entities and agreements that take counsel together against You, Your anointed and me. Please destroy all books and records of ungodly wars, and establish Your righteous counsel in all realms, domains, dimensions, spheres, grids and kingdoms.

I declare that You have won the victory through all the ages and dimensions, and have raised up Your church, which is Your body, to rule and reign with You and in You. Wisdom and counsel and might are ours in the dominion that You've granted through Your resurrection. Your Body is one and we reign with You.

Lord, please cause your grace to work with your mercy, for I understand that Your compassion and mercies endure forever. Please bring me into Your realms of mercy and grace so I can experience the totality of Your mercy and true grace.

Prayer to Release Joy

In the name of Jesus Christ, on behalf of myself and my family line.

I repent for relying on ungodly sources to generate joy in my life.

I repent for coming to you to receive joy but then disconnecting and trying to sustain or generate joy through self-effort.

God, I thank you that you are the true source of joy. I thank you that the Holy Spirit produces an endless supply of joy.

Jesus, I declare that I choose to abide in your love. I choose to come into agreement with your love.

Lord, please fill me up and surround me with your true joy.

Help me to mature in my awareness of your true joy.

Lord, please align the living stones that are part of my spirit. So that I am completely connected to you.

Prayer to Break off Kundalini

On behalf of myself and my family line, I repent for corrupting Your intention for the Seven Eyes of the Lord by pursuing or participating in the concepts of a chakra column and chakra points.

I repent for anytime I or those in my family line attempted to control or manipulate energy through self-effort or in partnership with the enemy.

I repent for attempting to control, manipulate or align chakra columns.

I repent for attempting to channel or redirect energy among chakra points.

I repent for anytime I or those in my family line came into agreement with kundalini spirits or any evil associated with chakras.

Lord please disconnect me and my family line from any influence of kundalini and from any other evil.

Lord please remove all contamination and bring Your Seven Eyes of the Lord into balance and alignment according to your original design.

Please bring all flows of energy into alignment and balance according to Your design.

Prayer to Reject Deception About Our Position in Christ

I reject the lie my ancestors believed, which said that God could not be trusted and we must trust only in our own endeavors and efforts because He did not come through for us.

I repent for my generational line and myself back to before the beginning of time for perpetuating that lie through all successive generations because it was taught and modeled by each generation:

- Claiming they believed but not practicing their supposed faith; thus teaching their children to do the same, and to operate in unbelief
- Not believing that we are more than conquerors
- Focusing our eyes on the things of the earth and its concerns, rather than on the Lord and His abundant provision in all areas of life, including financial, emotional and spiritual abundance, and physical health

I declare that I will turn my gaze from the things below, set it on things above, and take my seat in heavenly places.

Father, please focus my gaze upon Jesus, Who is the Way, the Truth and the Life. I choose to live my life from above, letting go of the log in the eye of Adam and the generational line, which is the knowledge of good and evil. I choose eternal sight instead of earthly sight. I declare that Christ will live in me and His light will shine out of my eyes.

Lord, please remove me from all places of entrapment and deception in the width, length, depth and height, and from all ungodly heavenly places, realms and kingdoms. I declare I will dwell only in the righteous heavenly places.

Prayer to Abolish Fear

Father, I come as your child, your heir, to repent on behalf of my generational line and myself for all of us who have failed to recognize our position and authority in Christ Jesus, choosing to be intimidated by fear rather than trusting you to be sufficient for all of our needs. Please forgive us for all of the times that we have set our eyes on the cares of the world instead of seeking You first.

I repent for any instance in which we have frightened others through words or actions, becoming fear mongers who spread false teachings and the deceitfulness of the world. I now declare the truth that You, Lord, are my light and my salvation; of whom shall I be afraid? You are the strength of my life so whom should I fear? You are my hiding place, my deliverer and protector, and I choose now to take up the full armor of God and use all of the weapons you put at my disposal to resist fear, knowing that it must flee in the face of faith.

In times when I am tempted to be afraid, I now choose to be strong and to let my heart take courage as I wait for You. I choose to change my thinking and set my mind on things above, looking to You as my deliverer, for I am persuaded that nothing in any physical or spiritual dimension is able to separate me from Your love.

Father, Lord Jesus, Holy Spirit; You are my perfect love and I trust You now to cast fear out of my life according to your promise, and I ask for a seven-fold return through the blood of Jesus of all that the enemy has stolen from me through fear and all of its by-products; I ask for your joy to well up within me and bubble over onto everyone I encounter; I boldly ask for the gift of faith to live with the assurance of things hoped for and the conviction of things not seen, faith to move the mountains in my life and to live in victory through Christ Jesus.

I declare that this is the foundation of my faith; God is real, His Word is true; Jesus said it so I believe it, and I must always seek Him first. My life is His; He is my refuge and strength, my place of rest, my peace and my hope; He meets my every need. With Him on my side, I willingly choose to join the battle!

Prayer to Break the Influence of the Father of Lies

Lord, in the name of Jesus I come before You on behalf of my generational line and myself. I ask that You apply all of the repentance and deliverance that occurs throughout this prayer from before the beginning of time to the present, and down to all of my descendants.

Father God, I recognize that the father of lies[36] has sown deception and all manner of unrighteousness into our genetics ever since the Fall in the Garden of Eden. We have believed the lie that You, God, are not good and that Your lovingkindness does not endure forever.

I acknowledge that:

- Idolatry on the land has defiled the land and me and it has especially defiled land specific to my physical birth and my new birth spiritually

- Idolatry on-and-in the water has defiled me

- Influence from the tree of the knowledge of good and evil results in a multitude of man's systems of philosophies, religions, and cultures, which conflict with one another and cause division

- The seven eyes of the Lord manifest upon me, and the eyes of my heart[37] have been contaminated, in part, by the ungodly branches

- Hope deferred has made my heart sick and has nurtured ungodly roots and branches

I repent for all of that evil and also for:

- Ungodly generational trading on the land, both by the fallen sons of God and the fallen sons of men who gave away that which belongs to my generational line and me

- Ungodly generational efforts for self-protection, ungodly soul ties, vows, curses, oaths and blood covenants; for I acknowledge that these sins established ungodly seeds, roots, branches and trees

- All intellectual decisions that resulted from past personal judgments as well as judgments made by my ancestors

- All the times we had blind and unbelieving hearts

- Coming into agreement with ungodly fruit

Lord Jesus, I break all ungodly ties between the land areas of both my physical birth and my spiritual new birth and me.

I choose to only be connected to You and Your Living Water, and I appropriate Your blood to cleanse and sanctify my consciousness from all dead works so that I may serve You alone as the Living God.

---

[36] John 8:44
[37] Ephesians 1:18

Lord, please:

- Remove the original seed of deception that the father of lies sowed into our genetics and generational line. Pull out the taproot that reaches all the way back through every branch of my generational line to the Fall

- Destroy all generational Asherah trees and poles

- Remove all of the effects of spiritual and physical parasites that have affected me

- Unlock the abundance of the seas, and the treasures hidden in the sand.[38]

- Disconnect me from all ungodly roots coming out of Adam and Eve; rightly connect me to You, Jesus, as The Root[39] and The Branch[40]

- Remove all ungodly seeds, roots, branches, leaves and fruit and destroy them; burn them up in Your furnace

- Release your anointing so the ungodly connectors are destroyed

- Connect all righteous roots to the righteous branches so that I am rightly connected to my generational inheritance

- Remove the idolatrous defilement from the water that has affected me; remove all defilement that has come into me either from the unrighteous river or any other unrighteous waters

- Disconnect me from all unrighteous water sources, and connect me to Your River of Life

- Cancel all ungodly treaties that enabled the enemy to successfully remove the birthright from any land area of my heritage in order to establish trading routes to pillage the wealth of the land, and destroy all evil that has empowered lack

- Remove all ungodly elders affecting the tree of the knowledge of good and evil, for I choose not to be tied to or aligned with any of that ungodly knowledge

- Disconnect any land area in my heritage from the ungodly trees and connect me to the tree of life

- Remove all ungodly seeds and branches that are tied to my experience with, and perception of, the seven eyes of the Lord

- Remove all contamination from the soil in which my generational line and I were planted

- Remove all ungodly roots that have come from generational and lifetime bitterness

- Disconnect me from the star, Wormwood[41]

- Destroy all of these ungodly branches and remove the contamination that affects the eyes of my heart as well as my perception and involvement with the seven eyes of the Lord.

---

[38] Deuteronomy 33:19
[39] Romans 15:12
[40] Isaiah 4:2; Zechariah 3:8
[41] Revelation 8:11

- Repair any damage to Kairos time, which has altered time and affected my connection to my earthly father; and which also has blocked the generational inheritance from coming down to me from my parents; restore that inheritance sevenfold

I cast off the works of darkness and put on the armor of light; I call upon You as the righteous Branch, asking You to bring order to my branches and produce the fruit that will bring glory to your name, Elohim.

Father, I thank You that Your seed abides in me.[42]

---

[42] 1 John 3:9

Prayer to Break Ungodly Connections Associated with Military Service

In the name of Jesus Christ, on behalf of myself and as a representative of my entire family line from before the beginning of time, I repent for all of us who were quick to violence instead of seeking God first.

I also repent for any of us who abused positions of military authority and I repent for any time that we cursed, gossiped, slandered or spoke in any ungodly way against others, including:

- Our superiors and those who have reported to us
- Citizens of countries to which we were deployed or visited
- Members of other religions
- People of other genders

Please forgive us, Lord, and remove the personal and generational consequences of our iniquity.

In the name of Jesus Christ, I cancel all curses, gossip and slander spoken against me for any reason, including my military position, my nationality, my faith or my gender.

Lord, please:

- Break all ungodly territorial connections between any place I've been deployed, lived, worked or traveled and me
- Clean up and return any part of me that has been lost, stolen or given away
- Remove anything from me that is not part of your plans for my life
- Put me back together according to your original design
- Cancel and cut off any spiritual retaliation coming against my family or me due to my military service or for any other reason

I now declare that I choose to dwell in the shelter of the Most High and I will abide in the shadow of You, Lord God Almighty, for You are my refuge and my fortress and I put my trust in You.[43]

God, please establish Your protection around my family and me. Please remove anything that does not honor You.

---

[43] Psalm 91:1-2

Prayer to Reconcile, Reunite and Restore Me to the Land Where I Live

Lord, I come on behalf of myself and the sins of my entire generational line back to before the beginning of time. I renounce and repent for all of us who engaged in ungodly sexual activities outside the will of God on the specific land areas where we lived. We have repeatedly broken your covenantal laws, clearly laid out in Exodus 20:14 and Leviticus 18:1-30, which instruct us not to:

- Have sex with any family member
- Commit adultery
- Have sex with someone of the same gender
- Have sex with an animal
- Abort our children, which is patterned after the burning of our children in the fires of Moloch

Lord, please forgive us for defiling the land areas where we have lived through infidelity, and through the murder of the next generation. I recognize that because we have been unfaithful to You, the land You betrothed to us has issued a divorce decree to us,[44] and I repent for our unwillingness to follow Your Word. From this day forward, I pledge my personal fidelity to You and the land where I live. Lord, please:

- Cleanse us of all defilement and guilt resulting from our unholy sexual activities and the murder of the innocent
- Sever every ungodly soul tie between me and the land areas where we have sinned sexually
- By Your grace and mercy, please burn up the divorce papers that the land served us, and cleanse by your blood every geographic area where we have lived

Lord, as the Lion of Judah, please release the sound and frequency of Your mighty roar and set free all generational spirit and soul parts that have been entrapped in the land; remove all parts from the ungodly length, depth, width and height.[45] I also ask You, Lord Jesus, to wield Your sword as the Son of Man and sever me and my generational line from the grip of the Rephaim, which show themselves as the dead ones, departed spirits or shades.[46]

Lord, please complete the process of reconciling, reuniting and restoring me to the land You have given us by destroying every ungodly generational library to which the enemy has access. This has resulted in us being spit out and/or has caused the lands where we live or have lived to come against us. Lord, I am truly sorry that we have wounded Your heart, and have giving the enemy the legal right to wreak havoc upon our families and the lands where we live.

---

[44] Jeremiah 3:8
[45] We have observed that the Lord often does this by sending out His chariots of fire and the horsemen of Israel across every land area where I/we presently live or have lived. It appears that "spiritual centripetal force" is applied.
[46] Isaiah 26:14

Lord, please release the authority that is available to me through Jesus Christ, so that I may advance Your kingdom in the land you have given me.

Lord, for me, my family line, and my descendants, please establish our connections to the land that are in accordance with Your original design.

Prayer to Remove Me from Ungodly Counsel

Lord Jesus, I repent on behalf of myself and my generational line for agreeing with the fallen sons of God[47] and their refuge of lies.[48] I agree that the heart is deceitful and desperately wicked, so who can know it?[49] I acknowledge that I do not comprehend the lies of my heart because I have been affected by this refuge of lies. Lord, please execute judgement on the fallen sons of God who have orchestrated their lies from hidden places in Sheol and the ungodly depth.

I repent for listening to the enticing speech of the harlot, succumbing to her seductive ways, and straying onto her paths that lead into hell and death.[50]

I renounce and repent for any way in which we have made agreements with the enemy because we have drawn our identity from mankind rather than from You.

I renounce and repent for coming into agreement with the enemy's counsel, and for trying to protect ourselves by making covenants with death. Forgive us Lord, for coming into agreement with Sheol so we could feel as if we were protected from danger, disaster and death.

I acknowledge that:
- The reason we listened to the counsel of the ungodly is that we wanted a sense of control and were unwilling to follow Your counsel
- Our families often attempted to usurp Your position as God in attempts to save themselves; we have tried to 'play God'
- We were afraid to trust Your counsel and would rather trust in our own efforts
- We have often believed the lie that if we place our trust in You, we will fall into nothingness and die

Lord, I renounce and repent for:
- Not inquiring of You to discover what You desire, but have instead listened to other spiritual and human voices for direction
- Not following the guidelines of scripture to stay on the Ancient Path[51] and abide by Your will
- Not seeking righteous counsel from those who belong to You

I declare in Jesus name, that I have obtained an inheritance because I have been predestined according to Your purpose to work all things for good according to the counsel of Your will.[52]

---

[47] The fallen sons of God are the Rephaim. A full discussion is available in *Exploring Heavenly Places, Volume 2; Revealing of the sons of God*
[48] Isaiah 28:17
[49] Jeremiah 17:9
[50] Proverbs 7
[51] Jeremiah 6:16
[52] Ephesians 1:11

Lord, please establish around me Your righteous elders,[53] who are tied to Your holy counsel; for I now reject all counsel coming from the enemy and/or from those who are wise in their own eyes. I declare that I will inquire only of You and will receive only Your counsel so that I will not stray from the Ancient Path. I now entrust my heart to You Lord and declare that I will not lean on my own understanding but will acknowledge You alone to direct my paths.[54]

---

[53] The righteous elders are mentioned in Revelation 4, 5, 7, 11, 14, 19
[54] Proverbs 3:5-6

Prayer of Release from the
Multi-Dimensional Zodiac System

Lord Jesus, I renounce and repent for all those in my family line and me, back to the beginning of time and from Adam and Eve forward, who entered into sexual sin and/or engaged in sex outside of marriage, which appears to cause your design for the Mazzaroth to go out of alignment. Lord, please restore any godly blessings have been block or diverted and blessings that were dispersed among the stars. Please clean up and restore any godly energy that has been used by the enemy for nefarious purposes rather than for the purposes of the Lord. Please disconnect my family line and me from any dimensional zodiacs. Please properly connect me to Jesus Christ and restore all godly associations to any dimensional Mazzaroth[55]. Please bring me into righteous alignment throughout Your dimensional creation.

Lord, I repent for ungodly joining to any other person or thing that has interfered with my righteous joining to You. Please remove all misalignment and ungodly joining, and join me to You so that I am no longer fractured. Please establish me as one, complete person I repent for anytime I or those in my family line refused to ask for Your Ancient Path or declared we would not walk in Your Ancient Path[56]. Help me to trust in You and please align me to You and establish my paths to align with Your Ancient Path; make this path straight so that Your life flows through me.[57]

In the name of Jesus Christ and by the power of His blood, I renounce and repent for all evil that has caused my family line and me to be disconnected from both the land[58] and the God-given electromagnetic fields of the earth.[59]

Father, forgive us for committing sexual sin on the lands in which you have positioned us. I repent for giving our hearts over to the enemy; thus allowing him to gain control over the electromagnetic fields and permitting him to ravish our hearts to the point where they are not connected to Your heart. Forgive us for allowing the enemy to usurp Your glory, and for giving the enemy the worship he longs to receive.

Father, I repent and ask Your forgiveness for any ungodly trading, and for seeking prosperity and protection from anyone or anything other than You. I confess that You are the true source, but we have sought these things from the enemy through ungodly trading. I also renounce and repent for placing our security in the desires of our flesh rather than in You.

Father, forgive us for sacrificing our children because of our selfish desires, and for contaminating the land with their blood; forgive us for aborting children, as well as for shedding their innocent blood and sacrificing children in the fires of Moloch.[60] Please retrieve all scattered spirit and soul parts entrapped in the ungodly depth, ungodly deep, and the dimensions within

---

[55] Job 38:32
[56] Jeremiah 6:16
[57] Proverbs 3:5&6
[58] Isaiah 62:1
[59] We have discerned that sin seems to affect our association with electromagnetic fields. The goal is to ask God to restore this association.
[60] Leviticus 18:21, Ezekiel 20:31

dimensions. Sever all connections between the ungodly star, Rephan,[61] and us. Please disconnect me from all ungodly, dimensional zodiacs that have been affecting the electromagnetic fields. Please disconnect my heart from every ungodly star, star system and constellation where I have been entrapped.

Lord, please:

- Forgive us for giving way to seductive and enticing spirits, and for seeking counsel from the ungodly council instead of seeking Your righteous counsel

- Disconnect me from any ties, chains, and ropes that have attached me to the ungodly council, and remove the evil consequences of those attachments

- Perform surgery upon my physical heart and remove all ungodly electromagnetic fields

- Disconnect me from all ungodly powers that have been fueling this ungodly activity; retune and recalibrate my heart to synch with Your heart

- Remove all ungodly worship of the enemy in my generational line

- Destroy all ungodly walls that were erected because of sin on the land, which have blocked my family line and me from other people

I now issue a divorce decree between myself and the enemy. Lord, as I am now being disconnected from all ungodly dimensional zodiacs, please correctly connect me to the godly Mazzaroth and marry me to the land.

I repent and renounce any partnership with all ungodly thought/belief systems and for acceptance of that which is not true. Lord, please release me from selling out to seduction and false mindsets.

Lord please:

- Disconnect me from the ungodly seven spirits of the enemy

- Take me out of all ungodly cycles of the multi-dimensional zodiacs, especially where my family line and me are trapped in any 7 ½ year ungodly cycle(s)

- Remove me from all twelve of the ungodly zodiac systems of houses, and rightly connect me to your Mazzaroth for I want to be only in Your House

- Correctly align the domains of my spirit with the correct Jewish months, Jewish tribes, and also with the correct constellations in the Mazzaroth

- Correctly adjust the sounds, frequencies and vibrations of my living stones to resonate correctly with Father, Son and Holy Spirit, so that I am aligned with Your Glory and holiness

---

[61] Acts 7:43

- Removed me from all evil-imposed ungodly calendars, especially those tied to the gods assigned to the days of the week, the months of the years, and the zodiac cycles that are tied to the gods of this age

- Remove me from any river of death, and disconnect me from all pollution and corruption that has come against my family line and me because of generational agreement with false wisdom, knowledge, and all ungodly world systems.

- Remove me from the ramifications of the corruption of light

Lord, I acknowledge that the ungodly seed of the enemy was grown into all kinds of defiled roots and branches that have negatively affected my life and inheritance. Please burn up all of these roots and branches in your furnace.

Lord please:

- Set me free from the bondages of this present age so that I may flow correctly in Your river and in correct space-time

- Remove all false prophecies, divinations, and enhancements that used the fallen stars as their information source

- Remove all projections and overlays of time lines that distort our time lines, such that times and seasons are changed to align with the enemy and not with You

- Set me free from the ungodly ordinances and rule of the zodiac, and establish me correctly with the righteous ordinances and rule of Your Mazzaroth

- Remove me from the path of the age of this cosmos, and establish me on your ancient path

- Take my family line and me out of the darkness of this age, and place us into your Kingdom of Glorious Light

- Remove all contamination off of the elemental spirits tied to my body, which resulted from the worship of all the ungodly star systems

- Disconnect me from all ungodly thrones and power structures that are linked with the fallen zodiacs

- Take back all the inheritances, blessings, anointings and giftings that were stolen or blocked by every ungodly system addressed in this prayer

- Disconnect me from all ungodly windows that were associated with every system mentioned in this prayer, and correctly align all righteous dimensional windows so that the full blessings You have for me are completely released and can flow without hindrance

- Return to me through Your blood all spirit and soul parts that have been scattered because of the generational and lifetime iniquity and sin mentioned in this prayer

- Destroy all walls that have separated my soul and spirits from each other and from me, and establish correctly in my spirit the twelve jewels

I repent for all of us who gave away our authority over the land in trade for prestige, power and comfort. Please restore our rightful authority over the land, dimensions, grid and the elements so that You can again be properly glorified. Please remove and erase all glory that has been given to the enemy through the generations, and return that glory a hundredfold to You, the true-and-living God.

Lord, please now break, shatter, destroy, and dissolve all ungodly magnetic fields attached to me; and release Your river to short circuit all ungodly powers, bringing life and health to the land and to me.

I declare my life is not a cycle, but flows with the River of God.[62] Thank You, Lord, that as I exit and disconnect from these ungodly cycles, I now able to enter into your rest and peace. Thank You that you are establishing me in your times and seasons as I am being removed from all ungodly clocks. Thank You that You are preparing me for the powers of the age to come.

---

[62] James 3:6

Prayer to Break the Influence of Fallen Sons of God Over My Family Line

In the name of Jesus Christ and as a representative of my family line, I repent for not coming into agreement with our positions as sons of God.[63] I repent for any actions that corrupted our faith or contaminated the inheritance we have through Jesus Christ. I repent for employing legalism and religiosity or for trying to make the law our guardian.[64]

I repent for participating in activities that were in agreement with the fallen sons of God or other evil entities. I repent for participating with, or allowing influence from, the fallen sons of God or other evil entities.

I repent for wasting resources and for being poor stewards of time and energy by focusing on conflicts and arguments, rather than pursuing godly unity.

Lord, I confess that many of us have:

- Taken unrighteous vows and made covenants against each other and against You
- Forced other members of the family to join into ungodly alliances, which furthered the disunity and caused internal wars combating one another in a familial civil war
- Lied about and/or slandered other members of the family.

Lord, I repent for:

- Any way that I have ignored, condoned or actively participated in this
- Not coming to You to verify accusations that were made against us and against others
- Every time I aligned with the enemy because I was angry
- Every time I strategized regarding any break in the family that could benefit me instead of grieving and praying it through

Lord please:

- Remove all records of wrong that are hidden in the ungodly libraries that are located in the ungodly heavenly places
- Bring spiritual, physical, emotional and relational healing to my family and my extended family
- Remove the ungodly council of fallen sons of God over my tribe and family
- Position my tribe and family correctly in the Kingdom of God and the Kingdom of Heaven
- Remove the distorted family timeline and place my family and tribe into your Kairos time

Lord, for my life and family line and the lives of my descendants, I ask that you now remove all impacts that resulted from discord and disunity. Please remove all blockages or distortions of blessings that were meant to come down our family line.

---

[63] Romans 8:14, Galatians 3:26. Also see *Exploring Heavenly Places - Volume 7: Revealing the Sons of God* by Paul Cox and Rob Gross
[64] Galatians 3:23

Lord, please heal and set us free from infirmity, loss, disunity, disfavor, heartache, sorrow, depression and anxiety. Please remove any negative affects against the land.

Lord please heal us from distressing thoughts and loss of sleep.

Lord please restore our godly inheritance.

Lord, please bless my children and all future generations with the benefits of these prayers.

Prayer to be Released from Ungodly Want, Need, Lack and Expectations

On behalf of myself and my family line, I repent for settling into a mindset of lack, of always wanting, needing and expecting something else, rather than trusting You. I repent for not believing that You are always good and Your lovingkindness endures forever. Lord, please take me out of the ungodly dimensions where want, need, lack and expect reside. Please place me into Your kingdom mindset, for I want to be a kingdom-oriented person who sees Your kingdom come on earth as it is in Heaven. I declare that I do not have to operate in lack; I don't always have to experience want or need regarding what I don't have; and I can expect You to always do what's right. I will not only be content, but also will contend for everything You want me to have.

Lord, I surrender any personal or generational resistance over to you. I give You permission to release into me a desire to create, to see those things that are not as they should be. Help me to comprehend Your desire for me to live in abundance, prosperity and fruitfulness through Your limitless design. Sanctify my imagination to call those things into place that You intend for me, my family, my influence, my creative finances and prosperity.

Enlighten the eyes of my heart, Lord, in Jesus' name.

Prayer to Remove the Effects of the Rebellion of the Ungodly Mighty Ones

Lord Jesus, I submit the following prayer, asking that You break all ungodly ties between fallen mighty ones[65] and me.

Lord, please:

- Release the sun of righteousness with healing in her wings[66] to burn up all ungodly roots and branches in the furnace of God[67]

- Disconnect from me all ungodly counterfeits of the Branch,[68] who is Jesus

- Disconnect me from all ungodly created beings that are called the mighty ones[69]

- Remove all ungodly access to the windows[70]

- Disconnect me from all ungodly watchers and fallen holy ones[71], and rightly connect me to your godly watchers and holy ones

- Remove all ungodly vibrations, sounds, frequencies, light and electrical impulses

- Totally dismantle all programming and foundations of programming that are rooted in the fallen mighty ones or any other evil.

- Disconnect me from all fallen and distorted attributes and names of God

- Administer eye salve to the seven eyes of the Lord and to the eyes of my heart

Lord, thank You for removing the shame of nakedness and clothing me in white garments[72]. I now choose to walk by faith, not entering into the distraction of my circumstances by saying that I am in want, need or lack, and that I can't have faith to expect your goodness and abundance.

Lord, please:

- Remove me from all fictitious places and illusions in regions of captivity

---

[65] Genesis 6:4
[66] Malachi 4:2, Statement is "in her wings" in original Hebrew.
[67] More information available in our teaching "The Furnace of the Lord" aslansplace.com/the-furnace-of-the-lord/
[68] Isaiah 4:2, 11:1
[69] Our understanding through discernment and prophetic revelation is that these beings originally carried the attributes of God, but have twisted those attributes.
[70] Our sense is that God's intention for our interaction with the windows of heaven has been interrupted through ungodly programming and manipulation of time.
[71] Daniel 4:13 – This scripture provides an example of godly watchers.
[72] Revelation 3:5

- Bring me back from all the places in the remotest parts of the heavens, and gather me to the place where You have chosen for my name to dwell; for I reject all false names given to me

- Destroy all remaining ungodly contracts made with the mighty ones that have filtered into this present age

- Disconnect me from all ancients[73]

- Disconnect me from death, and from all agreements with death and the place of death

Lord, I declare that I will not be in the place of LESS but in the place of BLESS

Lord, please:

- Resolve and remove all body and cellular memories that have kept me in bondage, and remove all evil off of my adrenals

- Disconnect me from all ungodly systems of elders associated with the fallen mighty ones

- Remove all injustice, unrighteousness and deception associated with the fallen mighty ones

By the power of the blood of Jesus and the cross of Christ, I cancel all codes and regulations that were written against me by the fallen watchers and fallen holy ones or from any other ungodly beings.

Lord, please:

- Release Palmoni[74] to bring to correct created order all vibrations, frequencies, sounds, and channels

- Uncover the Deep[75], remove the darkness from the face of the Deep, and release Light over the Deep[76]

- Let Your light come to dispel the darkness and reveal that which is hidden in darkness[77]

- Turn the land of the shadow of death without any order[78] to morning[79]

- Release us who have been held in chains in the darkness,[80] restoring our soul and spirit parts that have been trapped in darkness; let Your sure word of prophecy bring light into the dark places[81]

---

[73] Our sense is that these fallen beings are, or have been, manipulating time in the past, present and future.
[74] aslansplace.com/the-sound-of-the-lord-paul-l-cox/
[75] aslansplace.com/understanding-the-depth/
[76] Genesis 1:2l3
[77] Luke 8:17
[78] Job 10:22
[79] Amos 5:8
[80] Jude 1:6
[81] 2 Peter 1:19

- Break up the Deep by your knowledge[82] so that the knowledge of the glory of the Lord may cover the earth like the waters cover the sea[83]

- Remove the queen of heaven from being seated over the waters of my life[84] and cause the Holy Spirit to move over the waters of my life[85]

- Remove the coverings off of Sheol, Abaddon[86] and the bottomless pit and reveal your truth. Please restore the treasures of my soul and spirit parts from these places

I repent for the worship of and allegiance to the king of the scorpions, the angel of the bottomless pit – Abaddon, Apollyon.[87] Please cancel the legal rights of Abaddon to bring destruction and to bring formlessness and void, and remove me from the dominion of the king of terrors.[88] Please also:

- Unfold the heavens; unroll and spread them out[89] so the firmament is in its right place, and length, breadth, width and height[90] are restored to their proper measures and boundaries

- Rescue all soul and spirit parts that are trapped in utter desolation and judgment of formlessness and emptiness

- Remove me, including all of my parts, from the ungodly deepest deep, and integrate me so that I am one in Christ throughout my entire being of body, soul and spirit

- Remove the stones of emptiness and the lines of confusion[91]

- Remove all contamination that came upon the living stones of my spirit that have affected my spiritual, mental and physical health

- Restore us as living stones and call me out of darkness into Your marvelous light[92]

- Rightly position Mount Zion, the north over the formlessness and the earth over the void[93]

- Remove me and my soul and spirit parts from the ancient ones, the ancient places, realms, and from being trapped with the kings in the ungodly assembly, on Mount Saphon[94]

---

[82] Proverbs 3:20
[83] Habakkuk 2:14
[84] Revelation 17:1
[85] Genesis 1:2
[86] Job 26:6
[87] Revelation 9:11
[88] Job 18:14
[89] Job 9:8
[90] Ephesians 3:18
[91] Isaiah 34:11
[92] 1 Peter 2:5,9
[93] Job 26:7
[94] Isaiah 14:13 Mount Saphon – Baal's Mountain. Derek Gilbert, Veneration (Defender Publishing, 2019) page 19

- As in the days of old, I ask for the right arm of the Lord to come with your mighty sword;[95] to go to war against the ungodly ancient ones and reclaim Your realms; war against the ungodly spiritual beings Rahab[96], Behemoth[97], Leviathan[98] and the dragons, who live at the border of the worlds and shift the godly boundaries. What they have held captive in the depths, please release. With Your sword, please cut me out of the ungodly Rahab, Behemoth, Leviathan, the dragon and remove me from the associated realms, dimensions and universes. Remove the creatures that are affecting me from all realms that were not appointed for them, and take me out of the marshes and mires[99] of the transition between the worlds.[100] Stir up the sea by Your power, and divide the sea by Your mighty power; by your understanding, smite the ungodly spirit, Rahab[101]

Lord, please:
- Restore the godly boundaries between light and darkness,[102] water and land[103]
- Restrain the sea behind its proper limits and gates[104]
- Restore the circular boundary on the face of the waters where the waters meet the sky[105]
- Restore your firmament
- Restore the original intent of all creation, no longer allowing Behemoth to swallow the living water,[106] and release the life of God from the strongholds of Leviathan in the deep;[107] please dethrone him as king over the sons of pride in my life[108]
- Strike the twisting serpent and the cosmic snake in the sky[109]
- Rebuke the seven pillars of heaven,[110] the ungodly watchers, and restore the righteous pillars of heaven and righteous watchers
- Restore the brightness of the firmament[111]
- Restore to me the soul and spirit parts that the Rephaim have held captive under the waters.[112]

---

[95] Isaiah 51:9
[96] Job 26:12
[97] Job 40:21
[98] Job 41:30
[99] Psalm 40:2
[100] Behemoth and Leviathan are associated with marshes which are places of transition between worlds. The marshes were from dream from intercessor Rita Anderson
[101] Job 26:12
[102] Genesis 1:4
[103] Genesis 1:9
[104] Job 38:11
[105] Job 26:10
[106] Job 40:23
[107] Job 41:31
[108] Job 41:34
[109] Job 26:13
[110] Job 26:11 7 *apkallu* or watchers Derek Gilbert, Ancient Cataclysms Conference 2020
[111] Daniel 12:3
[112] Job 26:5

I declare that Mount Zion, the rule of Jesus,[113] is the meeting point of all the dimensions, realms where He holds all things together by the word of His power.[114] Lord, please remove any legal rights brought over from the ancient days, including all ungodly scrolls, words, prophecies, the seals of the ancient ones, crowns, kingdoms, scepters, inheritances, bloodlines, and liens.

Lord, please:

- Dissolve any word that is an ungodly binding, and the ungodly binding of the Pleiades[115]
- Cause the sword of Your word to establish godly boundaries between soul and spirit, bone and marrow[116]
- Close all ungodly time gates, energy gates, water gates and open the righteous ones so that the King of Glory may come in;[117] let the godly star gates be opened to allow the life of God into me and disconnect me from ungodly stargates
- Cleanse the stars associated with me
- Remove the ungodly thrones and thrones of iniquity,[118] elders and kings in the star gates[119]
- Remove the darkness from the stars, and command the light to shine out of darkness[120]
- Cleanse the power grid, and cause the ungodly ley lines in the grid to become pathways of righteousness and justice in the power grid of the Crystal Sea so that You may be enthroned on the foundation of righteousness and justice[121]
- Remove the ungodly government at my gates, including the ungodly judges and elders,[122] ancient ones, kings and thrones, doorkeepers and gatekeepers and watchers
- Graft Your power into my life, the resurrection power of Christ, and cause the grid to be powered by the life of God
- Remove me out of death and destruction; wake me out of slumber, and let the resurrection power of Christ revive me and bring my dry bones to life again[123]
- Release to me the treasures of darkness, the hidden riches of secret places; uncover the treasures and blessings of the Great Deep
- Release to me the precious things of heaven, the dew and the deep that crouches beneath, the precious fruit of the sun, the precious produce of the months, the best things of the ancient mountains, the precious things of the everlasting hills[124]

Lord, I repent for my belief in all false perceptions and revelation spewed by the fallen mighty ones, fallen elders, fallen cherubs, and any other ungodly being. Please:

---

[113] Psalm 110:2
[114] Hebrews 1:3
[115] Job 38:31
[116] Hebrews 4:12
[117] Psalm 24:7
[118] Psalm 94:20
[119] Jeremiah 1:15
[120] 2 Corinthians 4:6
[121] Psalm 89:14
[122] Deuteronomy 16:18
[123] Ezekiel 37:5
[124] Deuteronomy 33:13-15

- Take me out of the ungodly time line set up by fallen elders in collusion with the fallen stars and fallen mighty ones
- Remove all fallen angels that are aligned with the mighty ones that are coming against me
- Remove all personality disorders that have contaminated my family line for any reason, including because of the rebellion of fallen mighty ones, fallen watchers and fallen holy ones
- Disconnect me from all ungodly wheels within wheels and all ungodly cherubim
- Disconnect all parts of me from the ungodly holy ones and ungodly mighty ones,[125] and remove the fear, agony, anguish, war and torment that they have inflicted on me[126]
- Remove all ungodly thoughts, words, deeds, gestures, vows and covenants that I have taken in order to attempt to escape from the repercussions of evil mighty ones

I confess that we have been asleep to what has been caused by the ungodly mighty ones and ungodly holy ones, and passive to the deception, injustice and unrighteousness[127] that has flowed down through the generations from these evil beings. We have not taken up the sword against them, but have been complicit in their ways. I declare to my spirit and soul, "Awake oh sleeper, arise from the dead," and I acknowledge that Jesus Christ will shine upon me.[128] Lord please remove all parts of me from the ungodly deep and restore me to Your righteous deep. I recognize Your deep calls to the deep I am in because I pray according to Your word:

> *Give ear to my words, O LORD; consider my groaning. Give attention to the sound of my cry, my King and my God, for to you do I pray. O LORD, in the morning you hear my voice; in the morning I prepare a sacrifice for you and watch. For you are not a God who delights in wickedness; evil may not dwell with you. The boastful shall not stand before your eyes; you hate all evildoers. You destroy those who speak lies; the LORD abhors the bloodthirsty and deceitful man. But I, through the abundance of your steadfast love, will enter your house. I will bow down toward your holy temple in the fear of you. Lead me, O LORD, in your righteousness because of my enemies; make your way straight before me. For there is no truth in their mouth; their inmost self is destruction; their throat is an open grave; they flatter with their tongue. Make them bear their guilt, O God; let them fall by their own counsels; because of the abundance of their transgressions cast them out, for they have rebelled against you. But let all who take refuge in you rejoice; let them ever sing for joy, and spread your protection over them, that those who love your name may exult in you. For you bless the righteous, O LORD; you cover him with favor as with a shield.[129]*

Lord, I declare that even the parts of me trapped in the deep or other places of captivity will be rescued when they cry out to You, so that they will also praise You. Please:

---

[125] Isaiah 13:3
[126] Joel 2:6, Isaiah 13:7-8
[127] Psalm 82
[128] Ephesians 5:14
[129] *The Holy Bible: English Standard Version.* (2016). (Ps 5:1–12). Wheaton, IL: Crossway Bibles.

- Remove all ungodly coding and coating that was placed upon my generational DNA, RNA, and mitochondrial DNA by or through the fallen mighty ones or any other evil

- Release the hidden wisdom of the DNA, RNA and mitochondrial coding that You have predestined before the ages for our glory [130]

- Remove the generational programming of the doubt, deception, lies and twisting of the DNA and RNA when I was woven in secret in the depths of the earth. [131]

- Break the authority of the ungodly mighty ones over my DNA, RNA and mitochondria, and rightly align my DNA, RNA and mitochondria DNA so that I am returned to your original creative design

I renounce and repent for myself and my generational line for all of us who promised the enemy our souls and those of future generations in order to acquire wealth and possessions. I admit that this is the trading of souls, which is condemned in the Word of God. [132]

I declare that my soul and spirt will be will be rightly aligned to God's ancient path and my mind will be transformed and renewed to the mind of Christ, [133] that I will make the Lord my trust, [134] and I will go beyond the fears that have previously captivated my spirit and soul. Lord, thank You for removing me from the miry clay [135].

---

[130] I Corinthians 2:7, 16
[131] Psalm 139:15
[132] Revelation 18:13, Genesis 14:21, Ezekiel 27:13
[133] Romans 12:2, I Corinthians 2:16
[134] Psalm 40:4
[135] Psalm 40:2

Prayer to Release the Joyful Sound

I renounce and repent on behalf of myself and my family line back to before the beginning of time for:

- Listening to and aligning with ungodly sounds

- Coming into agreement with dissonance and disunity in any way

- Buying into or accepting the enemy's corrupted version of the seven Spirits of God or the seven Eyes of the Lord

- Honoring God with lips while our hearts were far from Him

- Any participation in ungodly worship through music, rhythms or dance

- Listening to ungodly worship

- All use of music as part of ungodly sacrifices

Father, Son and Holy Spirit I acknowledge that you are the Master Conductor and that You determine the time signature of the sound movements of my life, and the composition of the notes of my life. Lord please:

- Remove any contamination off the righteous seven eyes as they manifest through my life so that the sound of the Lord may go through the ends of the earth

- Recover my birthright of righteous light sound that has been stolen and trapped in ungodly stars, false sounds, frequencies and cycles

- Retune, realign, and/or replace the sounds and vibrations of any of the three chords connected to parts of my body, mind, and soul which are out of tune

- Remove all ungodly 'star sounds' in my body, soul and spirit, and correct all ungodly dissonance so that my body, soul and spirit now emits the correct sounds that are to the Praise of Your Glory

- Release palmoni[136] to set the correct vibrations in my body, soul and spirit back to Your original created design

- Cause my living stones to vibrate to your original created design, and restore Your proper chord structures in my life and family line

- Break all ungodly ties between me and ungodly beings that were established in any way including through ungodly worship

- Replace ungodly beats and rhythms with Your heartbeat

---

[136] Palmoni is Hebrew for a certain holy one, numberer of secrets; key scripture, Daniel 8:13

- Align my God given song to the symphony of Your body so that we are of one accord.[137]

- Release into me the correction of sound that took place at the Cross

- Release into me the sound of every word Jesus spoke on earth

- Remove all ungodly powers that have encapsulated every musical star chord

---

[137] It is our understanding that this will bring healing to the land

Prayer of Repentance and Release for Those of Jewish Ancestry

Lord, on behalf of myself and my generational line back to before the beginning of time, I renounce and repent for the sins of the priesthood as represented in Malachi 2:1-9.

I repent for:

- Not listening as the priesthood and not taking to heart and giving honor to Your name
- Willingly bringing the curse upon ourselves and our children
- Not believing You and fearing Your name when You said you would curse our blessing; taking your words lightly
- Willingly taking on the rebuke of our offspring because we did not want what You wanted, choosing to what we thought was best
- Willingly receiving the curse of the Lord; living outside of the fear of the Lord
- Despising the covenant of life and peace, the covenant of Levi
- Refusing to fear Your name, and stand in awe of Your name
- Abandoning Your true instruction
- Speaking falsely
- Turning away from peace and uprightness, while turning toward iniquity; and turning others away as well
- All who didn't guard knowledge about You, and led others into deception.
- Hiding godly instruction
- Killing the messenger of the Lord of Hosts
- Turning aside from the righteous way and causing many to stumble through false instruction
- All corruption of the covenant of Levi
- Choosing to become despised and abased before all the people
- Not keeping Your ways and showing partiality in our instruction

Lord, in the name of Jesus, Yeshua Hamashiach[138], I renounce all of that evil and ask that You remove and reverse the curse.

According to Your promises, I declare and decree on behalf of the descendants of Abraham, of whom I am one, that You will raise a signal to continue his righteous inheritance among the Jewish people. I ask You to set things right and to raise up the tribes of Jacob; bring them back, and make them a light for the nations that Your salvation may reach to the end of the earth.[139] Lord, please remove us from any ancient, ungodly dimensions.

---

[138] Yeshua Hamashiach means "Jesus the Messiah". We feel it is important to acknowledge that Jesus is the Messiah.
[139] Isaiah 49:6

I also renounce and repent for myself and all those in my family line who:

- For any reason, including persecution, rejected Your plan for their lives and chose to give into fear instead of trusting You

- Rejected You and Your covenant, not turning to You in times of suffering

- Did not choose to lay down our lives for You, but instead chose to hide ourselves and our identity in order to preserve our lives

- Chose to hide by becoming oppressors, inflicting the same oppression that we received on others

- Enslaving others, and hiding our identity in self-hatred; choosing a life of lies, oppression and hatred instead of You

- Knew You, the God of Abraham, Isaac and Jacob, but because of fear for their lives, turned their backs on You and embraced false religions, false gods and false traditions

- Cursed You and blamed You for allowing our children to be kidnapped, proselytized and indoctrinated; causing their hearts to turn away from You into other religions

- Rejected their heritage and their identity within the tribes of Israel, and chose to allow fear, self-hatred, and loss of identity to be imprinted in the DNA

- Instead of looking for and to You, chose self-effort to bring about self-preservation.

Lord, I come to you in humility and ask for the return of my birthright; for the identity that You imprinted on our generational heart. I ask for the gifts, the callings, and the fearlessness we were meant to have; I ask You to disentangle fear from my identity, my DNA, RNA, cellular and molecular parts, and to imprint Your holy, rock-solid gift of faith in their place. I ask for restitution and healing for all those we have hurt through our fear; and for generational healing, not only for us but for all those whose identities we stole.

Thank you Jesus, for Your love toward me and my family line. I choose this day to honor You in Your redemptive plan for my family and my own children and their children's children for thousands of generations so that we may take our place in history as the ones who followed You to the death, laying down our lives at all costs for the love of You, rejecting all else but You, and finding our lives and our identity only in You.

Lord, I confess the truth that if anyone is in Christ, that person is a new creation; the old has gone, the new has come,[140] and I thank You.

---

[140] 2 Corinthians 5:17

Time Prayer

Lord, please heal me from any time my spirit experienced fear.

Lord, please retrieve all parts of my spirit that were scattered before or after conception in any dimensions or any dimensions of time. Please put me back together according to your original design.

Lord, I acknowledge that fear can result in parts of me splitting off and leaving the ancient path and going my own way. Lord please clean off all scattered parts as they are being returned to me. Please restore me to Your ancient path. Lord Jesus, please close all ungodly doors and gates that were opened when this happened to me. Lord Jesus, please open all doors that should be opened so that righteous gates can never be closed again.

Lord Jesus, on behalf of myself and as a representative of my family line I renounce and repent for:

- All the times we chose to align with man's times, cycles, seasons and festivals and not yours

- Altering the markings of time to honor ungodly beings or celebrating those ungodly being's high dates and places.

- Every occasion in which I became impatient and refused to wait for your appointed times

- Moving the ancient boundaries of time

- Refusing to take action in your time

- Delaying obedience in your time

- Participating in sacrifices to establish ungodly times and seasons.

- Not permitting our families to operate in their God-given times.

- Aligning ourselves to ungodly calendars.

- Misusing, ignoring or corrupting God's timing or wasting God's time.

- Participating in violence, strife and iniquity that altered our timelines and birthrights.

- Allowing our times and seasons to be governed by the zodiac or astrology

- Honoring leaders or nations that did not follow God's timing or did not allow us to follow God's timing.

- Participating in ungodly practices and trading to change our timelines or trade away portions of our timelines

- Refusing to be in synchronization and alignment with God's Kairos times and seasons.

- Attempting to manipulate birth for ungodly purposes or selfish reasons

- Disrupting God's sequences of time and time markers in our life

- Walking in the fear of man to honor man's timing and not God's time.

- Submitting to spiritual leaders who were out of Your time

- Fearing man and submitting to his spiritual affirmation, approval and promotion rather than waiting for yours

- Preempting Your time of death by suicide and euthanasia

- Trying to control time, the flow of time, and ungodly time travel

- Trying to become like God or to become immortal

- Pursuing war or confrontation out of God's timing for any reason, including to prove our point or demand our own rights from personal confrontation to corporate confrontation.

- Not coming from a place of compassion and love.

- Forcing our own timing in relationships, instead of pursing Your timing, Lord

- Trying to fulfill promises and prophetic words outside of God's timing

- Worshipping or establishing covenants with ungodly beings of time or fate

Lord, please:
- Correct any ungodly vibrations of the windows. Return the vibration of the windows to Your original creative design.

- Cleanse memories attached to times of trauma and remove any ungodly memorial stones in our spirit, soul and body that mark times of trauma.

- Retrieve, cleanse and restore all parts of me that are trapped in time and trauma memories

- Reestablish memorial stones that celebrate the times of Your blessing and goodness towards us

- Disconnect me and my family line from ungodly clocks and cycles of stars and zodiacs. Please retrieve, clean and restore all parts trapped in clocks, cycles and star dates

- Help us to walk in your wisdom and to pursue Your timing

- Cleanse and heal our timelines, repair and bridge bruises and gaps in our timelines so that Your life and glory may flow down our timelines

- Remove all ungodly clocks, calendars time measures, time frequencies and clocks and reset all our clocks, calendars, measures, frequencies and cycles to their original design

- Remove us from the ungodly wheel of time and ungodly houses of the zodiac

- Establish Jesus Christ as the One who was, is and is to come, the Alpha and the Omega as the origin of my space and time

- Remove ungodly alignment between my family line and I from any evil trees and branches.

- Disconnect me and my family line from ungodly rings of time, wrong government, wrong branches and wrong legislation

- Remove me and my family line from all ungodly time signatures and bring me fully into Your time signature

Prayer to Enter the Kingdom of Heaven

Lord, on behalf of myself and my family line back to before the beginning of time, I repent for:

- Ungodly access of the heavens, ungodly travel in time and in the dimensions.

- Using occult practices, drugs or alcohol, and ungodly connections with the eyes of the Lord

- Stealing from the storehouses of heaven

- Any time I or my ancestors established ungodly trades or covenants with the fallen sons of God for any reason, including to gain access to the heavens, lay claim to the heavens, or to build our kingdoms there

- Building structures, portals, and the Tower of Babel[141] to access the heavens through Freemasonry, the occult, witchcraft, deception, fear or coercion

Lord, please cancel these covenants and take back the heavens that belong to You alone.[142] Please remove all ungodly structures, including the Tower of Babel and its manifestations through the ages. Please remove the chaos in the waters,[143] sea monsters, dragons, octopuses and ungodly Leviathan[144]. Please remove or correct any ungodly order, laws, and operations that were imposed on the waters and restore everything to Your original design.

I repent for:

- Idolatry, including the worship of the host of heaven and fallen sons of God

- Agreeing or participating in the rebellion of the fallen kings and rulers against You.[145]

- Our iniquity on the earth, which was reflected into the heavens,[146] defiling them

- Mapping the heavens on earth – earth grids, tunnels and mounds – in order to manipulate the heavens

- Building temples, altars, blood sacrifices at key points[147] on the grid[148]

Lord, please:

- Remove all heavens of bronze and ground of iron and restore rain and godly fertility to the land[149]

- Remove the transplanting and comingling of souls and stealing of bodies[150]

---

[141] Gen 11:4
[142] Psalm 115:16
[143] Gen 1:2
[144] Psalm 74:13,14
[145] Psalm 2:2
[146] Hosea 2:21
[147] Stonehenge, Chichen Itza, Giza Pyramids, Angkor Wat
[148] It is our sense that these activities empowered evil dominions to use soul and spirit parts to take over grids and ley line sections
[149] Deuteronomy 28:23, 24
[150] Ezekiel 13:17-20

- Remove ungodly fractals, multiples, derivatives, and images of the heavens and its storehouses and vaults

- Remove trading lines of slavery

- Remove unrighteous kings, including the King of Tyre and the queen of heaven, and the whore of Babylon from the governmental seats[151]

- Remove their ungodly authority and dominion over many waters,[152] the seven mountains,[153] the trading routes, chessboards, trading ports, platforms and marketplaces[154] of the heavenly grids of the waters

- Remove levies, taxes and gate control of the kings and rulers

- Sorceries, enchantments,[155] ungodly kingdoms[156] of the queen of heaven, and their multiplication, images and fractals from the grids of the heavens

- Remove trafficking of birthrights, inheritances, blood, DNA, bodies, souls, sex and identities

- Remove raiders of ungodly kingdoms and their multiplication more than the stars of the heavens[157]

- Remove violent ones who think they can take the kingdom of God by force[158]

- Remove from the waters any patterning and imprinting of the un-holy spirit and the ungodly seven spirits

- Remove strongholds of logic, logic gates, and everything that has elevated itself into the governmental heights and mountains that exalts itself against the knowledge of God[159]

- Remove mirrors and lattice frameworks

- Close the ungodly gates, doors, windows, portals,[160] lattices and grids of the heavens that need to be closed, and open those that need to be opened to allow the waters – the life of God to flow into our lives.

- Remove ungodly lines upon lines and unrighteous precepts upon precepts at every level of the foundations[161]

- Remove ungodly lines, measures, sounds of injustice, and wormwood[162] from the firmament

---

[151] Ezekiel 28:2, Ezekiel 28:5
[152] Rev 17:1,
[153] Rev 17:9
[154] Ezekiel 27:12
[155] Isaiah 47:9,12
[156] Isaiah 47:5, Nahum 3:4
[157] Nahum 3:16
[158] Matthew 11:12
[159] 2 Cor 10:5
[160] Genesis 7:11, Malachi 3:10
[161] Isaiah 28:10
[162] Revelation 8:11

- Remove the ungodly plumb stones and alignments of unrighteousness[163]

- Remove ungodly laws, testimonies, statutes, commandments, fears and judgments[164] from every level of the foundations; and at every level of organization of quarks, protons, neutrons, electrons, atoms, molecules, and all fiery stones

- Remove ungodly organizations and bindings and restore their godly creation according to the mind of God

- Cleanse the elemental spirits of the foundations

- Remove the ungodly womb of the dawn

- Restore the highways of holiness

- Restore the soul, spirit and body and inheritances that have been lost, stolen or traded away

- Remove any ungodly binding or any corruption of Your word and thoughts[165] and restore me to Your original design when I was knit together in the depths of the earth.[166]

- Restore my godly frame that was designed by Your thoughts towards me

- Cleanse the power lines, networks, and connections of the grid of the heavens and the earth

I repent for agreeing or aligning with ungodly power sources and structures in my life, and for covenants that drew power and life from networks of the world systems rather than from the life of God.

Lord, please:

- Dismantle the fallen kingdoms of the heavens, their eternal fractals and closed systems

- Remove ungodly records, memories and false witness[167] that are stored in the heavens or any other location

- Cleanse and heal trauma memories

- Remove, any warping of spacetime[168]

- Restore the godly separation of the waters above and the waters below,[169] and the separation of the higher dimensions and the lower dimensions

- Establish the heavens according to Your understanding[170] alone

- Restore the doors and bars of the seas to Your decreed location[171]

---

[163] Isaiah 28:17
[164] Psalm 19:7-9
[165] Hebrews 1:3, Psalm 139:17-18
[166] Psalm 139:15
[167] Isaiah 65:17, Deuteronomy 30:19
[168] Our sense is that the fabric of spacetime is associated with a lattice structure within the crystal sea mentioned in Ezekiel 1:22-23
[169] Genesis 1:6
[170] Proverbs 3:19
[171] Job 38:8-10

- Cleanse the first particles[172] and restore and establish the foundations of the earth[173]

- Close the fountains of the ungodly deep, the abyss, and the windows and mirrors of the ungodly heavens[174]

Lord, I repent for allowing my thinking to enable mindsets of fear, blindness, limitation, poverty, lack, pain, doubt, unbelief and hard-heartedness. I acknowledge that these limit my perspectives of You in my life, and prevent me and others from entering the unlimited riches and possibilities of the kingdom of heaven.[175] Please help me to become like a little child in order to enter the kingdom of heaven.[176]

I repent for walking in the spirit of the sons of disobedience according to the lusts and desires of the flesh; and for walking according to the age of this cosmos, according to the prince of the authority of the air.[177]

Lord, please:

- Dismantle any ungodly authority structures, hierarchies and frameworks

- Restore Your grace, favor and blessings

- Reveal Your creation of new heavens and a new earth and let even the memory of former things be removed[178]

- Deliver Your mighty grace, and remove any ungodly governmental mountains and temples, inverted mountains, and the ungodly all-seeing eye

- Establish Jesus as the tried-and-tested Cornerstone, Foundation and Capstone[179]

- Restore the correct latticework, dimensions and organization of the crystal sea[180]

I repent for anytime I or those in my family line rejected Your justice and righteousness, which are the foundation of Your throne.[181] I choose to walk in the way of your righteousness and Your paths of justice.[182]

Lord,

- May the righteous kings be in righteous authority in the seats on the waters

- May godly wisdom be the organizing principle of the pillars of heaven, the fiery stones and our lives in God

- May Your wisdom be at all the locations you designed it to function, including star gates in the grid of the heavens and at the meeting of the ancient paths[183]

---

[172] Prov 8:26
[173] Psalm 104:5
[174] Genesis 7:11
[175] Matthew 23:13
[176] Matthew 18:3
[177] Eph 2:2
[178] Isaiah 65:17
[179] Isaiah 28:16
[180] Ezekiel 1:22
[181] Psalms 89:14
[182] Proverbs 8:20
[183] Jeremiah 6:16, It is our sense that decisions are made where ancient paths meet

- Please fill in the valleys, level the mountains, make the crooked places straight, and make the rough ways become smooth for the King[184]

- Cleanse the ley lines so they can be highways of holiness for the King

- Repair and restore the generational timelines. Please remove the ungodly clocks and timekeepers

- Rightly connect the seven eyes to the pathways of the firmament[185]

- Cause Your wisdom to become the stability of my times

- Release and clean all soul and spirit parts trapped in sanctuaries and places of captivity in the grids of the heavens,[186] power systems, batteries, voltages and currents

- Release and heal trapped memories and energy in the systems and gates on my body, and establish Your ancient pathways[187] of the flow of the life of God

I acknowledge that the heavens declare the glory of God, and the firmament shows the works of His hands.[188] I thirst for the true waters of the life of God, which satisfy me deeply.[189]

I come into agreement with the fact that you are building Your church upon the Rock, which is Jesus.[190]

I come into agreement with the judgement of the Ancient of Days, which was made in favor of the saints of the Most High. Lord, may Your time come for the saints to possess the kingdom.[191]

Lord, please restore the dew[192] and the precious things of Heaven, and the storehouses of the heavens[193]

Father, I come into agreement with the truth of Your image[194] that You have placed in us before the foundation of the earth.[195] I declare that Your image is timeless, and this is eternity in my heart.[196]

Lord, please:

- Remove all evil operators and coding, and disconnect me from all fallen angles, elders, rulers, fallen sons of God, kings, watchers, or any other evil systems that are enabling the contaminant of the seed, which affected how I reflect the true image of God

- Remove all efforts of influence of the enemy that took me off of the ancient path and led me into deception, fear and disbelief of the heart

---

[184] Isaiah 40:4, Luke 3:5
[185] This line in the prayer comes from prophetic revelation
[186] Mark 13:27, Nehemiah 1:9
[187] Jeremiah 6:16
[188] Psalm 19:1
[189] Isaiah 55:1,2
[190] 1 Peter 2:6
[191] Daniel 7:22
[192] Deuteronomy 33:13
[193] Deuteronomy 28:12
[194] Genesis 1:27
[195] Ephesians 1:4
[196] Ecclesiastes 3:11

- Unlock my heart so that my representation of the image of God can be fully restored and repurposed in me

- Disconnect me from the father of lies

- Remove all coding and seeding that has been intermingled in the fabric, DNA and RNA of my life by the father of lies, or any other evil

- Remove all contamination and ungodly structures that have been set up on the living stones

Lord, on behalf of myself and my family line, I repent for:

- All ungodly fellowship of the saints that birthed disunity and destruction

- The setting up and participation in created, ungodly storage facilities and vaults in time and/or space to lock away parts, identity, representation of the image of God, places in my heart, anointings, gifts, inheritances and other resources that You have given me to steward

- The use of ungodly rituals, sounds or chanting of any kind. Including any attempts to undo the very fabric of time, or attempts to use time as an ungodly storage facility

- The creation of all false images

- All generational manipulation of light and sound

Lord, please remove all fallen watchers of time, and return all stolen portions of time; establishing the correct boundaries of the portion of time. Please restore all righteous beings to the positions in which you've designed them to function.

I repent for all personal and generational worship of ungodly images.

Lord, please:

- Remove all ungodly seraphim and ungodly tents of meeting

- Remove all evil that has inhibited the godly function of the golden pipes[197]

- Disconnect the golden pipes from all ungodly places and from ungodly time

- Remove all junk DNA and RNA implanted by the enemy

- Remove all ungodly libraries and data of any kinds from me, including that which may be tied to the ungodly firmament

I reject the false book of life, which promises eternal life apart from Elohim. Lord, I choose Your actual book of life, and I take back all portions of time that You, Lord, have established for me.

---

[197] Zechariah 4:12, It is our sense that the golden pipes receive God's power through the firmament.

Prayer of Release from Sororities and Fraternities

In the name of Jesus Christ, on behalf of myself and my ancestors I repent for and renounce:

- Participating in ungodly oaths and covenants

- Placing a priority on secrecy instead of pursuing godly truth

- Being part of ungodly councils and ungodly assemblies

- Secret counsels, ungodly wisdom and restriction of knowledge to access and retain power.[198]

- Being part of the ungodly or false families

- Replacing intimacy with intellectualism, control, legalism, slavery and false religion

- Worship of and pledges to the false trinity, ungodly patrons, saints, founders

- Disconnecting attributes such as wisdom and knowledge from God and forsaking relationship with Him for elevation and worship of attributes of God rather than God Himself

- Trying to bypass Jesus and God's standards through theft and robbery or for trying to lead the flock astray [199]

- Elitism[200] and being ungodly chosen ones

- Ungodly offices of consul, kustos, pro-counsul, annotator, magister

- Ungodly stations, challenges, passwords, keys, signs and salutations

- Ungodly recognitions, mottos, principles, values, ideals,

- Ungodly initiations, altars, shrines and symbols

- Ungodly obligations, examinations, tests, false cleansings, qualifications, admissions

- Shutting out God's light by accepting the darkness and deception of ungodly blindfolds and hoodwinks

- Ungodly salvation and crosses

- Ungodly seven candlesticks, darkness of false enlightenment, false fountain of Greek and worldly wisdom

- Twisting of Scripture and the nature of God and His teachings

- Using man's wisdom in the disciplines of learning, teaching, aims, and virtues

---

[198] Job 15:8,9
[199] John 10:1
[200] Romans 10:12, Galatians 3:28

- Ungodly robes, masks, shields, heraldry, insignia, and jewels

- Redefining gender, masculinity and femininity and the roles of men and women in society

- Allowing worldly values and culture to define our identity and positioning

In Your name, Jesus, please:
- Restore my true belonging – spirit, soul and body to You[201] and your family[202]

- Remove, return and clean all soul and spirit parts from the ungodly councils and please undo the union of my glory with the ungodly assembly.[203]

- Break the bands of the wicked from off me and my line[204]

- Cancel the covenants made to all ungodly sororities, fraternities, divinities

- Cancel ungodly oaths (even those considered unbreakable by man), rituals, spells, magic potions, illusions, sacramental meals.

- Set me free from false philosophies and deceit. Please remove all ungodly influence of elemental spirits[205]

- Remove the ungodly bonding of the false holy spirit in ungodly unions

- Remove me from all false families, false brotherhoods and sisterhoods and false friendships

- Remove all sources of false light

- Break any curses, backup curses, time curses and reinforcement of curses in allotted timeslots that may come upon me or my family as a result of what we've broken off today

---

[201] Psalm 100:3
[202] Ephesians 2:19, 3:15
[203] Genesis 49:6
[204] Psalms 119.61
[205] Colossians 2:8

Generational Prayer Model
Aslan's Place, Apple Valley, CA

Step 1   Briefly get to know the person you are about to pray for.

Step 2   Briefly introduce self (i.e. your background, history, etc.).

Step 3   Provide a brief explanation about generational strongholds.

"The LORD passed in front of Moses, calling out, 'Yahweh! The LORD!
The God of compassion and mercy! I am slow to anger and filled with unfailing
love and faithfulness. I lavish unfailing love to a thousand generations. I forgive
iniquity, rebellion, and sin. But I do not excuse the guilty. I lay the sins of the
parents upon their children and grandchildren;
the entire family is affected — even children in the third and fourth generations.'"
(Exodus 34:6-7 NLT)

Step 4   Provide a brief explanation about the gift of discernment from Hebrews 4:15

a. Touch (Acts 12:7)
b. Smell (Psalm 45:8)
c. Hearing (2 Samuel 5:22-24)
d. Taste (Job 6:30)
e. Sight (Isaiah 6:12)
f. Evil default (Acts 16:18)

Step 5   Open in prayer: Holy Spirit I invite you to cleanse (person's name) generational
line. In the name of Jesus, I command all evil to leave (person's name) family line
and go to the feet of Jesus!

Step 6   Determine the generational issue

Ask the person if they have had:
a.   A recent or recurring dream.
b.   If they haven't, ask them if they have had a childhood memory of anything
that has troubled them over the years.

Note: A recent or recurring dream or troubling memory will be the starting point
of the generational prayer process. For example, if the person has had a dream or
memory about lust there is likely a stronghold of sexual impurity in their family
line. If the person remembers their childhood being very lonely, loneliness may be
something the enemy planted in their family line. Note: The Lord may give you a
strategic dream the morning of your appointment that reveals the stronghold.

Step 7   Determine when the stronghold began

Ask: Lord, how many generations back was (generational issue) empowered in (person's name's) family line?

Note: The Holy Spirit will give the person you are praying for (and you) and other team members, the numbers of the specific generations when the enemy empowered evil in the person's family line. The Holy Spirit will do this by giving you an impression or vision, etc. Note: As the Holy Spirit gives different numbers when lust or loneliness was empowered and re-empowered in the generational line be cognizant of any sensory confirmation ("hits" in the Spirit) on your body. Clue: The stronger the sensory confirmation the greater the presence of evil in that particular generation.

Step 8   Determine the country

Ask: Lord, what country was (the generational issue) empowered in?

Step 9   Determine what happened

Ask: Lord, what happened (i.e. an event) at this generation to empower (i.e. lust or loneliness) in the family line?

Wait on the Lord to show you "how" the enemy infiltrated the family line.

Step 10   Start with the biggest number and ask the Holy Spirit: Lord, what happened at (such and such's) generation to empower (i.e. lust or loneliness) in the generational line?

As soon as you have prayed this prayer, "wait" on the Lord to give you a "word of knowledge," "impression" or "vision" as to what happened in this specific generation to empower (i.e. lust or loneliness) in the generational line. For example you may hear the words "prostitution", "orgies", etc.

Step 11   Then pray: In the name of Jesus I come against all evil that has been given the legal right to establish the stronghold of lust in (person's name) family line. I break, shatter and destroy lust from the (start with the generation you determined in step 7) and demand that (root of generational issue i.e. lust) go to the feet of Jesus! Note: (Wait for the evil to leave. (We find most often that you will sense this through your evil default on your head.)

Step 12   Have the person pray through "Renunciation of Sins in the Family Line" from Aslan's Place "Prayers for Generational Deliverance."

Note:As the person is praying this prayer take careful note of any impressions, sensations, visions you have. As they come to mind command them to leave (for i.e. say "lust leave." "Sexual impurity leave." Etc.) Be sure to explain that when

253

you are telling the strongholds to leave that it does not reflect upon them personally but is the evil leaving their generational line.

Step 13   Once the person has finished renouncing the sins in their family line go to the next lowest number. (Remember you started with the highest number) Pray: Lord at the (nth generation what re-empowered (i.e. lust or loneliness) in the family line

Step 14   Wait on the Lord to show you which prayer to have the person pray from Aslan's Place prayer manual. Keep in mind that the Holy Spirit does something different in each deliverance session. Because of this you can't rely on set prayers for every session. Some of the most commonly used prayers are:

- "Prayer Breaking Ungodly Ties Between a Person and the Dimensions"
- "Prayer of Renunciation for the Misogynistic Spirit"
- "Prayer to Release One from the Ungodly Depths"
- "Prayer of Release from Chronic, Physical, Mental and Spiritual
- Disorders"
- "Prayer to Release Supernatural Favor to Proclaim the Favorable Year of the Lord"

Step 15   Continue on to the next lowest number and repeat the above prayer process until you come to the present generation. At this point pray: From the present generation to (person's name) descendants to a thousand generations.

Next, ask the person to close their eyes and ask the following questions:

1.   Can you see yourself as a creative spirit before God's throne (mention Jeremiah 1:5)?

2.   Did you want to join your mother and father's sperm and egg at conception?

3.   Did anything happen to you between leaving God's throne and conception?

4.   Ask: Lord, did, any ungodly trades occur?

- See Ezekiel 27:13 (ESV) Joel 3:3, Revelation 18:13 (ESV)

Note: Ungodly trades occur when unborn children are "dedicated" to false altars. For example, parents could dedicate their future child to an animal in the Zodiac (the snake, the dragon, etc.). Ungodly trades also occur when blood is shed.

Step 16   Ask the Lord to remove all idols and false altars from the family line.

Step 17   Have the person pray the following prayer:

Lord, I repent for those in my family line who traded human souls with the enemy for present favor. I repent for this and I demand back from the enemy all parts of my spirit, soul and body that were scattered. I declare to my spirit, soul and body that I will yield to the Holy Spirit. I repent for all blood sacrifices and offerings of blood in my family line that gave the enemy the legal right to scatter parts of my spirit, soul and body among the ungodly stars. I now, declare that I will rule and reign over the gates and doors assigned to me and my family line! Please remove all evil that tried to prevent me from being conceived. Amen!

Step 18   Have the person pray the prayer, "Ruling and Reigning with Christ."

Step 19   Follow the Rapid Healing Model in the Prayers for Generational Deliverance.

Step 20   Conclude the prayer session by blessing the person by speaking Numbers 6:24-27 and Isaiah 11:2-3 over their life.

May the Lord bless you with many gifts! May the Lord guard you with a hedge of protection! May the Lord illuminate the wholeness of His being toward you to bring order to your life! May the Lord beautify you! May the Lord lift up His wholeness of being and look upon you and set in place all you need to be whole and complete! May the Spirit of the Lord rest on you! May the Spirit of wisdom and understanding guide you! May the Spirit of counsel and might move mightily through you! And may the Spirit of knowledge and the fear of the Lord encounter you at all times. In Jesus' name, amen.

Index of Prayer Topics

favorable year of the Lord · 62
Fear · 214
Fear of the Lord, restoring · 80
female, hatred of · *See* misogyny, renunciation of
financial freedom, release into · 39
fraternities · 250

G

generational evil, renunciation · 13
Generational Prayer Model · 252
generational roots, removal of ungodly · 9

H

hard heartedness, breaking of · 42
healing, emotional · 114
healing, evangelistic, release of · 52
heart, breaking hardness of · 42
heart, removing curses · 12
heart, retune and realign · 89
height, ungodly · 157
Hinduism, renunciations for · 122
Holy Spirit, fullness · 26
homosexuality, repentance for · 1, 20, 56, 157

I

inadequacy, freedom from · 11
Incubus · 56
inertia, changing · 2
influence, release into God given · 46
inheritance · 188
inner healing, prayer for rapid · 27
intercession, ungodly · 74
intimacy with the Lord, release into · 36

J

Janteloven iniquities · 11
Jewish ancestry · 239
Jews, agreement to bless · 31
joy, release of · 211

K

Kairos · 112
kingdom of heaven, entering · 244
kings and priests, establish as · 148
kundalini · 212

L

lack, ungodly · 229
land · 219
land, repentance of misuse · 166
learning disabilities, healing from · 22, 24
length, ungodly · 157
lies, father of · *See* father of ;lies
light, worship of · 206
living stones, cleaning contamination · 199
living stones, establishing as · 44

M

magistellus · 56
male, hatred of · *See* misandry, repentance of
man, hatred of · *See* misandry, repentance of
Mare (nightmare) · 56
marriage, prayer for · 25
mazzaroth · 157
medical field, trauma associated with work · 156
memory · *See* cellular memory prayer
mental disorders, release from chronic · 34
might ones, ungodly · 230
military service, breaking ungodly connections · 218
mind of Christ, receiving · 10
misandry, repentance of · 168
misogyny, renunciation of · 109
Moloch · 157
Morning Star, release the · 96

N

need, ungodly · 229
Nephilim · 56, 157
nightmare · *See* Mare

Made in the USA
Columbia, SC
01 July 2024

37931861R00146